THE BEST OF GLOBAL SITE DESIGN

WEBS!TE GRAPH!CS NOW

BY THE EDITORS OF MED!AMATIC

Thames & Hudson

COPYRIGHT

First published in Great Britain in 1999 by Thames and Hudson Ltd, London

First published in paperback in the United States of America in 1999 by Thames and Hudson Inc.,
500 Fifth Avenue, New York, New York 10110

Copyright © 1999 BIS Publishers

British Library Cataloguing-in-Publication Data
A catalogue record for this book is available from the British Library

Library of Congress Catalog Card Number 98-75077

ISBN 0-500-28119-X

Printed and bound in Singapore

WEBSITE GRAPHICS NOW
TABLE OF CONTENTS

LEARNING FROM HOLLYWOOD

It has become customary to start a preface for a book on Web design by stating how computers have changed our world, how we live in a media age, suffer from information overload, face paradigm shifts, have to rethink design, etc. All these phrases are true but mean nothing any more for those of us who spend a large part of our time actually designing websites. We know that storage gets cheaper and processors faster; we have long since given up trying to download the latest update of all the software clogging up our hard disks; and I know that whatever I might want to say about any cool new stuff — Flash, Shockwave, you name it — may be well out of date by the time you're reading this. There is, however, one thing we can be sure of: people always like to read, browse, flip between pages, compare, be amused, astonished or enlightened. If you just want to grow older by two hours without any immediate danger to your health, you watch TV. But if you want more than that, an exciting alternative even for the laziest couch potato is checking out websites, surfing the Internet, whatever you want to call it. What used to be just page after page of badly presented electronic data has now become a medium that fulfils one of our most basic needs: storytelling. We humans have a very deep desire to find out what happens with other humans. Do we watch movies because we're afraid of dying stupid? Do we go to the theatre or the opera just to wear our tuxedos? Do we read books because we get paid for it? No, we want to find out how other humans cope with life, or suffer from it just as we do.

The archetypal stories of love, glory and suffering have been known since the Greeks paid actors to perform in public. And although, from Kurosawa to John Ford or Wim Wenders, these stories have been retold thousands of times, we cannot get enough of them. A giant industry has sprung out of repackaging the ancient stories, catering to that human need for storytelling. This industry, symbolised by Hollywood, is about to merge with the publishing industry. Together they'll be much more than mere shifters of data. They'll be purveyors for our hopes, fantasies and dreams as well as for our information needs and hunger for facts.

We see that convergence happening when we look at websites today, or at least those which are represented in this book. A good website has to tell a compelling story, lest it bore any but the hardcore information seeker. As in the movie industry, the producers have to hire a whole team of specialists to come up with the goods. And just as your regular cinema-goers don't want to know anything about cameras, lights or editing suites, our websurfers couldn't care less whether the designers are using cool code, slick software or awesome animation. They just want to be carried away by a good story well told.

Learning from Hollywood therefore means bringing together the right people: storytellers, visualisers and technicians. Producers pick the teams and make sure they're paid. Writers provide storylines, editors fit them to the medium. Designers set the scene and keep the audience's attention. And the director holds the vision of how the story will finally appear. Anyone who's ever worked in the same room as programmers and designers knows that these two cultures are not a natural mix. It takes effort to create a common understanding, and the best way to get there is to share that vision.

The film industry has managed to bring all these different attitudes, backgrounds and aspirations together. The aim is a seamless result which gets us into their cinemas, keeps us there and makes us tell our friends about the experience afterwards. And what works for the movies, will work on the Web. Give us the necessary facts, but don't bore us in the process. Tell a good story and we will listen. Make it look good and we will keep our eyes on it. And make it work well, so we won't switch off before the Happy Ending.

The stuff in this book is proof of the fact that our industry is beginning to get beyond code for code's sake and away from self-indulgent design which serves no purpose but to fulfil designers' vanity. We now have teams just like in Hollywood, all working to a common goal, serving the audience. Or do we call the spectators 'participants'?

However we refer to our end-users, like most of them, I'm not concerned whether the makers of a website used dhtml, Flash or Hot Water, as long as I find what I need, get what I didn't expect and have a good time doing so.

Erik Spiekermann

THE LAST OF THE VIEW SOURCE PRINCIPLE

For several years, the main tool for learning new tricks and skills in Web design has been the 'view source' option in your browser. Until recently, Web design has resembled a massive ongoing research project where everyone was sharing their new insights, their latest discoveries, simply by allowing others to have a look at their source code. But recent developments in extending browser functionality have allowed more and more sites to close off this creative back door with such tricks as the 'pop-up' window, or by excluding the tool and navigation bar thus removing the option to open the source code. From the designer's point of view, these new browser features help to concentrate the viewer's attention on the site's content, since they do away with the sources of distraction and escape. They also provide the longed-for control over content, which until now has only been partly possible in html using devices such as tables. Sites produced in Macromedia Flash or Shockwave are a different matter altogether. When viewed across the Web, there is no way of finding out how they were made.

The ongoing commodification of information is playing a major role in these developments: website design work is shifting to reflect the increasing complexity of visualising, controlling and interacting with large amounts of dynamic information. Tailored software code is becoming a vital part of many a new website. In fact, now some sites don't even exist as such until the user starts using them! Coming to terms with this invisibility, and with code-driven sites such as those that use transactions (both from the designer's and the user's point of view), form the subjects of two of our introductory articles. In his article, Paul Kahn argues for the importance of visualising the invisible part of websites. Site maps have always provided a sort of meta-look at a site's structure. Recently, mapping devices and metabrowsers have provided a different look at the Web in general and sites in particular, and may point to a future, visual way of dealing with the information on the Web. For his part, Nathan Shedroff explores the development of interaction and transaction, and their importance in today's websites.

Website Graphics Now presents a selection of sites that showcase different facets of this transitional development. Several sites still make the best of 'classic' Web design strategies and techniques, while many others now employ Flash and Shockwave to create engaging interfaces with the digital content, and still others explore the new features of dhtml, java script, and java programming. Unsurprisingly, we've found that splitting up websites across different categories has proved increasingly difficult. Websites now tend to be extremely hybrid in what they offer, as well as in what they try to accomplish. A site like Fabric8, for instance, was set up both as a site for e-commerce and as a showcase for the design company. Yet it also has an important function in representing a local community of designers and artists to the world at large. This schizophrenic nature characterises many of the sites we've chosen. In our first category are the artists and designers who are increasingly attempting to break the rules and boundaries of contemporary Web design, reflecting on the nature of such work online, on how it relates to the medium (as seen in the work of Jodi), and on more traditional art spaces (like, for instance, Rhizome who attempt to curate online art to gain a wider audience). Design studios are also creating interesting sites. Fork and Lateral are pushing the possibilities of communication design in innovative ways in this area. Our education category shows how the Web is becoming a significant source of research information and learning. Schoolteachers can easily create their classroom courses from the information found on the Web. A good example of the way a TV programme is supplemented by an outstanding collection of information is the BBC's Windrush site, perfectly representative of educational resources on the Web.

Obviously, one of the most widely used functions of sites on the Web is the promotion of products or companies. We've come across a lot of 'one-off' websites, sites especially created to launch one particular product, for instance New York-based Razorfish's G-Shock site for Casio (which is only loosely connected to the Casio mother site). Our promotional category also features a few early examples of 'multimedia' productions: self-contained Flash-based animations for companies and businesses stream across the Web as if they were running off a CD-Rom. Doing business on the Web, or serving users/clients in other ways, also calls for a carefully considered series of transactions and interactions. Personalisation and customisation are keywords for the sites presented in this category. From the sales of handcrafted, custom-made products in Fabric8 to the personalised online banking facilities in Mediamatic's Rabobank site, these sites are potential precursors of a new generation of websites.

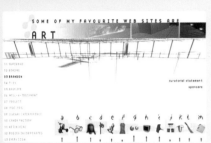

From the beginning, magazines have been the primary source of experimentation for formats in digital publishing. Our e-publishing category presents a wide range of digital publications, from the hardcore html pages of De:bug to the visual communications of Volumeone. E-zines are also becoming more sophisticated. Atlas magazine, for instance, has some of the most extensive dhtml programming of any sites in this book, despite its subtle, crafted style. Finally, three sites exemplify a characteristic that underlies more sites in this book than immediately meets the eye. What these sites have in common is that they thrive on, or foster, a sense of community. The DIY site, for example, has arisen from the UK rave community and continues to be one of their main sources of information. Platform shows the rise of so-called portal sites which, as well as offering a collection of information and music on their own, also serve as a springboard to an entire collection of related sites as a service to their interest group.

Website Graphics Now marks this moment of transition — the steady coming of age of a medium with all its attendant problems, shifts and possible directions. In the world of the Internet there's not much we can be sure of, except of course change itself, change that will take us into a more dynamic, more customisable, more engaging and definitely more multimedial era of the Web.

Noel Douglas, Geert J. Strengholt

While 'interactivity' is a fairly new word, it is a phenomenon which is older than anyone can determine. Only an industry as simultaneously arrogant and ignorant as the computer industry could possibly believe that it has invented something as important as interactivity. The truth is that interactivity has been part of human culture since time immemorial. Conversations, storytelling, playing football, painting a picture, creating a sculpture, an afternoon of shopping with a friend, raising a child — interactivity is all around us and forms a deep

or proudest moments. More likely than not, these experiences are emotionally and financially valuable precisely because they share elements that make them interactive. Online media that can tap into these elements, that can begin to compete with real-world experiences, have the ability to become valuable and memorable to people.

Another thing to understand about interactivity is that it forms a spectrum, from passive to interactive. There is no demarcation between passive and interactive experiences, no dividing line. Experiences flow along this spectrum, making it difficult to

WHAT'S SO INTERACTIVE ABOUT INTERACTIVITY ANYWAY?

part of our lives. It is merely new to electronic media. The good news about this revelation is that we already know a lot more about interactivity than we think we do, and we can use this information to accelerate its growth in computer media — especially online media.

So why is interactivity important at all, and why is it important to computer media? Looking at other media, such as television, print and film, it isn't immediately apparent that interaction is an important ingredient to successful media. But what makes the computer medium unique is the fact that it is an interactive medium. Aside from direct human-to-human experience, it is the only medium which provides the opportunity to be interactive and which has the ability to create interactive experiences.

Interactive experiences have a high correlation to value. That is, interactive experiences tend to be more sought-after by audiences, and audiences are willing to pay more for them than for other types of experiences. For example, an admission ticket to a theme park costs (and is correspondingly worth) more than a ticket to a film. A quick meal is never worth as much as one in a restaurant, which is an opportunity for fine conversation and a special experience. In general, the experiences that tend to be more interactive are most memorable to us. You can prove this to yourself: call to mind your most intense memories, your happiest

differentiate. This is what has caused so much confusion and misunderstanding. But there are a number of components to experiences along this spectrum, and these are the very elements that designers and developers can use to enhance their creations, to create truly interactive experiences.

These components are not unique to computer media. In fact, they are most often present in non-computer media, that is, real life. This is important in understanding interactivity: computer experiences — whether interactive or not — are not only competing against other computer experiences. The truth, which many developers and manufacturers have learned the hard way, is that they compete against all life experiences. Therefore, the components of interactivity form the basis for successful, valuable experiences in people's lives, no matter what the medium. These components include:

• Feedback
• Control
• Creativity
• Productivity
• Communication
• Adaptivity

All media have their strengths and differences along this spectrum, and the differences only highlight the need to play up the strengths of different media — particularly online media such as the World Wide Web.

The problem with online and other computer-based interactive media is that these disciplines are still so young that there are few interesting examples worth highlighting or emulating. In the years to come, almost none of what has already been produced will be worth looking back at, except for a retro sense of nostalgia about our naïvety and quaintness. This said, there are some

position of the cursor. It is actually a fairly easy trick, but a highly effective one, and one that's very well done here. The sound cues (more feedback) definitely enhance the experience.

PlumbDesign's Visual Thesaurus (http://thesaurus.plumbdesign.com) is perhaps the most seductive experience you can find on the Web today. This thesaurus builds an interactive network of word meanings, connected in a beautiful and surprisingly easy-to-use interface. The words, which flow either towards or away from you based on your choices, allow you to navigate meaning in a way so original

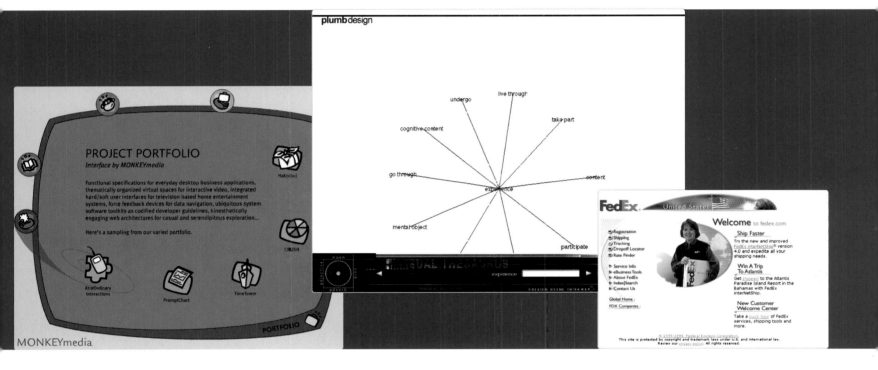

examples which can be examined now, but be sure to understand that these only scratch the surface, and achieve only a fraction of what this medium is capable of. Anything you see on the Net today, or in this book, still pales in comparison to a real experience. So with these caveats in mind, here are some interesting examples of the above-mentioned components.

Feedback and Control Feedback and control are simply ways of keeping the audience/user/participant/customer informed about the state of the experience, and of helping him or her to feel some sense of control over it. Higher levels of feedback and control make an experience feel more interactive and also tend to facilitate the other forms of interactivity mentioned below.

Realise that there is a difference between action, reaction and interaction. Perhaps a computer will never be truly interactive. It may only be possible for it to be reactive (to the user), but these examples display innovative means of making the system feel more seamless and easy to use, more dynamic and more interesting.

MonkeyMedia (http://www.monkey.com) has an interesting way of navigating that makes it feel like the site is dynamically reconfiguring itself based on the user's choices. The visual interface grows and shrinks, hides and reveals, according to the

and fluid that you can barely pull yourself away.

Creativity and Productivity While these two words initially seem like different things, they are actually both the same: they speak to the skill (and value) inherent in making something, be it for work (productivity) or for play (creativity). Perhaps this is a bit of an oversimplification, but there is nothing fundamentally different between the two. Furthermore, the ability to make something of interest has always been one of the most valued in society. From parents' pride about their children's drawings, to handmade gifts from family or friends, to application software that allows us to extend our abilities and learn new skills, making something has proven to be worth a lot of time, money and emotion. Using the Net for being creative or productive is a very new phenomenon and thus there are few examples. However, the following sites make use of the medium in ways that help people to be more productive.

Though tracking a package is certainly not the be-all and end-all of existence, when it is important, there is no substitute for the ability to track things yourself. Federal Express (http://www.fedex.com) provides just that ability. All bank and financial services sites are now striving to create tools that allow their customers to manage their finances, pay bills and move their money around electronically. These are clearly productivity tools that will become much more important in the future. The Bank of America (http://www.bankamerica.com) is a good example.

While most shopping sites simply allow people to buy items, a few are beginning to realise that shopping is more than just a transaction. Being able to buy something is inherently productive, but how the site is organised, and what people can do there, makes all the difference. Ultimately, simple purchase transactions will only be effective for products that people don't need to touch

between people, and instead worry too much about the content of their website. The reality is that, when it comes to communication, online media are no different from any other media. Treating online communication as something other than a conversation short-changes both community hosts and community members by depriving them of valuable interactive experiences.

If you want to see some successful online communities, the best so far are those created for kids. Purple Moon software has created a busy, large, energetic and viable community (http://www.purple-moon.com) where young girls can share in

or see before buying. What will be more successful are new kinds of products and personalised products. Examples of these can be seen at the sites of iKhakis (http://www.ikhakis.com) and Fabric8 (http://www.fabric8.com), where customers can not only purchase new clothes, but can also tailor them in several ways so that they fit exactly. This isn't something they can do in most stores.

Communication
Allowing people to talk to others is an easy way of creating some interactivity, since it essentially connects two people (who are both interactive) via a medium that is as neutral as possible. In this way, the medium seems to be an interactive one, while it is actually only a conduit. Unfortunately, most often this connection is anything but neutral, and creates interface problems that hinder the communication between people. This is where many forms of online communication (like discussion groups, chat systems, video conferencing, etc.) fail. Perhaps the most important and successful example of communication on the Internet is e-mail.

Good communication is the most important ingredient in any community. The reason most communities on the Net fail is either that they have not set up any means of communication, or that they lack a subject which is of interest to many people. In fact, most online communities do a poor job of creating conduits

'Friendship Adventures', find postcard pals and set up their private homepage. Despite purposely making it difficult for its members to communicate, in order to maintain security and privacy, Purple Moon's site buzzes with interactive exchanges.

Adaptivity
Perhaps the most important — and valuable — aspect of interactivity is that it can create experiences that change in order to suit different audiences' needs, interests and behaviours. The basic premise of adaptivity is that experiences which are different are seen as being more interactive, whether this is based on customisation (the tailoring of an experience from a limited number of pre-built choices) or personalisation (the fine-tuning of an experience based on personal information that is not necessarily predetermined). Aside from this, experiences might also adapt to user behaviours, the time of day, the location (of either user or server), or technological data (such as the type and version of browser, operating system or computing device). Unfortunately, this is difficult and expensive to create, and there are few examples so far on the Net.

My Yahoo (http://my.yahoo.com) is one of the most popular personalisation sites on the Web. My Yahoo is a good start when it comes to creating a customised homepage. CNN Custom News (http://customnews.cnn.com) is one of the most sophisticated news systems yet developed and offers a quick and easy way to customise based on pre-built 'profiles', so that users who don't fully understand the concept can still see some benefit. Even these users can further tune their profiles to be more responsive to their interests. Note as well the Dutch Rabobank site (http://www.rabobank.nl) in this book.

Adaptive experiences are extremely valuable and are virtually taken for granted in human social interaction; anyone who tries to carry on a conversation following a pre-built script is not viewed as a very good conversationalist. Here, too, is an example of real-life

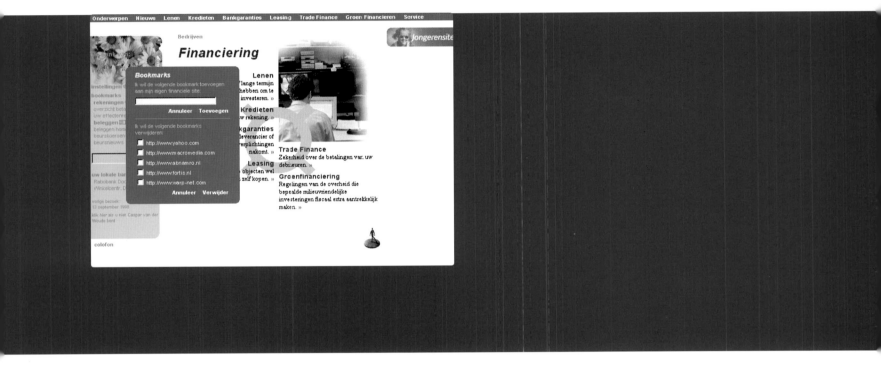

experiences serving as a model for interactive, computer-based ones. We've always recognised the value and importance of adaptive experiences in our personal lives, but it's only recently that a few companies have translated this understanding into their computer-based products and services.

A good source of techniques and ideas for further codifying human interactions into computer logic might be a study of improvised theatre and comedy. I've not only found a lot of ideas from these disciplines, but have also gained a lot of understanding about how conversations, stories and other interactions start, develop, flow and end — which is exactly what websites have to do as well.

Nathan Shedroff

At http://www.nathan.com/thoughts/ Nathan Shedroff maintains a list of resources about computer-based interactivity.

VISUALISING WEBSITES

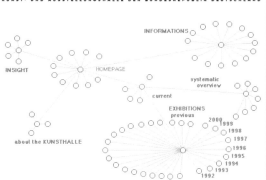

Since the Web has become part of our daily media landscape, graphic designers have been applying old and new techniques to its design, trying to visualise its structure. When it comes to classic publication design, no one questions the need for an underlying structure and logic. The structure of the page guides the eye and reassures the reader with regular patterns, rhythms and visual relationships. A similar underlying structure is also needed when designing a website. In this respect, the mutation of html's table tags, from tools for tabular material to a mechanism for controlling screen layout, has improved Web design far more than any other factor.

However, no matter how we improve our control over the design of individual screens, the Web presents an enormous lack of physical context. Beneath the structure on the screen is the structure of the website as a whole. A website's scope, its overall shape and boundaries — these factors are invisible! The website exists somewhere out there on the Net, perhaps distributed across machines that reside on different continents, perhaps on a tiny sector of a disk no larger than a credit card tucked inside a small black box. A website has no physical context, no apparent beginning and end, no covers, visual boundaries, weight, smell or physical texture. A Web designer must somehow express its structure and visual pattern to support comprehension, navigation and interaction.

While print publications can be read in a non-sequential way, they are designed, and their content is presented, as a sequence. The division of a publication into chapters, sections, subsections, parts, etc., helps the reader grasp the logical grouping of the content. An effective visual analogue of this section/subsection and sequential structure is an indented outline. The content of a website, however, is inherently non-sequential. Structuring and then visualising the information can play a crucial part in defining clear relationships between the various parts of the website's content. A sound 'information architecture' is needed. The author (sender) needs it to plan and organise the content to match the user's needs. The designer needs it to create the interface that will allow the user to interact with, and navigate through, the website. Finally, the user needs a visualisation to obtain an overview of the site. The traditional table of contents may not be the best visual form of representation for this task. Fortunately, there are other models we can turn to.

Representing the Real World Maps are a special form of visual communication, a representation of the three-dimensional world in a coded two-dimensional form. Maps serve many purposes. The map is a form of code, a geometry to feed the visual imagination. 'The map is a help provided to the imagination through the eyes,' stated Henri Abraham Chatelain in the early eighteenth century. Since then we've developed many visual conventions to transfer our experience of the real world into codes that conveniently fit onto paper. The Mercator projection of the world is an example of a conventional distortion which we've all come to recognise as 'real'. In fact the world doesn't look like a wall map, but we all know that, and anyway it's hard to fit a globe into a book. Such conventions are an agreement between the designer and the viewer. To help us grasp the abstract topology of a website, there are more conventions at hand.

This fifteenth-century German road map is a useful model.

'THE MAP IS A HELP PROVIDED TO THE IMAGINATION THROUGH THE EYES'

Henri Abraham Chatelain
(early eighteenth century)

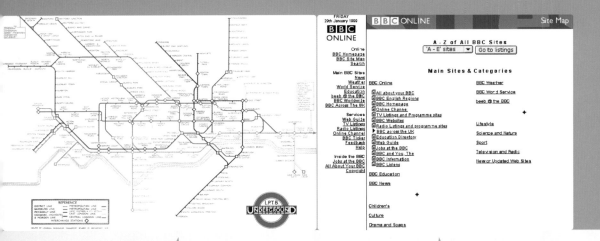

Essentially it is a node-link diagram, where every town is a node linked by a series of dots representing distance in miles. The distance between towns that are not linked is unimportant. Since this map radiates from a central town, there is a single road or link that connects each point. The map of the Kunst- und Ausstellungshalle der Bundesrepublik Deutschland website, created about five hundred years later, follows a similar strategy. The distance between the clusters of pages is unimportant. The lines connecting the circles, and the name for each cluster, make up the visual information that tells the viewer how the website is organised, and how it can be travelled by following links.

Two other classic examples of maps as 'information graphics' are worth pointing out. The Turgot plan (named not for the designer, but for the administrator who commissioned it) is a marvel of eighteenth-century design, showing the streets, buildings and land usage of the city of Paris in the 1730s. The richness of detail still dazzles the eye, but the lesson we need to learn is the usefulness of a projection applied by the map makers using a raised point of view and parallel lines. This information graphic is rendered in what computer graphics now refers to as two-and-a-half-D rather than 3-D. Architectural height is shown without a vanishing point, creating the minimum of distortion. In exchange for photographic realism, the mind receives a much more complete picture. Finally, Beck's map of the London Underground dates from the 1930s and was just as revolutionary. His alignment of the lines (and the river banks!) in a grid creates a visual harmony. The bold colours make it easy for the eye to separate the lines. The distortion of distances between the stations makes the map easy to read. After all, the distance between two stations is less important than their names.

Mapping the Virtual World of Websites
The visualisation of a website can take on two basic forms: the planning or analysis diagram and the site map. Each has its own distinct audience and function.

The site map is for the visitor who is presented with the opening page of a website. Of course, it's just as likely that he'll find himself looking at a page deep within the website's structure, discovered by following a link or doing a search. The visitor wants to be oriented: he needs some combination of a website overview and a sense of how what he's looking at fits into a larger structure. The site map is a floor plan or a navigation aid, an overview which provides a sense of what the site contains and how it is organised. How much does the map need to show? For many websites, everything is too much. The important information is contained in the organisation of the first two levels, the main sections and subsections. This information can be presented in any one of several visual codes.

The simplest site map is obviously the indented outline, where the distance of each item from the left margin indicates its level in the website. This is the familiar shape of a table of contents, familiar in form and simple to maintain. Yet expanding outlines can become very long, and the visual distance between first-level items makes the top-level organisation difficult to grasp. One strategy for avoiding this problem is to take advantage of the Web's interactive nature and utilise progressive disclosure. The BBC site map is a good example, where the initial view of the map is a two-column list of the first-level sections. Clicking on a section reveals both the sections and the subsections beneath it, while keeping the other first-level sections in view.

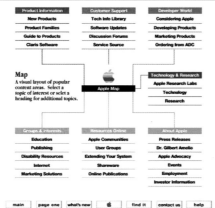

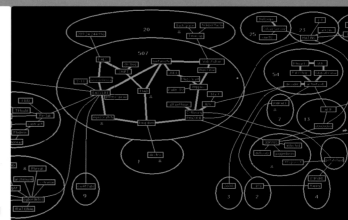

A common alternative to the indented outline is the horizontal/ vertical list, a strategy well-suited to a two-level site map. The horizontal axis usually represents the first-level structure, with the second-level items organised in vertical columns. The Adobe site map is a classic example of this, having maintained the same basic design for several years.

A circular organisation can add visual interest to a site map and also de-emphasise the hierarchy of sections. There is less of a sense of a 'first' section in a circular organisation, though the general rule that a viewer reads a screen from top to bottom, left to right, gives prominence to the upper-left position. A circular site map graced the Apple Computer website for several years until it was replaced by a more utilitarian multi-column list in 1997. That circle map used colour to distinguish the seven first-level sections and centred text to indicate second-level sections. The detail was limited but the overall scope of the site was easy to grasp in one view. Of course, simplicity and clarity are not always the goals when presenting the visitor with a site map. The map of www.Jodi.org is a large pattern of ovals, boxes and lines, showing some grouping relationships among art websites around the globe. The lack of pattern and hierarchy is the information that is being communicated.

Valuable lessons for visualising websites can be learned from studying the abundance of site maps that have appeared on the Web in recent years. The most successful maps seem to use colour and relative positioning, rather than lines and arrows, to express relationships. When a site map begins to look like a wiring diagram it tends to lose its utility.

The planning/analysis diagram is for the author, the builder of

the website. Before revising a site or attempting to add features or sections, the author needs a clear account, an under-the-hood look at what's already there. And if an existing website is hard to imagine, largely invisible as it is, it's even more difficult to visualise a website that is still in the making. Following the architectural model, we need a set of structural drawings and plans to serve as blueprints for the creative team. The builders need analysis, detail and strategy expressed in a visual form.

A well-crafted map can represent several facets of a website simultaneously. The planning map for the Nature Neuroscience website uses a combination of colour, position and symbols to show site structure, page type, click depth and user access rights. Dynamic pages are shown connected to the databases from which they are populated. Combining many facets into a single diagram helps the author visualise the relationships and dependencies being created. Once the initial version of the site is created, planning and analysis diagrams are the basis for the ongoing development, expansion or reorganisation. In this case, a flattened and simplified version of the planning diagram also serves as a site map to orient the visitor within the final website.

As dynamic websites become the technological standard for presenting content drawn from databases, planning diagrams can be used to visualise the relationships between the collections of data and the front-end interface design. The map of a dynamic website is less an account of individual pages (there may be thousands of stories in a magazine archive, or tens of thousands of items in a catalogue) than it is a representation of data types and relationships among them. Often some portion of a dynamic site, such as a registration or personalisation feature, is

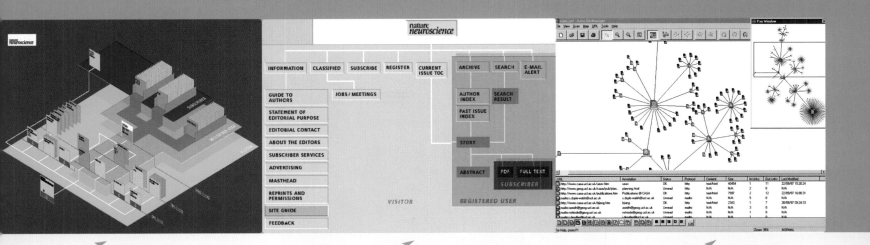

essentially a software application. As the user fills in forms and makes selections, various programs are run to select and populate a page. In such cases, the author is best served by a map that represents both the flow of control and the visual details presented to the user.

Dynamic Maps and Diagrams Recently a number of tools have been developed to chart a site's information and link structure, each producing dynamically its own visual site maps or diagrams. A map generated by such a program can be a tool for maintaining a website, as well as a navigation aid. As with the previous distinction between planning diagrams and site maps, the tools for visualising websites range between products that produce a map for the Web administrator, such as Astra Site Manager, and those that produce a map for the visitor.

The greatest problem in creating a map of a website by automatic means is determining how to represent the order and organisation of the links. The Web is a network of linked documents, with no inherent priority for links between any two documents. Any mapping program must first visit the documents by following links to determine what the website contains. The simplest technique is to organise the link structure of a site as it is discovered. But how should the program position nodes in the map? Which links should be shown and which should be pruned? Where should a page be placed within the map — where it is initially located or where it 'belongs' in the structure?

There are no definitive answers to these questions, and the tools available today offer rather primitive solutions. The most important thing to remember is that a website is not a file system.

Solutions that make a website appear to be another set of files on the computer desktop are going in the wrong direction. Experience shows that a map which tries to show how everything is connected to everything else is also doomed to failure. There is no inherent topology in a hypertext. Large hypertext networks resemble a plate of spaghetti from whichever angle they are viewed. On the other hand, a program that accounts for everything on a website, including checking all link destinations and reporting on errors, is a wonderful tool for maintaining a website's integrity. In this case, the visualisation technique is less important than the kinds of reports available to the Web administrator.

There are several visual strategies for representing a hypertext network that can be used to create a navigation map by automatic means. The most obvious one is the tree diagram, organised either from the top down or from left to right. The disadvantages of this kind of diagram are similar to those of the expanding outline already mentioned above. Representing the links as a set of radiating circles creates a pattern similar to a field of dandelions. The Merzscope program (see www.Merzcom.com for product details) which is used to create the map for the Kunst- und Ausstellungshalle der Bundesrepublik Deutschland uses this technique.

Another visual strategy is based on the fish-eye view, where items rapidly shrink as they move away towards the periphery of a circular focus area. By arranging the hierarchy tree in a circular fashion and shrinking items on the basis of their distance from a selected node, this kind of diagram can present more information in a small space than can the traditional tree.

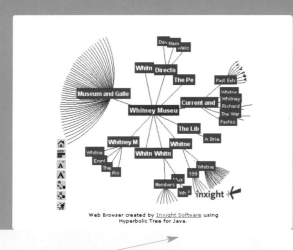

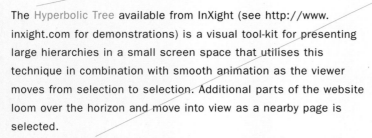

Web Browser created by Inxight Software using Hyperbolic Tree for Java.

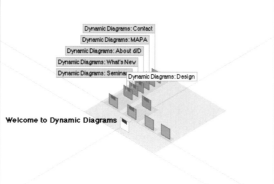

The Hyperbolic Tree available from InXight (see http://www. inxight.com for demonstrations) is a visual tool-kit for presenting large hierarchies in a small screen space that utilises this technique in combination with smooth animation as the viewer moves from selection to selection. Additional parts of the website loom over the horizon and move into view as a nearby page is selected.

Finally, the MAPA system adopts a visual strategy inspired by the Turgot and Beck maps, placing three levels of a hierarchy on an isometric grid and grouping these linked pages, by colour and position, in a two-and-a-half-D space. This diagram always represents three levels of a website: the selected page, the 'children' of that page and the 'grandchildren' behind each child, as well as the 'ancestors' of the selected page back to the homepage. The viewer can move up and down through the hierarchy of a very large website by selecting a new focus page from the diagram. Animated transitions help the viewer see the relationship between the current map and the new map as it is created.

The Future: Customised Site Maps and Meta-browsers? In the future we can hope for a richer set of definitions and conventions for defining a website. Some definition of the boundaries of a website, as well as a classification of link and page types, would make automatic mapping tools practical and worthwhile. The support for XML in Web browsers should encourage designers to use this more structured markup language, and that additional structure would help the visualisation effort.

We can also look towards visualisation tools that will help the

viewer get a personal view of where he has been, a form of visual memory which combines browsing history and bookmarks. The Web is a sea of information concerning both the content being offered to the viewer and the viewer's own interactions with the content. Bookmarks, visited link colours, history lists — these are the beginning of a personal view of the Web. Metaviews of websites and the Web at large, like I.O.D.'s Webstalker, are on the rise. Combining a road map of how a website is inter-connected, with information on the traffic patterns of how those connections are used, will give both the viewer and the administrator an interesting perspective.

In the 1930s, the advent of microfilm gave rise to H.G. Wells's image of the 'World Brain' and Vaneevar Bush's 'Memex'. Today, the Net causes us to imagine the world's information connected in infinite ways through the tiny portal of our Web browser. What form could a map of this enormous Web assume? It may resemble a transportation diagram, a star map, a CAT scan, or some image we have not yet seen.

Paul Kahn

TODAY, THE NET CAUSES US TO IMAGINE THE WORLD'S INFORMATION CONNECTED IN INFINITE WAYS THROUGH THE TINY PORTAL OF OUR WEB BROWSER.

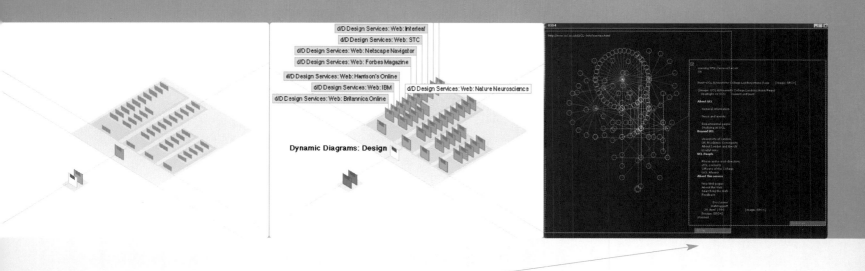

Dynamic Diagrams: Design

Illustration References:

German Road Map, Nuremberg, early 15th century, found in
Josef Müller-Brockman, *A History of Visual Communication*,
Switzerland: Verlag Arthur Niggli, 1971, pl. 54, p. 50.

Turgot map is published in Bernard Rouleau (ed.), *Le Plan de Paris
de Louis Bretez dit Plan de Turgot*, Nördlingen: Verlag Dr. Alfons Uhl, 1989.

Beck London transportation map is published in Ken Garland, *Mr. Beck's
Underground Map*, Middlesex: Capital Transport Publishing, 1994.

The planning diagram and site map for the Nature Neuroscience site
were created by Krzysztof Lenk (art direction) and Chihiro Hosoe (design).

The **main menu** provides access to the main information about The Remedi Project (on the right) and the individual contributions (below). These two screens show how a mouse-over on the numbers below loads the title and an image for each project, in this case those of Annette Loudon and George Larou.

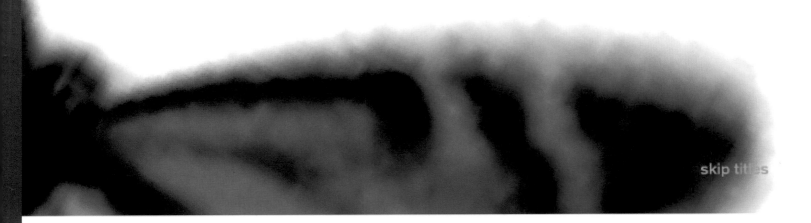

Annette Loudon's 'Skyline' presents a continuous panoramic scroll. Two buttons determine the direction of the scroll, left or right, and one can temporarily stop its flowing motion.

TITLE OF THE SITE The Remedi Project ❧ **COPYRIGHT OWNERS** All rights to The Remedi Project are owned by Josh Ulm, except artwork which is copyrighted to their respective artists ❧ **PLACE AND DATE OF DESIGN** San Francisco, April 1998 ❧ **CLIENT** Self ❧ **LANGUAGE** English ❧ **CONTRIBUTORS** Permanent Contributing Artists: Annette Loudon, Matt Owens, Terbo Ted, George Larou, John J. Hill, Andy Slopsema, Kleber, Jimmy Chen, Ammon Haggerty, Josh Ulm ❧ **LIMITED EXHIBITION ARTISTS** Fall 1998: Future Farmers, Bullseye Art, Shannon Rankin. Winter 1998: Eric Rodenbeck, Daniel Jenett, George Shaw ❧ **SOUND DESIGN** Josh Ulm ❧ **EDITORIAL** Josh Ulm, Michael Gough, Foreword Stephen Bloom, Copy Editor ❧ **SCREEN DESIGN** Josh Ulm ❧ **PRODUCTION** Josh Ulm ❧ **OFFICIAL URL** http://www.theremediproject.com ❧ **AWARDS** Communication Arts Site of the Week, Macromedia Site of the Day 1998, New Media Envision Award Gold Recepient, 1998 ACD web 100 Award ❧ **ANIMATION/GRAPHICS** Kirk Clyne, Josh Ulm ❧ **INTERACTION DESIGN** Josh Ulm ❧ **APPLICATIONS USED** Photoshop, InfiniD, Flash ❧ **PLATFORM USED FOR DESIGNING THE SITE** Macintosh 100%

THE REMEDI PROJECT

http://www.theremediproject.com

What do Web designers do when they get home after a hard day's work at the studio? You guessed it: they sit down behind their computers and start fiddling with the Web once again. As a platform for these after-hours Web experiments, Josh Ulm initiated The Remedi Project. 'Remedi?' you ask. 'Remedi for what?' The Remedi Project aims at REdesigning the MEdium through DIscovery, offering a cure for, or at least an alternative to, the wild growth of bland websites which clutter our global communications. It features a wide variety of experiments by some of the most innovative designers, whose professional handiwork you'll also discover in some of this book's other sites.

The Remedi Project's centre-piece is a Flash-based environment designed by Ulm which acts both as a menu and as a source of contextual information for all the projects. A roll-over menu on the side of the screen gives all the background information on the site's concept. A horizontal menu below loads the title and a preview image for each individual project. Clicking one of the options in this menu will bring up a short introduction by the designer and some information about the required plug-ins. Yes, 'required' because these Remedi projects are plug-in intensive and require Shockwave, Flash, Quicktime (VR), Beatnik — you name it, they need it.

But once you're fully equipped, you're in for a treat. In a take on advertising's graphic language, for instance, George Larou's 'Ultra Clean' takes on the spectacle of consumer culture, turning the vernacular of adspeak back onto itself. Using Flash, Larou creates a series of spoofish, interactive ads for Ultra Media™, a collection of 'clean design' products like Ultra Clean Screen, Virtu-sheen and Ultra Clear which are destined to brighten your day. Supported by a '50s piece of ad muzak, you can have your screen wiped squeaky clean, or experience the clarity that Larou's Ultra Clear font brings to your screen designs.

Josh Ulm's 'The Family' (excuse the lack of phonetics here) presents an interactive graphic environment in which the user can play around with pieces of spoken and written text. By browsing them, the user creates complex messages based on their own free associations. In three interlinked Flash movies, Ulm experiments with linking textual messages to speech feedback by means of roll-overs. 'Mixing messages', a statement pronounced in the 'Da Mu'ter' section, seems to cut right to the project's core. It forces the user to slow down, take his time to get involved and experience his own role in the creation of meaning.

In 'Skyline', designer Annette Loudon uses dynamic html to create a sheer, endless, panoramic experience. She combines a horizontally scrolling collage of façades with a collage of friends' short statements in which they describe their fascination with the sky. Her engaging, virtual skyline — sometimes reminiscent of the futurist visions of Metropolis — leaves you with a strange sensation of so many buildings holding up the sky. Your daily trips through the urban environment will never be the same again.

Obviously, not each and every contribution to The Remedi Project can be discussed in these pages, even though the variety of work demands you browse them all to get a good impression of the overall undertaking. Sixteen projects have been featured so far, but The Remedi Project will continue to serve as an open platform. More projects should be added in the future boldly going where few designers have gone before. Whether it will ultimately redesign the medium or reshape the way we use it to communicate remains to be seen.

by Geert J. Strengholt

George Larou's interactive ad for Ultra Clean media products combines some **interactive fun and excellent audio feedback** to make a poignant critique of contemporary advertising culture. The bubbles on the right serve as the main interface. Clicking for one of the ads, 'Ultra Clean' engages the user in a clever game of reversal and connection. After spraying your screen from the inside, your mouse hooks up with the sponge to wipe you monitor screen squeaky clean.

browse the artist statements below.

01.
02.
03.
14.

15.
00.

0.

josh ulm **da fam'ə lē** 13.

the remedi project redesigning the medium through discovery

04. 05. 06. 07. 08. 09. 10

Introduction screen and project screens

from Josh Ulm's 'The Family'. Subtle roll-overs across the texts/words will cause them to be read aloud for you. The apparent randomness of these messages triggers personal associations with the user, drawing him into the process of constructing meaning.

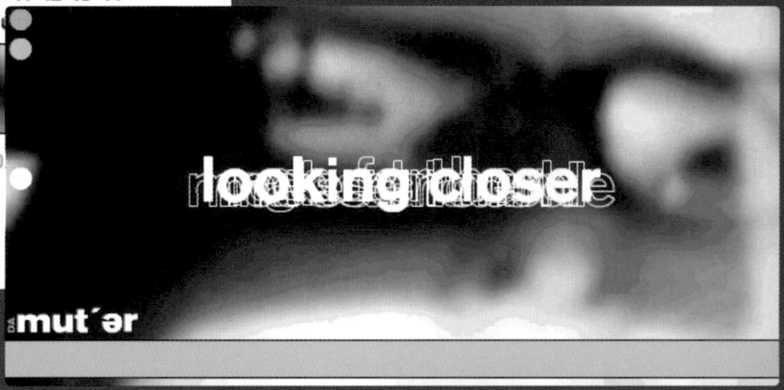

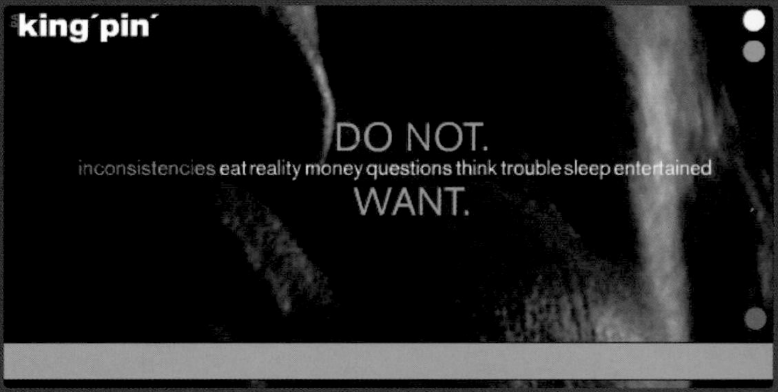

looking closer

mut'ər

jest'er

post violent gris inficolass.coloration

can't stand   leaves behind misplaced

a good haiku gravy

king'pin'

DO NOT.
inconsistencies eat reality money questions think trouble sleep entertained
WANT.

ok! ultra cleansing bubbles
of blue phosp
ULTRA CLEAN SCREEN™ is enhanced with VIRTU-SHEEN®
me on... scrub it

it's as easy as... 1
2
3

scrub your screen
then pop #2

it's simple it's

U L T R A
clear

and...

one SOLUTION for all your design needs

one application results in Ultra Clear™
typography set entirely in Ultravers 55®
with 57 character column widths in a

Through a series of **graphic Shockwave animations** Jimmy Chen's 'Untitled' makes an elaborate attempt at sinning against every convention of contemporary Web design.

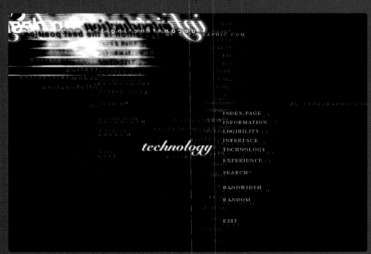

Shannon Rankin's 'Flesh' (get it?) consists of a series of **engaging graphic collages**. Like bodies intertwining, these images, texts and processed sounds can be rearranged, mingled and triggered at will by clicking various hot spots or moving across the roll-over grids.

View source

The main menu for The Remedi Project was created in **Flash**, presenting the user with an interface and meticulously timed animations. The animated butterfly that flutters by, unannounced, fills the empty space perfectly between both menus while the user ponders his or her options. The buttons in the menu respond to roll-overs by presenting navigational clues, and can be clicked to dig up further information or to launch a particular project in a separate window.

The individual projects use a variety of tools and techniques, but currently most of them turn to either Flash or Shockwave. Obviously these tools allow them to employ all of their graphic abilities in an interactive environment. From the complex and layered collages of images and typography in Jimmy Chen's 'Untitled' to John J. Hill's bashed-up document clippings in 'Transmitting Agencies', the Remedi projects display a wide range of enhanced graphic experimentation. Coupling graphic elements with sound bites, as in Josh Ulm's 'The Family' or Shannon Rankin's 'Flesh', adds another dimension altogether. Rankin's piece, in particular, takes advantage of Flash's sound capabilities. In Flash, **sound samples** can be linked and triggered very precisely. You can even use the same sample in multiple ways, or even parts of it, without consequences in terms of file size or quality.

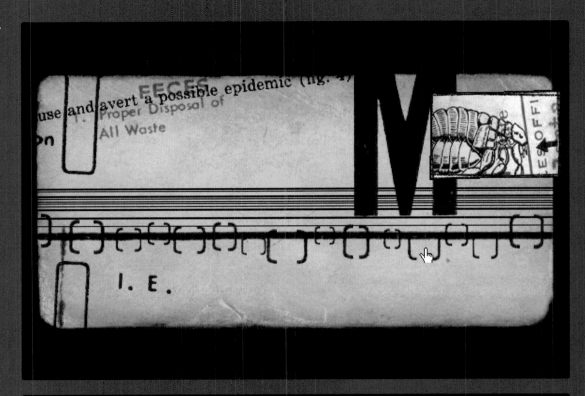

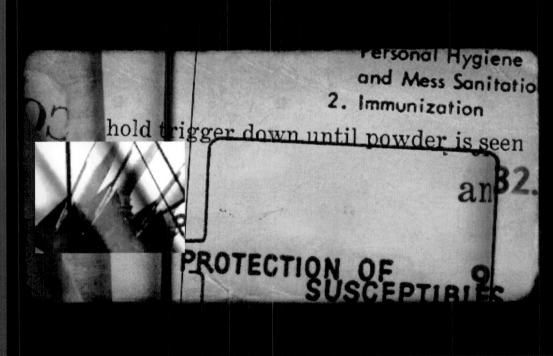

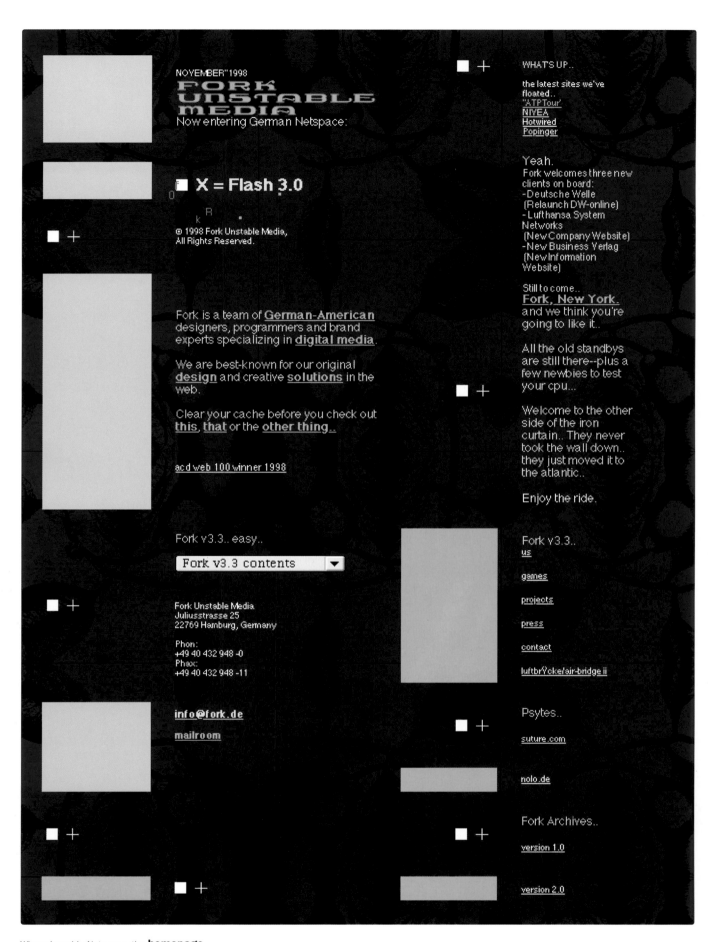

NOVEMBER "1998

FORK UNSTABLE MEDIA
Now entering German Netspace:

X = Flash 3.0

© 1998 Fork Unstable Media,
All Rights Reserved.

Fork is a team of German-American designers, programmers and brand experts specializing in digital media.

We are best-known for our original design and creative solutions in the web.

Clear your cache before you check out this, that or the other thing..

acd web 100 winner 1998

Fork v3.3.. easy..

| Fork v3.3 contents ▼ |

Fork Unstable Media
Juliusstrasse 25
22769 Hamburg, Germany

Phon:
+49 40 432 948 -0
Phax:
+49 40 432 948 -11

info@fork.de

mailroom

WHAT'S UP..
the latest sites we've floated..
"ATPTour'
NIVEA
Hotwired
Popinger

Yeah.
Fork welcomes three new clients on board:
-Deutsche Welle
(Relaunch DW-online)
- Lufthansa System Networks
(New Company Website)
-New Business Verlag
(New Information Website)

Still to come..
Fork, New York.
and we think you're going to like it..

All the old standbys are still there--plus a few newbies to test your cpu...

Welcome to the other side of the iron curtain.. They never took the wall down.. they just moved it to the atlantic..

Enjoy the ride.

Fork v3.3..
us

games

projects

press

contact

luftbrŶcke/air-bridge ii

Psytes..

suture.com

nolo.de

Fork Archives..

version 1.0

version 2.0

When viewed in Netscape, the **homepage**
uses a java script to encircle the mouse
pointer with bee-like letters which spell out
the word 'F O R K'.

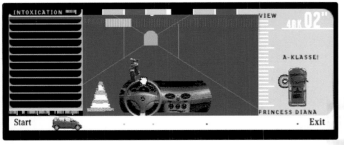

FORK UNSTABLE MEDIA V3.3

http://www.fork.de

Somewhere in the Fork website it says, '100 ideas a second'. Now take all those ideas and add the magic of some great experimental interface design and a strong graphical sensibility. Check your bandwidth and plug-in capabilities — the Fork site is bandwidth intensive — and you can enjoy one of *the* most interesting, cutting-edge, multimedia websites of its kind.

Fork is characterised by its makers' sense of rootlessness in the modern world. A recurring theme throughout the site is the questioning of the notion of 'home', and, in turn, related notions such as nationhood. The studio combines the talents of both American and German designers, a fact which is constantly alluded to and played with, whether it is the homepage telling us that we're entering 'German netspace' or that the site itself comes from the other side of the Iron Curtain (which apparently never came down, but was simply moved to the Atlantic)! To fit this schizophrenic 'cold war' mood, the press section of the site uses some clever java applets to turn the navigation into something resembling a flight simulator. It even comes with gun target which you use to 'shoot' links to different documents. Alternatively, it can be viewed as an html layout — the only thing to work out now is which version is meant to be the USA and which one is the Russians! Alongside the military themes, there is also a general mood of irreverence towards authority figures. These feature most strongly in the site's large games archive. Accessed from three lists entitled 'bread', 'butter' and 'freshmilk', these archives contain a range of Shockwave delights, including a game where you have to feed the mind and body of former German Chancellor Kohl to keep him from starving. In another game you take on the role of the intoxicated chauffeur of a Mercedes driving a certain, now deceased, member of the British royal family through an infamous French tunnel while simultaneously being hounded by press photographers! Here again, military themes abound. One delightful game called 'Cold War' lets you either give a scrolling row of soldiers bunches of red roses with angels flying out of them, or simply machine-gun them to death. The site also features a great deal of audio: most pages have a 'soundtrack' that contains fragmentary blends of what sound like TV or radio reports. Some are English, some German, but all are mixed with subtle techno noises and general electronic noise disturbance. As you surf through the site, these soundtracks evoke feelings of listening surreptitiously to illegal broadcasts, which sits well with the general playful multimedia mood.

To give them all due respect though, Fork aren't all just about a cool, knowing postmodern cynicism. They have their humanist side, too, best exemplified in a section entitled 'Hotel'. Designed as an interface experiment using a combination of java and Flash, 'Hotel' uses key words which scroll past you at high speed, as if the browser were suddenly a train window. When clicked upon, these words start a process in which you explore personal narratives based on the theme of what 'home' might mean. This is an example of Fork's philosophy that, in an unsettled world, where we come from is not so important. Instead, what we share is our common humanity, and this is actually our 'home'. It is ultimately this positive message that wins out, delivered in an impressive, experimental and bold website.

by Noel Douglas

TITLE OF THE SITE FORK Unstable Media v3.3 ❧ **OFFICIAL URL** http://www.fork.de ❧ **PLACE AND DATE OF DESIGN** Hamburg, August 1998 (redesign) ❧ **CLIENT** self-promotion ❧ **LANGUAGE** English ❧ **COPYRIGHT OWNERS** FORK Unstable Media **PRODUCTION** Nicole Kengyel, Sascha Merg, Jan Studt, Harald Oefverholm ❧ **EDITORIAL** David Linderman ❧ **CONTRIBUTORS** Manuel Funk ❧ **SCREEN DESIGN** David Linderman ❧ **INTERACTION DESIGN** Jeremy Abbett, David Linderman, Sascha Merg, Andrea Mittmann ❧ **SOUND DESIGN** Sascha Merg ❧ **ANIMATION/GRAPHICS** Jeremy Abbett, David Linderman, Sascha Merg, Andrea Mittmann ❧ **PLATFORM USED FOR DESIGNING THE SITE** Macintosh 75%, Wintel 25% **APPLICATIONS USED** Macintosh: Fireworks, Photoshop, BBedit, Freehand. Wintel: 1-4all, Homesite, Jdk

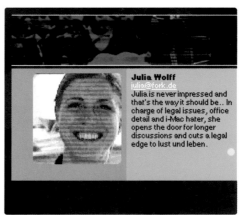

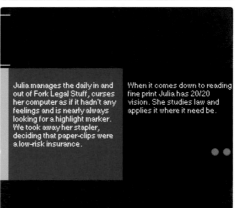

Clicking on the names in the Fork site's **staff list**, this small window pops up. Clicking on the dot in the right-hand corner of the screen makes the whole page shift right to left so that you can read more biographical information on your chosen employee.

Julia manages the daily in and out of Fork Legal Stuff, curses her computer as if it hadn't any feelings and is nearly always looking for a highlight marker. We took away her stapler, deciding that paper-clips were a low-risk insurance.

When it comes down to reading fine print Julia has 20/20 vision. She studies law and applies it where it need be.

The designers at Fork also have small sites where they experiment with layouts and graphics. Here are a few screenshots from the **'No-live-Operator'** site.

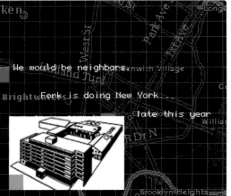

Fork are soon to set up an office in New York so, instead of just telling us about it, they've created a delightful small **Shockwave map** that scans over the city as you direct the mouse in a chosen direction. The translucent orange squares produce radar-like red dots as you go over them (complete with radar 'blip' noises) suggesting that information is available. And sure enough, clicking on the square unfurls an image and caption of various aspects of the city that we would share with Fork if we lived there too!

java applications   site navigation ▶ fork ▼

progress... manuel ++ david ++ jeremy ++ ralf ++ nicole ++ sascha ++ chris ++ anne ++ andrea ++ jannik ++ jan ++ anna ++ julia ++ room +++

View source

Fork programmed their own *java applet* to provide a different way of viewing the 'press reviews' section, aside from the html. This applet performs like *a browser within a browser*. Its interface works in the same way as a flight simulator. It can take some getting used to, but then not everyone's a pilot! When you're over a review, the line-drawn rectangular areas in the 'landscape' fill in and can then be clicked to access the review text. This is interesting, as it shows how applets can allow us to redefine the way we navigate through information within the same browser framework.

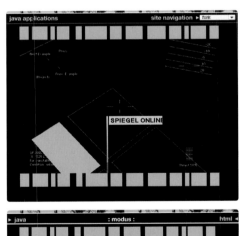

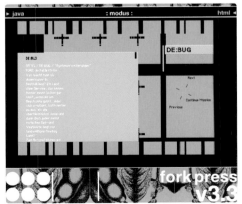

ART AND DESIGN EXPERIMENTS

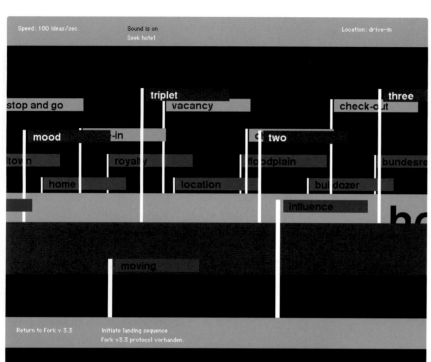

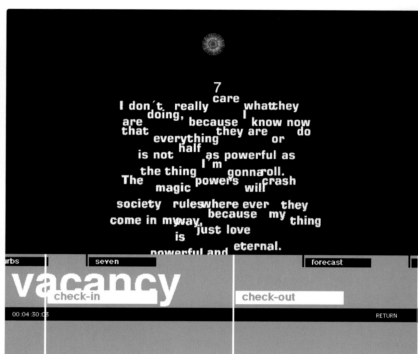

'Hotel' is an **innovative interface** where a series of layered 'flags' scroll past the browser window at high speed. With a good connection speed, this is highly effective as the interface is scalable to different screen sizes. Targeting a keyword on a flag takes you into one of the designer's personal narratives, which are mini-interactive pieces in their own right.

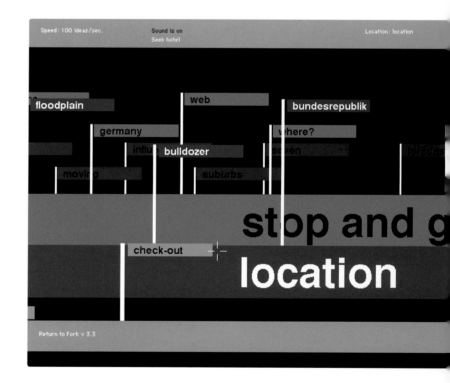

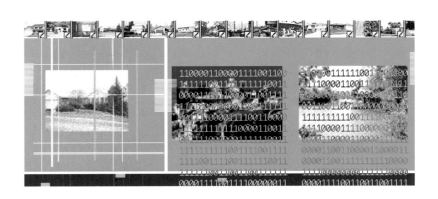

now i live in hamburg, germany
- in the bundesrepublik -

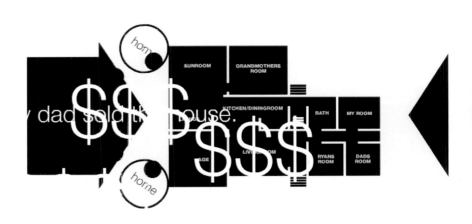

my dad sold the house.

$$$
$$$

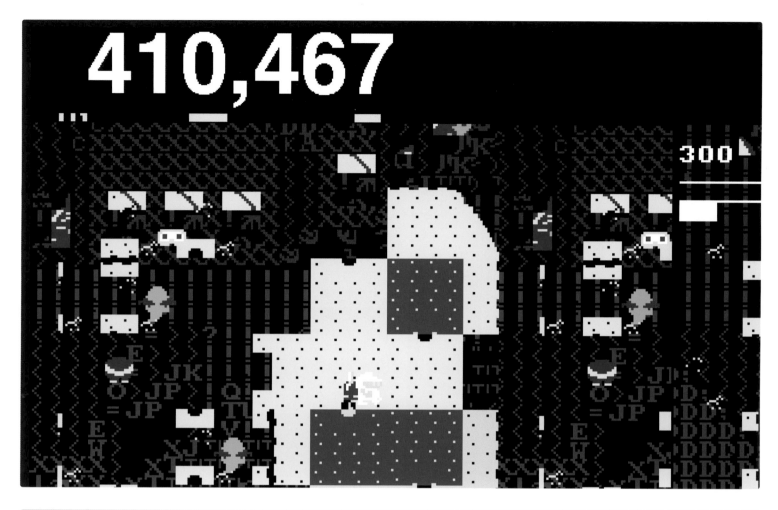

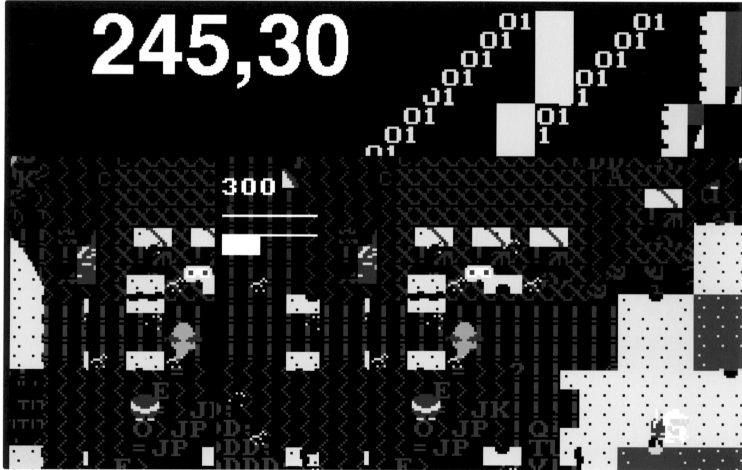

Jodi.org's design incorporates elements from the crash screens of a wide set of machines. This page, '100', with its wildly undulating 'score' figure at the top, evokes the impression of a **haywire arcade game**. What Jodi.org relies upon here, and throughout, is the resonance that such images have. Most of us have watched a video game crash, staring uncomprehendingly as its sprites dump to the screen in a sudden flurry, and thus the idiom is instantly set.

Other pages of '100' examine notions of space and mapping on the Net. These compromised **Cartesian grids**, accompanied by network and socket connection symbols, are covered by arrows pointing up towards **oblique vectors** and co-ordinates which seem to shift arbitrarily. Is '100' asking whether space on the network can be mapped, or is it again pointing out that, without a basic understanding of the network's operations, one representation is as useless as another?

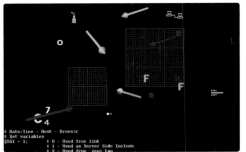 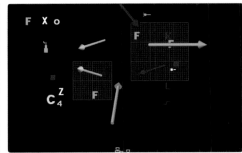

TITLE OF THE SITE Jodi.org ➤ OFFICIAL URL http://www.jodi.org ➤ PLACE AND DATE OF DESIGN http:// from:1995 ➤ CLIENT <!-no client-> ➤ LANGUAGE .html ➤ COPYRIGHT OWNERS Jodi ➤ PRODUCTION Jodi ➤ EDITORIAL Jodi

SCREEN DESIGN Jodi ➤ INTERACTION DESIGN Jodi ➤ SOUND DESIGN Jodi ➤ ANIMATION/GRAPHICS Jodi ➤ AWARDS www.rhizome.org/query [jodi] ➤ PLATFORM USED FOR DESIGNING THE SITE Macintosh 90%, Wintel 10%

JODI.ORG

http://*www.jodi.org*

Jodi.org positions itself as a thoroughgoing critique of Internet practice, deploying the familiar glyphs and signs of Internet protocol both as central components of its look and feel, and in order to test the conventions of coding, design and the organisation of 'content' on the Web. The site is assembled around the conceit of the malfunctioning interface, with the index pages taking their cues from crash screens all too familiar to many Net users. The front page, for instance, offers an ersatz 'Transfer Interrupted' message as a hyperlink; upon clicking, the visitor is taken to one of three wilfully obscure index pages, all of which take shape around a degraded, corrupted Cartesian grid, offering arbitrary hyperlinks with impenetrable and unhelpful titles such as 'MAP' or '404' (from the notorious '404 Not Found' error). It's a navigational system which mimics and parodies the often nebulous modes of sorting and accessing information on the Web at large, where visitors are left clicking more or less at random, not really knowing where they're going next.

What Jodi's oblique hyperlinks reveal, in fact, is a series of acute dissertations on the aesthetics and aestheticisation of the network's various transmissions. In '400' [http://www.jodi.org/400], the shivering lines of text which fill screen after screen once again play on the outward signs of machine meltdown; this is the other side of the Web, the side filled with error messages and hung systems, miles away from the gloss and polish of java-powered, Shockwave-enabled, style sheet-friendly browsing. Clicking (assuming that you can find the hyperlinks) just moves the visitor through page after page of incomprehensible script, which may or may not be real system error messages, java script, C++, or PERL. This use of code, or the semblance of code, plays upon the visitor's ignorance: we know that this is what makes the Internet work, but we don't quite know how. This can make a hunk of esoteric alphanumerics seem at once beguiling and threatening. Is it a sign that things have gone wrong, or that we're somehow seeing through into the workings of the Net? Jodi.org never lets on.

This same unparsable, corrupt code is also the central component of '404' [http://404.jodi.org/bcd/], which seems to lampoon the transmission of web-based bulletin board systems. Here, the visitor is presented with a long page of other visitor's posts, messages which lapse in and out of comprehensibility — not unlike, in many cases, the real thing. 'The secret is to write like this:' someone has written, 'v#w$ls ~r$ v#w$ls ~nd ...' — some secret. The 'Re.' button poised at the bottom of the page then asks visitors to respond to a code for which there is no key, to add their views to the garbage already up there — whereupon a (hidden) script quickly turns the response into gobbledigook. This critique of the threaded bulletin board system, which despite the rhetoric of interactivity that surrounds it is often put to work hosting unbelievably banal interchanges, is all the more amusing for its harsh unforgivingness. In fact, this is true of the whole site: while its scope does not extend to the offline world, Jodi.org is unfailingly acute in documenting and commenting upon the excesses, and the structured absences, of the networked domain.

by Jamie King

Another central component of Jodi.org is the use of IP addresses. Here, network information is displayed about what seems to be a LAN **(Local Area Network)**, complete with various routers and nodal points. But again, this is the aestheticisation of technical information, a schematic which relates to nothing, and which seems to laugh at our inability to decode it.

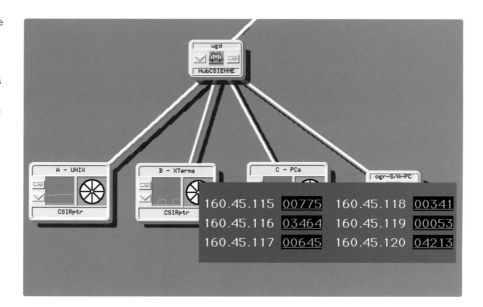

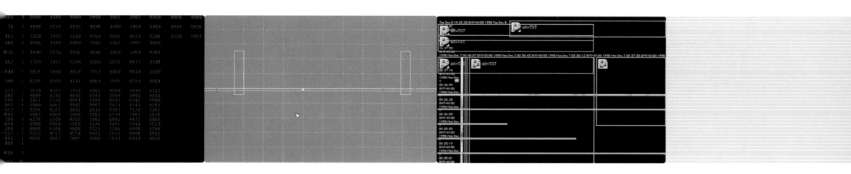

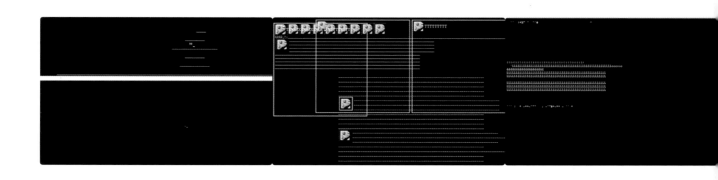

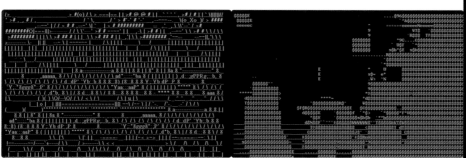

In 'location', the **aestheticisation of code** is played upon again, with the blocks of alphanumerics taking the form of archipelagos and islets, or stanzas.

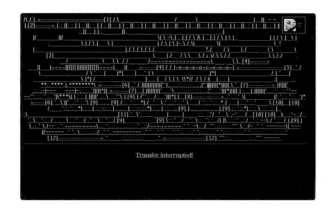

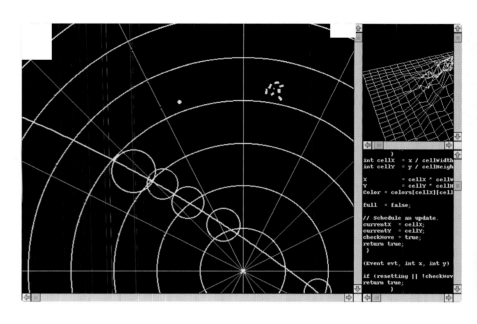

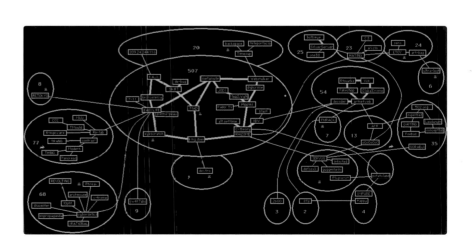

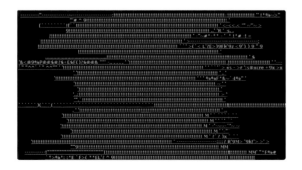

View source

The total **inversion of page and code** is exemplified in these ASCII drawings, which serve as source code for the rampant green type running across the screen.

The 'J-Buyers' site featured in the 'Play' section has a **moving navigation bar** that 'creeps' into the screen, reaches a certain point and then zooms back out at double speed. This makes connecting to the other screens in the site something of a challenge, particularly to the unsuspecting first-time user!

> LATERAL

Play*
Work~   *~;
Us;

Lateral Net Ltd > Winchester Wharf > Clink Street > London SE1 9DG > T: 0171 378 1011 > F: 0171 403 4586 > studio@lateral.net

Perhaps the funniest part of this section is entitled **'Benjy the Wonderdog'**, a small story of how one of the Lateral workers got booked by the police for carrying Benjy on his motorbike! The site also gives a good excuse for publicising the Battersea Dogs Home which Benjy comes from, and whose website Lateral has designed.

TITLE OF THE SITE Lateral ❧ OFFICIAL URL http://www.lateral.net ❧ PLACE AND DATE OF DESIGN London, Aug - Sept 1998 ❧ CLIENT Lateral Net Ltd ❧ LANGUAGE English ❧ COPYRIGHT OWNERS Lateral Net Ltd

PRODUCTION Lateral Net Ltd ❧ EDITORIAL Lateral Net Ltd ❧ CONTRIBUTORS Lateral Net Ltd ❧ SCREEN DESIGN Lateral Net Ltd ❧ INTERACTION DESIGN Lateral Net Ltd ❧ SOUND DESIGN Lateral Net Ltd

ANIMATION/GRAPHICS Lateral Net Ltd ❧ PLATFORM USED FOR DESIGNING THE SITE Macintosh 100%

LATERAL

http://www.lateral.net

In the dark days of the early to mid-nineties, before java scripts, dhtml and style sheets, Web design studio Obsolete was producing some of the first websites to combine cutting-edge interactive techniques with a street-smart visual graphic style. Lateral.net arises from the ashes of Obsolete. Thankfully, their studio site maintains and develops the high standards set by Obsolete by being not only an excellent portfolio of work, but also an interesting site in its own right.

Upon entering the site, a simple and clear introductory screen gives the user three basic options: Work, Play, Us. These are fairly self-explanatory: 'Work' shows a selection of sites completed by Lateral, 'Play' contains an assortment of personal sites, games, art and illustrations, while 'Us' contains a brief mission statement, contact information and a map of where they're located geographically.

Clicking on one of the options takes you into the site proper. The whole website works 'laterally', in a horizontal arrangement of three frames. The main frame in the middle always scrolls from left to right. Navigation is quite logical throughout: the bottom frame always contains contact info and links to the sections not being viewed. The top frame has links to the other sections of the part of the site which is presently being viewed in the main, middle frame. Each showcase site is opened in a new window when clicked. The 'Work' sites range in scope from cutting-edge dhtml experiments (such as in one of the Levi's sites) to more standard frame/html site designs (such as those of the National Gallery).

This is all interesting enough, but the real heart of the Lateral site is the 'Play' section, where the designers and their friends get to express themselves, experiment and generally play around. The work in these sections relates to the site as a whole in the same way that a sketch-book relates to finished artwork. It is at turns funny (as with the 'Benjy the Wonderdog' site), touching (parts of the 'J-Buyers' and 'Muthafuka' sections), interesting (a selection of games and toys made by Lateral) and experimental (for example, 'Sneaker Builder'). Here designer Siaron Hughes lets her trainer fetish get the better of her to create a game where you can build your dream trainer. Clicking on the various parts of the shoe allows you to choose the style, and clicking again chooses a colour. There is an artists' portfolio, where fellow artists and illustrators whose work sometimes features in the commercial side of the studio get to show their work. For instance, there are some excellent bold images from Tom Barwick and Pete Fowler that were featured in the sites created for Levi's. Surfing through the 'Play' section, you come to realise how important experimentation, be it visual or technical, is to the Web. It also shows how interesting it is to see this process exposed and given as much status as work for clients, which, to be fair, in Lateral's case can be just as experimental and playful as the 'Play' section — if it fits for the client.

It is this open, friendly and funky approach to the technology — as aware of its limits as of its potential — that makes Lateral stand out as a design studio. They treat design as a whole process, not just a finished product, and, to boot, they have an intuitive understanding of Web technology. The fact that they, like Obsolete before them, maintain this level of experimentation and put it to real use both at 'work' and at 'play' shows how technological and design innovation are as much about the 'attitude' as they are about the know-how.

by Noel Douglas

Introduction

Everything we do has something special about it.

What we produce wins awards, meets deadlines, fulfills pre-defined objectives, creates a big impact and keeps clients very happy.

Levi Strauss & Co.

Lateral were asked by Levi Stra & Co. Europe to rethink their e presence on the web. Since there have been a whole serie innovative launches that have firmly established the site as a effective marketing tool in its right.

T > 0171 378 1011 F > 0171 403 4586 studio@lateral.net

Lateral Net Ltd > Winchester Wharf > Clink Street > London SE1 9DG

Mail Play Work Us

>LATERAL

One of Lateral's interesting aspects is that while they very much use the latest techniques to accomplish their goals, they also aren't afraid of utilising older computing standards, **mixing the high- and the low-tech** together, and seeing what comes out. Here, good old ASCII text is used for the intro title to a selection of games and toys that Lateral have built.

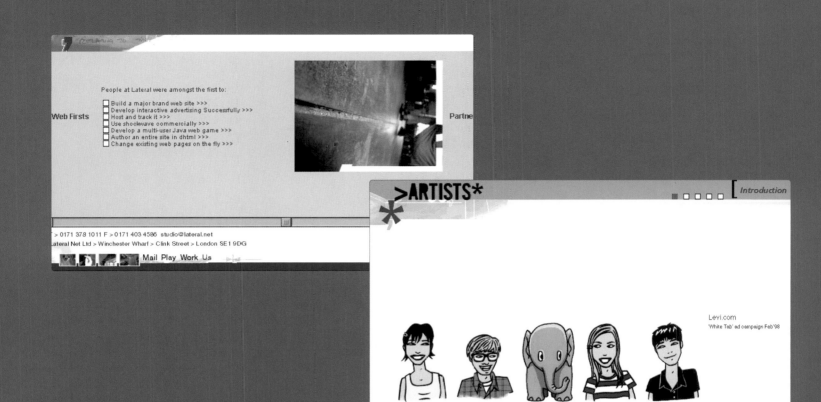

People at Lateral were amongst the first to:

- Build a major brand web site >>>
- Develop interactive advertising Successfully >>>
- Host and track it >>>
- Use shockwave commercially >>>
- Develop a multi-user Java web game >>>
- Author an entire site in dhtml >>>
- Change existing web pages on the fly >>>

Web Firsts

Partne

> 0171 378 1011 F > 0171 403 4586 studio@lateral.net
Lateral Net Ltd > Winchester Wharf > Clink Street > London SE1 9DG

Mail Play Work Us

>ARTISTS*

Introduction

Levi.com
'White Tab' ad campaign Feb '98

J-Japan < 1 > < 2 > < 3 > < 4 > < 5 > < 6 > < 7 > < 8 > < I have this feeling it's time to go home >

Another part of the 'Play' section, 'Muthafucka.com', presents an **intimate travelogue** of a trip to Budapest and the designer's thoughts on returning home to England, all accompanied by a user-controllable ambient soundtrack.

'Para-site' is a working proposal by Lateral for **a new Web advertising concept**. Users click on standard Web banners, but instead of being taken to the advertised brand's website, they are taken to a game page. From there, a back button appears to lead the user back to the 'original' site, but hidden from the user, the 'Para-site' has appropriated the code of the page and produced its own mock-up version! Altered of course, with advertising of the client's brand.

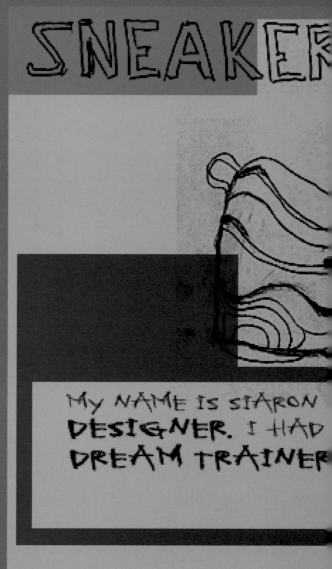

>ARTISTS*

Introduction] ■ □ □ □ □

Levi.com
'Tremor' ad campaign Feb '98

j-buyer
'Tom's Fe
Dec '97

DIGITAL STILL CAMERA DSC-F1

T > 0171 378 10 11 F > 0171 403 4586 st.dio@lateral.net
Lateral Net Ltd > Winchester Wharf > Clink Street > London SE1 9DG

Mail Play Work Us

>LATERAL

>> BUILDER >>

...HES, AND I'M A THINKER/SCRIBBLER.
...E IDEA TO DEVELOP YOUR ULTIMATE
...MAKING THE 'SNEAKER-BUILDER'.

View source

Java script *is used extensively in the Lateral site. Like their predecessors, Obsolete, they deploy it in the website in many interesting ways. Throughout this site, for example,* **navigation** *through the portfolios can be automated by clicking on roll-over buttons in the top right-hand side of the frame. When clicked, they whisk the middle frame automatically to the correct position, using some clever java scripting that works by tagging the middle frame in different places with co-ordinates that correspond to different positions in the frame; these then, in turn, refer to the different sites on view. One further touch is providing* **transportation functions** *with relative speed, which is based on the proximity of your desired site to the frame, relative to your current position.*

ART AND DESIGN EXPERIMENTS

Hygeia Revisited

In order to view *Hygeia Revisited* properly,
you need Netscape 4.05.
For the best result, please resize your screen
640 x 480 Hz before starting.

with special thanks to:
Chris Csikszentmihályi, Graham Frood,
Daniel Joliffe, Iliyana Nedkova, Peter Ride
& Mare Tralla

Supported by:

Hygeia Arcade

Beauty		Video
White Wash		Super Market
Happy Homes	**?**	
Feedback		Bridal Flesh

What is this?

The Hygeia Revisited site makes excellent use of java script to launch
the small 'Arcade' window — from here you can access the whole site, including
the clear 'What, how, who' section, which describes how the site originated.

Step Inside - Towards Ideal Beauty

These pages give a good feel for the fact that the site was originally conceived as a 'public' art piece. Here, passers-by use the touch screens to flip through the different sections, interacting directly through the shop window.

a b c d e

Telewest communications
all photos by Mare Tralla   See Manchester

a b c d e

Telewest communications
all photos by Mare Tralla   See Manchester

TITLE OF THE SITE Hygeia Revisited ➤ OFFICIAL URL http://www.channel.org.uk/hygeia/ ➤ PLACE AND DATE OF DESIGN London, UK / Tornio, Finland Jan. – Aug. 1998 ➤ CLIENT Commissioned by Channel / Artec (Arts and Technology Center), London

Supported by AVEK, Finland, Isea '98 / FACT (Foundation of Art and creative Techology), Liverpool, Root '98 / HTBA (Hull Time Based Arts), Hull, Arts Council of Finland ➤ LANGUAGE English ➤ COPYRIGHT OWNERS Tapio Mäkelä and Susanna Paasonen

PRODUCTION Godot oy / Tapio Mäkelä ➤ EDITORIAL Tapio Mäkelä and Susanna Paasonen ➤ CONTRIBUTORS Tapio Mäkelä and Susanna Paasonen ➤ SCREEN DESIGN Tapio Mäkelä and Susanna Paasonen ➤ INTERACTION DESIGN Tapio Mäkelä and Susanna Paasonen

ANIMATION/GRAPHICS Tapio Mäkelä and Susanna Paasonen ➤ PLATFORM USED FOR DESIGNING THE SITE Macintosh 100% ➤ APPLICATIONS USED Adobe Photoshop 4.0, Simple text, Netscape Communicator and Netscape 4.05, Macromedia Dreamweaver

HYGEIA REVISITED

http://www.channel.org.uk/hygeia/

Some of the most successful recent art projects on the Web have attempted to bridge the gap between a more traditional public art 'audience' and a Web audience. Projects like Susan Collins's 'In Conversation' and Simon Poulter's 'Hyperphilaterly' are but two examples that come to mind. Hygeia Revisited is a project by the Finnish-based media artists and researchers Tapio Mäkelä and Susanna Paasonen, originally commissioned by Channel and FACT in Liverpool as part of the ISEA revolution98 festival. It was intended to be seen in a 'series of seductive shop windows' in UK city centres, as well as on the Web.

The title refers to the 1876 utopian novel Hygeia — City of Health, in which Benjamin Ward Richardson suggested 'revolutionary solutions for abolishing the wretches of Victorian slums'. This information, which is easily found on the site, is important, perhaps indicating that Mäkelä and Paasonen's passion, at least with this project, may lie more with their activity as researchers than as media artists. The site sets out to question how issues such as ethnicity, gender and consumerism are constructed in a city space. It does this through a playful use of historical commercial images that centre around ideas of 'cleanliness', 'purity' and the overriding theme of 'whiteness'.

Generally, the site is designed with great clarity, employing simple java scripting to launch a small separate 'menu' window. It also supports the presentation of several series of images: interactive slide-shows based on themes such as 'Bridal Flesh', 'Happy Homes' and 'Beauty'. In addition to these slide-show sections, the site provides a section for feedback, a gallery showing the work as installed in Liverpool and Manchester, and a well-written introduction and information section. The photographs showing the piece installed with touch screens in Cyberia Manchester and Telewest Communications Liverpool give us some idea of how the work looked 'on the street'. Perhaps one criticism I would make of the project online is really pre-empted by this section — the choice of images and the way they've been manipulated is perhaps a little too repetitive and, at times, obvious. Yet seen in the context of a busy shopping street, among other shop advertising, they would probably work extremely well.

The work has obviously been thoroughly researched and was clearly laid out in a site plan. Good use of roll-overs in the slide-show sections make leafing through the images very entertaining. The manipulation of the images and the use of text obviously work better in some cases than in others. The user is at times drawn in by the humour of the work, but at other points is made to feel uncomfortable through clever use of interaction.

Mäkelä and Paasonen have spoken about the problems artists face while trying to deal with these kinds of 'cross-platform' public art sites. In answer to this, they've expressed their intent to develop further the site's feedback section. This would seem to be a potentially excellent development for the work — by showing feedback sent in throughout the project, the site's obsessive and entertaining 'archiving' could continue. At the bottom of the feedback page, the user is given the opportunity to send messages directly to the kind of companies that the site is attempting to question. Again, this move to extend the work beyond the actual site space into a more public arena further enhances its potential to question, narrowing down from the general theme of 'consumerism' to more interesting specifics and, in fact, pushing the onus back onto the user to continue the questioning process.

by Nina Pope

Each of the themes in the 'Arcade' offers a whole series of images which change as you run your mouse over them — either with contrasting images or the addition of texts. Clicking carries you through to the next in the series. These images are taken from the **'White Wash'** area.

North American handicraft tradition:
~ GRAB HER KNEES WITH YOUR MOUSE (OR CUT THEM OFF FROM THE CARTON)
~ DRAG THEM TO HER BOSOM, THEN DROP
~ LAUGH AT THE CLEVER TRICK, SHOW PROUDLY TO YOUR FRIENDS

North American handicraft tradition:
~ GRAB HER KNEES WITH YOUR MOUSE (OR CUT THEM OFF FROM THE CARTON)
~ DRAG THEM TO HER BOSOM, THEN DROP
~ LAUGH AT THE CLEVER TRICK, SHOW PROUDLY TO YOUR FRIENDS

North American handicraft tradition:
~ GRAB HER KNEES WITH YOUR MOUSE (OR CUT THEM OFF FROM THE CARTON)
~ DRAG THEM TO HER BOSOM, THEN DROP
~ LAUGH AT THE CLEVER TRICK, SHOW PROUDLY TO YOUR FRIENDS

Broaden up her
perspective with
a merry golliwog!

You can't bring up
a child in a safe

The addition of text to the images, as well as
the changes that occur as you roll around,
often provides a **humorous lure** into the
more serious questions behind the site.

At times, the apparent **'humour'**
involved in the interaction makes the
user feel even more uneasy about
the chosen material.

View source

Hygeia stretches the use of **layers**, a
feature of Netscape 4.x, to the limit,
while at the same time showing how the
limited use of one effect can work well
given good content. Effectively the layers
technique works by having some of the
images 'hidden' in layers around the
main screen image: moving your mouse
over a portion of the main image triggers
the script to reveal the hidden images,
thereby creating the impression that they
appear out of nowhere, when in fact they
were there all along.

MIRROR, MIRROR ON THE WALL..

make me fairest of them all

Let your mirror tell the story of beautifully fair hair. Use Hiltone and see how it makes your hair as fair as fair can be. See how Hiltone picks out the highlights and sets them dancing.

See, too, how natural your hair looks after using Hiltone. Hiltone your hair for the fairest beauty of all! For home users, 7/3. Obtainable from chemists and hairdressers everywhere.

To be perfectly fair

Hiltone YOUR HAIR

*The future opens up in front of you ~
an endless, joyous dance of matrimony*

*Make her happy -
Give her a HOOVER*

*How about some
feedback?*

Hygeia Revisited

Are you ready for tender Romance?

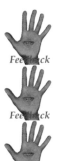

send feedback to:

The Hygeia Team

In all issues concerning the project: all suggestions, reactions, comments are very much welcome. The feedback recieved since September the 2nd will be published on October the 9th during Photo98. Please add your input and help us build *Hygeia Revisited* into a dialogical space of debate and shared ideas.

To Corporations and organizations

Some of the companies that have inspired our project are reachable online. You can also use this channel to give feedback to corporate representatives in issues of ethnicity, gender and marketing.

Robin Rive Gollywogs / Dolls & Bears   Paper   International Gollywog Collectors Club

The addition of a **feedback area** adds a further dynamic to the Hygeia site, especially when you notice that feedback can be sent to the corporations and organisations that 'inspired' the project, as well as to the actual Hygeia team.

"Why should I feel lonely while my husband is at work? After all, with this new fridge by my side, I am envied by all other housewives in this suburbia."

A happy user declares:
"This is a partner to be proud of!"

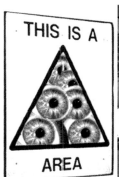

Make it White ...

Deep, Dark & Delicious!

Deep, Dark & Delicious!

Oh happy *future!*

Deep, Dark & Delicious!

THE WORKS

some of my favourite websites are

ART

CLICK HERE TO BEGIN

R H I Z O M E

Entrance to the site.

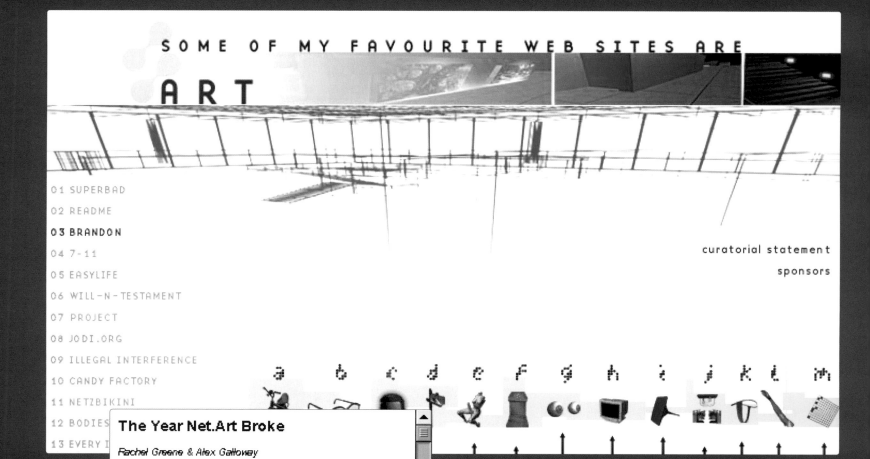

SOME OF MY FAVOURITE WEB SITES ARE

ART

01 SUPERBAD
02 README
03 BRANDON
04 7-11
05 EASYLIFE
06 WILL-N-TESTAMENT
07 PROJECT
08 JODI.ORG
09 ILLEGAL INTERFERENCE
10 CANDY FACTORY
11 NETZBIKINI
12 BODIES
13 EVERY

curatorial statement

sponsors

a   b   c   d   e   f   g   h   i   j   k   l   m

The Year Net.Art Broke

Rachel Greene & Alex Galloway

Our theme, "Some of my Favourite Web Sites are Art," captures an important truth about art in the twentieth century: for all the art criticism, museums, and galleries, it is still difficult to understand why something is called "art." Indeed it might seem that a web site is an unlikely candidate for this description. Considering internet art in general, we felt that even the most enthusiastic art fans might be turned off by the technical tedium of viewing art on the internet--sitting in front of a computer, dialing up the modem, launching a browser and waiting for plug-ins to load. The computer, net art's main tool, is an intersection of many different activities, from researching and word processing, to sending email and surfing cyberporn. Also, unlike painting or sculpture, internet art is not found in galleries, museums, or in rich people's houses. There are many aspects of this medium that seem out-of-line with our ideas and fantasies of what art is.

So then, perhaps the first thing to say is welcome to the underground! This is degree zero for the first new artistic medium since video. "Some of my Favorite Web Sites are Art" has an exciting mix. There are art projects that treat the internet as a canvas for creative expression, others that use it as a space for political activity and still others that treat the internet as one big Disneyland.

The duopoly of painting and sculpture is long dead. Today's net art, like offline art around it, has grown in response to the major developments of our times, including digital technologies, mass culture, visual media, biotechnology and the new capitalism.

Think of some of Warhol's famous images from the sixties, particularly the banality of his consumer products and newspaper clippings. Internet art has its parallels with Warhol's pop art: both tend to be defined by their mode of distribution and production;

Main screen. The gallery's virtual space is rendered through the scattering of lines and vectors throughout. Here, brief glimpses of the fantasy gallery space are presented in the ray-traced graphics at the top of the screen; below, the parameters of a vast virtual architecture are sketched in. Within this metaphor, the work on display is represented by three-dimensional objects: this sense of spatiality and depth is central to the site's strategy. Java-scripted roll-overs highlight the icons as well as the artists' names that link to the project-pages.

The **curatorial statement** is presented in a new window over the main page.

TITLE OF THE SITE Some of my Favourite Web Sites are Art ➽ **OFFICIAL URL** http://www.alberta.com/unfamiliarart/ ➽ **PLACE AND DATE OF DESIGN** Designed by Ken Lozowski. Produced by Rachel Greene. April- June, 1998. Project was conceptualized and created via remote

correspondence between Ken in Edmonton and Rachel in New York ➽ **CLIENT** n/a ➽ **LANGUAGE** English ➽ **COPYRIGHT OWNERS** The Works, Rhizome Communications ➽ **PRODUCTION** Rachel Greene and Ken Lozowski with Festival Executive Production by Vince Gaspari for The Works

EDITORIAL Rachel Greene and Alex Galloway ➽ **CONTRIBUTORS** jodi.org, Heath Bunting, Vanessa, Beecroft, Olia Lialina, Superbad, John Simon, Jr., Technologies to the People, Victoria Vesna, Eva Grubinger, 7-11 mailing list, Alexei Shulgin, KOGO/Candy Factory, Shu Lea Cheang.

SCREEN DESIGN Ken Lozowski ➽ **INTERACTION DESIGN** Ken Lozowski ➽ **ANIMATION/GRAPHICS** Ken Lozowski ➽ **PLATFORM USED FOR DESIGNING THE SITE** Wintel 100% ➽ **APPLICATIONS USED** Adobe Photoshop, Adobe Illustrator, Kinetix 3D, Studio Max, Ulead gif animator studio,

HTML – UltraEdit, Hexmac Typograph

SOME OF MY FAVOURITE WEB SITES ARE ART

http://www.alberta.com/unfamiliarart/

Some of my Favourite Web Sites are Art describes itself as 'a survey of Internet art'. It's a project which employs the spatial metaphor of a notional gallery space to organise a set of hyperlinks to net-based artworks. The value of the site's aestheticisation of the nominally neutral links page (surely familiar to even the novice websurfer) is immediately obvious: by ushering the visitor through a series of portals, the project succeeds in framing and contextualising the sites it points to, both by presenting them as objects within the spatial metaphor of the gallery, and — rather more slyly — by ensuring that the visitor at least glances through the texts by Rachel Baker and Alex Galloway which accompany the works on display.

This, in the final analysis, is the chief mechanism by which the site distinguishes itself from the wealth of links pages that already exist on the Web. Its merits lie in its ability to slow and shape the usually frenetic gaze of the websurfer (a similar effect, one realises, is achieved by spacing and layout in a 'real life' gallery) so that the works on display are granted an aura of significance, one which seems to exceed that of usual Web content. The basic formula of the site — offering relatively few hyperlinks of high content value, rather than (as with most links pages) many links of a relatively lower content value — should be one that will prove valuable to other web-based archiving projects. Links pages are, amongst other things, ad hoc exercises in curation, and offline galleries inevitably still have a few tricks to teach their online counterparts.

However, there is real a sense in which a project such as Some of my Favourite Web Sites are Art tests the notion of a 'real life' gallery, mainly through its obviation of the instrumentality of space in offline curation. One can feel this site's designers struggling to maintain a semblance of space through the vectors and lines which are used to designate plateaux and contours, interiors and exteriors — the gallery's virtual environs. One also senses those designers' reluctance to cede control of the work they're archiving: placing the linked-to sites in new windows (sans toolbars) ensures that the gallery space is shuffled to the back (and thus not left behind entirely) when visitors scrutinise the work.

Yet in spite of, or perhaps because of, these assiduous attempts at preventing gallery-clickers from escaping into the web-at-large, it seems inevitable that curatorial practice on the Internet must cede such control once the visitor clicks the final link. At this point, everything — the spatial metaphor, the textual analyses, the whole notion of the gallery — is left behind. Which, this exhibition leaves you thinking, can't really happen offline, where the works remain rooted in space, organised and structured according to the agendas of this or that curator. Of course, this is one of the many facets of the offline art experience that the Net artists have hoped to circumvent with their work online. I'm sure many of the artists featured here will be wondering how they've managed to end up in a gallery again, but in these early days of online curation, Some of my Favourite Web Sites are Art holds valuable lessons for future attempts: importantly, it is also a more-or-less precise snapshot of Net art as it is practised today.

by Jamie King

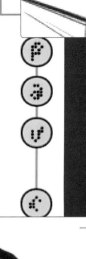

brandon

03 BRANDON

BRANDON
artist: Shu Lea Cheang

Brandon is an extremely ambitious and far-reaching project about living in one's skin (virtually, physically, or psychically). Over the course of one year, Brandon will be constantly 'processing': it has been designed with holes and loops, and with events and venues that will allow participants from all parts of the world and netspace to shape and author the project.

Brandon's central themes, the complex ecologies of gender, sexuality, are threads taken from the life of Brandon Teena/Teena Brandon, a (real) woman who lived and loved as a man in Falls City, Nebraska, USA. Brandon was raped and murdered in 1993 by two local men who discovered that "he" was a "she." Brandon (the project) will explore a range of spaces, from online multiple user spaces (like chatrooms or avatars) to offline spaces like the Theatre Anatomicum, a Dutch new media _____ experimental surgeries on prison ____

Brandon also has a certain symbo ___ site to be commissioned by the ____ production might signal a new ___

Portal page to Shu Lea Chang's **Brandon project**.
An animated GIF presents a rotating zoom-in on a virtual gallery building.

These final **portals** to the artists' work foregrounds texts by Alex Galloway and Rachel Greene. Though visitors are not obliged to read it in order to view the works, it certainly looms larger than the typewritten cards which usually accompany gallery exhibits. Offline, this practice might seem overbearing and bombastic, but online it serves to slow and focus the usually frenetic gaze of the websurfer.

Clicking one of the triangular icons above or below the central image will set a transitional flow of images in motion. The first image is deconstructed to give way to a ray-traced version of the next project's image. Mouse-overs will let you rub the fully rendered image into vision. The pages here represent **'Seven-Eleven'**, a collaborative e-mail project, and **'Easylife'** by Alexei Shulgin.

seven-eleven

7-11
artist: collaborative mailing list

Email is among the most important of all Internet developments for its ability to connect people around the world quickly. Email is generally the first Internet technology that people use, and is as such a basic, and increasingly common, mode of communication. Unsurprisingly, Internet art has a strong relationship with email–people who make Web art projects often participate in online forums to commune artistically, socially, and intellectually. 7-11, a spontaneous email project that started in September 1997, is such a community.

Email-based communities or discussions, also referred to as 'mailing lists,' work by having a central robot ('bot') to which all members of an email list address their posts (e. g. 7-11@mail.ljudmila.org). Whenever the bot receives an email, it is distributed to all those subscribed to that list. The bot also generates a header in an email's "subject line." For 7-11 the header [7-11] allows subscribers to distinguish 7-11 email from other correspondence.

7-11 subscribers share an interest in Internet art. A free-form, social ____

04 7-11

easylife

EASYLIFE
artist: Alexei Shulgin

Immediately upon visiting Alexei Shulgin's EASYLIFE, one gets the sense that he is very much at home on the Internet. Welcome to his house — don't worry about wiping your feet — the directive here is more ideological "You Better Subvert Yourself." The placards Shulgin has erected to "sponsors" Wired and Microsoft are faux and ironic — much of Shulgin's work satirizes Internet culture. Here, he takes aim at these two icons of market-driven Internet culture: he is after all a young Russian artist who, working and socializing online, can't avoid these American commercial.digital.culture giants.

Shulgin has always reminded me of a POP artist like Warhol or Lichenstein in that his work is consistently banal, light, conceptually strong, and generally media-centric — one of my favorite projects of his is WWWART (no longer available), an awards page that gave special awards to random Web sites that were not art projects but had an arty feel — similar perhaps to 20th century art's appropriation and recontextualization of quotidien images (think of Duchamp's urinal, Warhol's Soup Cans, etc.).

Shulgin doesn't rely on light aesthetic protocols or weighty ideas —

05 EASYLIFE

SOME OF MY FAVOURITE
WEB SITES ARE ART.

SOME OF MY FAVOURITE
WEB SITES ARE ART.

05 EASYLIFE

05 EASYLIFE

05 EASYLIFE

05 EASYLIFE

View source

The makers of this online exhibition have gone to great technical lengths to create a state-of-the-art gallery for Web art. The most eye-catching gizmo, of course, is the way each project's illustrations are built up while loading the info and are then deconstructed during the transition to the next project. This is accomplished by some advanced **java scripting in dhtml**. Looking at the source code, it seems that a little script called 'crazypieces' is responsible for the apparent movement of the image pieces. A roll-over then switches each image over to a fully rendered version.

All the **scrolls** in the site are automated by java scripts so as to avoid scrollbars within the actual screens. Most buttons are activated by roll-over scripts, loading extra info elsewhere onscreen or simply giving the user feedback by changing colour or shape. Even though the scripting is not completely bug-free and the site can wreak havoc on your browser when Web traffic is getting heavy, this site remains one of the more interesting examples of what java scripting can accomplish.

Apart from the java scripting, the use of a **restricted colour palette** should be mentioned. It's this choice of a limited number of colours that assures the crisp and clear appearance of the site under all circumstances.

jodi.org

JODI
artists: Joan Heemskerk and Dirk Paesmans

Still the oldest and best of the "browser artists," Jodi continues to crash, bang and boom around the insides of the internet. Jodi is the web site that makes you wonder if your computer is broken. Jodi loves the look and feel of raw code, using it often in their work. Joci.org projects are dominanted by text, and when images appear, they tend to disorient (or reorient) the user. Jodi's raw materials are text and image fragments, their templates the syntaxes of computer code.

Is Jodi just a bunch of hostile nonsense? I should hope so. If you look closely at the blinking screens, "system error" bombs and wildly animated images, you will see a keen interest in the browser itself as a focal point and structuring framework for art making. Jodi reflects directly on the nature of the web by using the web as art, not just the vehicle for art. Jodi pages are like machines that run on their own.

Jodi has two presences, web and email. In fact, since the beginning email intervention has been nearly as central to Jodi's artistic agitation as their well known web sites. Email bombs on usenet are old hat for Jodi. Cryptic, distracting, and sometimes chaotic, email

08 JODI.ORG

SOME OF MY FAVOURITE WEB SITES ARE ART.

The portal pages to the work of Jodi.

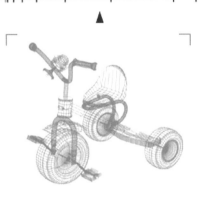

superbad

SUPERBAD
artist: Ben Benjamin

When I first went to Superbad I was stunned. How does he do that? I saw things at this site that I didn't think were possible without high-end browser plug-ins and a fast connecti... javascript or...

You will see ... culture, eme... And of cours... "browser ar... your web br... highly visua... viewer's att... programming... projects. It...

01 SUPERBAD

The portal pages to Superbad by Ben Benjamin.

01 SUPERBAD

05 EASYLIFE

05 EASYLIFE

05 EASYLIFE

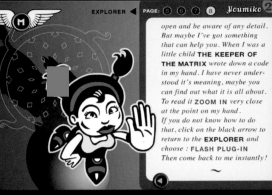

The menu page. Most buttons have two behaviours which can be accessed by either clicking on them or clicking and holding. The latter will normally reveal extra dialog boxes or speech bubbles.

THE SECRET GARDEN OF MUTABOR

http://www.yenz.com/menue/garden/

What do a crying squirrel, a fish with Pacman-shaped eyes, a bunch of snap rabbits and a beautiful queen have in common? Enter The Secret Garden of Mutabor and you will find out. This site, created by German designer Jens Schmidt, was born from a 'wish to create a webpage which allows things which are not usual for the Web, such as full-screen animations and big images, without the problem of bad Web resolution'. The chosen solution to this problem has been to use Macromedia Flash technology, the only feasible way a site with this quality of graphics could work over the Web and not fry your modem!

Upon entering The Secret Garden of Mutabor, we are confronted by 'Youmiko', our introductory guide into this beautiful and expressive puzzle game. It is here she tells us of the plight of the Secret Garden, and how its central source of life is the 'Heart of Desire', which cannot control its emotions and therefore must be kept in the only place where the heart will not overheat — the 'Castle of Ice' at the 'Frozen River'. But now the river is melting, which means that everyone could perish. Your task is to save the Secret Garden by finding the four pieces of code that will open the 'Gate of Serpent Zoom' while solving, in the process, the mystery of why the river is melting.

The Secret Garden uses clear, simple navigation and an extensive help system throughout, and though at times this can seem a little overbearing, on balance it makes the navigation clear and understandable. As Henry Ford once remarked, nobody ever lost money by underestimating the public! The Flash environment allows the site's users to forget the browser and become more immersed in the game. Buttons are reinforced by small sound samples, many of which are voices, and all of which have a feel that enhances the Asian, storybook-like quality of the illustration work.

Unlike many of the Flash sites on the Web, The Secret Garden has made good use of the extra element of depth available in the navigation by utilising the zoom in/out feature. This allows 'hidden' elements, such as clues and comments from the Garden's characters, to enrich the narrative while simultaneously creating a curiosity about the screens — What will I find if I look here? What happens if I go there?

Of course, making good use of prevailing tools is not enough to make a great site, and what really makes this site stand out is the beautiful and complex illustration work. It displays great use of colour and composition, which really bring the story's characters to life while at the same time managing to steer clear of the more clichéd uses of computer-rendering. This results in a warmth and richness that truly make it a visual feast. All of these factors combine to create a site that really stands head and shoulders above many others.

Although you get the feeling that the site is aimed at a younger audience, the fact that the help system is comprehensive and the level of difficulty is not too high means that adults could easily spend time with this and enjoy it. And without wishing to spoil your enjoyment of this site, it has to be said that in the end, the puzzle packs a cynical punch which belies its 'naïve' style!

by Noel Douglas

TITLE OF THE SITE The Secret Garden of Mutabor **✈ OFFICIAL URL** http://www.yenz.com/menue/garden/ **✈ PLACE AND DATE OF DESIGN** Milano, March 1998 **✈ CLIENT** Personal Project for my own pleasure and for advertising my work **✈ LANGUAGE** English and one audiopiece in Chinese **✈ COPYRIGHT OWNERS** Jens Schmidt (yenz.com) **✈ CONTRIBUTORS** Klaas Kielmann for help on HTML programming **✈ EDITORIAL** Jens Schmidt **✈ PRODUCTION** Jens Schmidt **✈ SCREEN DESIGN** Jens Schmidt **✈ INTERACTION DESIGN** Jens Schmidt **✈ SOUND DESIGN** Jens Schmidt **✈ ANIMATION/GRAPHICS** Jens Schmidt **✈ AWARDS** 1. Prize Adobe European Student Challenge 'Me my Idea' in the section 'New Media' 1. Prize (Absolute Winner) In the contest '36 ore di creatività' an Italian contest about Graphic Design, Webdesign, Illustration and CD-Rom-production 'The Lobby award, Best Creative Site' of the dutch online-magazine Lobby **✈ PLATFORM USED FOR DESIGNING THE SITE** Macintosh 100% **✈ APPLICATIONS USED** Macromedia Flash2, Macromedia Freehand, Soundedit 16, Adobe Illustrator, Adobe Photoshop

A comprehensive **help system**
backs up the whole of the site. Here,
the zoom tool help system is itself a
mini-tutorial, which teaches by doing!
But there are no dry, boring lessons
here, as 'learning' in this site still
manages to convey the humour as well
as the sense of play and discovery
found in the rest of the site.

View source

Interactivity and **narrative** are
often strange bedfellows. Normally one
discounts the other; if you interact, you
break a narrative flow. And yet, in The
Secret Garden, it seems that they've
achieved what generally shouldn't be
possible!

Using the **zoom-in** and **zoom-out**
functions to find some of the clues
within the site makes for a flowing
interaction which, instead of disturbing
the narrative, actually creates it, or
rather makes it visible. It's also amazing
to see how much depth this can lend to
two-dimensional illustrations (albeit, in
this case, some very well done two-
dimensional illustrations). It's not hard
to imagine this technique truly coming
into its own if it eventually becomes
more seamless, as Web connection-
speeds continue to increase. Altering
the depth of field could in fact be an
alternative to navigating through
different screens, and it all seems to
beg the question of why this function,
which potentially could be so rich, isn't
utilised more in other websites.

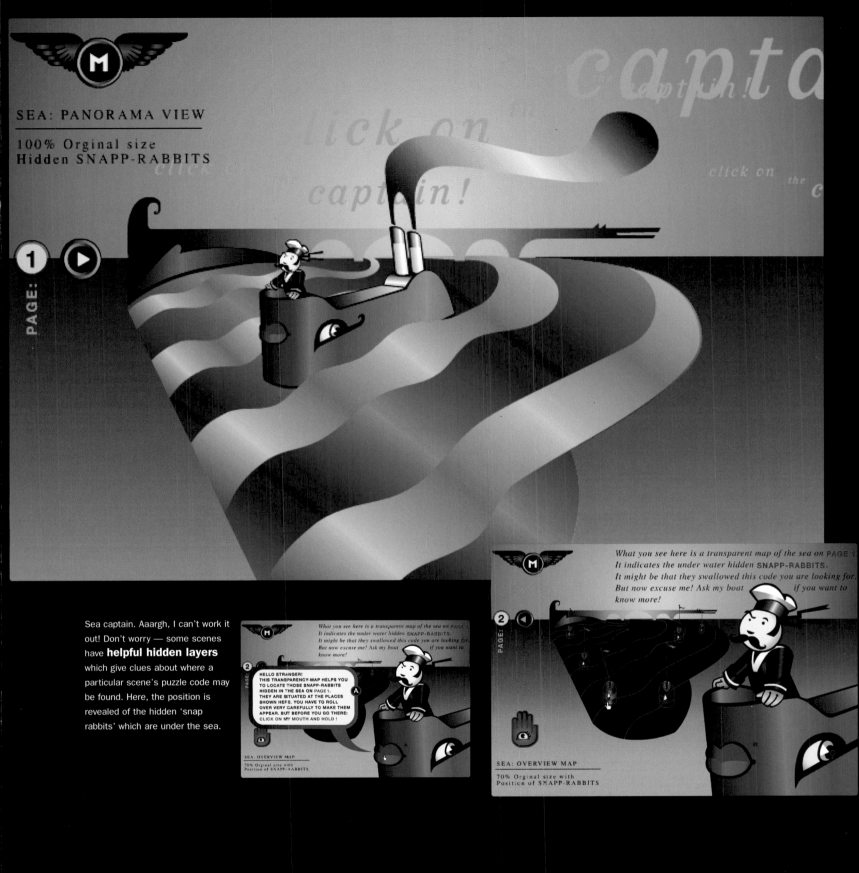

SEA: PANORAMA VIEW

100% Orginal size
Hidden SNAPP-RABBITS

PAGE: 1

Sea captain. Aaargh, I can't work it out! Don't worry — some scenes have **helpful hidden layers** which give clues about where a particular scene's puzzle code may be found. Here, the position is revealed of the hidden 'snap rabbits' which are under the sea.

What you see here is a transparent map of the sea on PAGE 1. It indicates the under water hidden SNAPP-RABBITS. It might be that they swallowed this code you are looking for. But now excuse me! Ask my boat if you want to know more!

PAGE: 2

SEA: OVERVIEW MAP

70% Orginal size with
Position of SNAPP-RABBITS

HELLO STRANGER!
THIS TRANSPARENCY-MAP HELPS YOU TO LOCATE THOSE SNAPP-RABBITS HIDDEN IN THE SEA ON PAGE 1. THEY ARE SITUATED AT THE PLACES SHOWN HERE. YOU HAVE TO ROLL OVER VERY CAREFULLY TO MAKE THEM APPEAR. BUT BEFORE YOU GO THERE: CLICK ON MY MOUTH AND HOLD !

SEA: OVERVIEW MAP

70% Orginal size with
Position of SNAPP-RABBITS

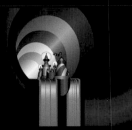

The Ice Castle page. By using Flash's **zoom-in and zoom-out** features, clues which are not readily apparent at 1:1 scale become visible; by zooming into

The **'Map' page** is the screen which allows access to the Garden's concluding scenes, provided that you find the correct codes within the other scenes. The code then has to be input correctly on the buttons in the middle of the page.

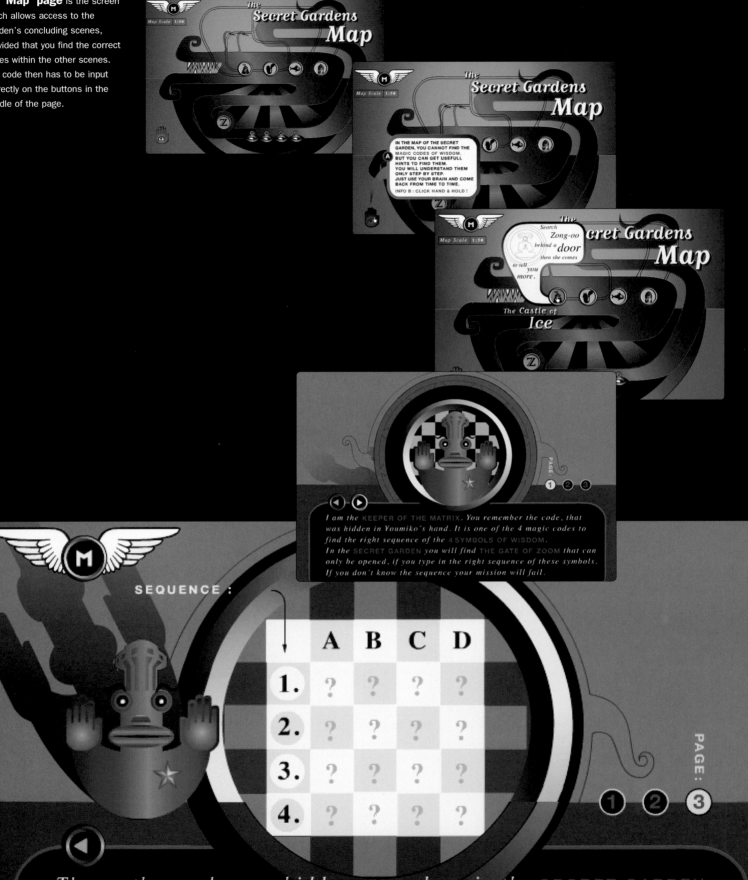

Three other codes are hidden somewhere in the SECRET GARDEN.
Find them, and come back to search the corresponding symbols!
Then go to the GATE OF ZOOM *and touch the* SNAKES EYES *in the*
right sequence to open the GATE OF ZOOM.
The MATRIX *already told you that you have to start with the first*
symbol "Yon" ⊗ . *Now leave me to find the missing codes!*

Why is Squirrel Scoiattolo crying? And how can you stop him? Well, you're gonna have to work to find out! Yes, it's time to **zoom in and out** again! This section is a good example of how 'layered' the site can be; the zoom is combined with dual behaviour roll-over buttons, animation and sound!

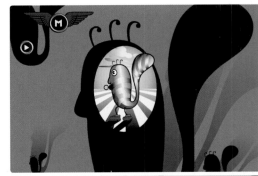

Click this button, to get the reward for saving the Secret Garden!

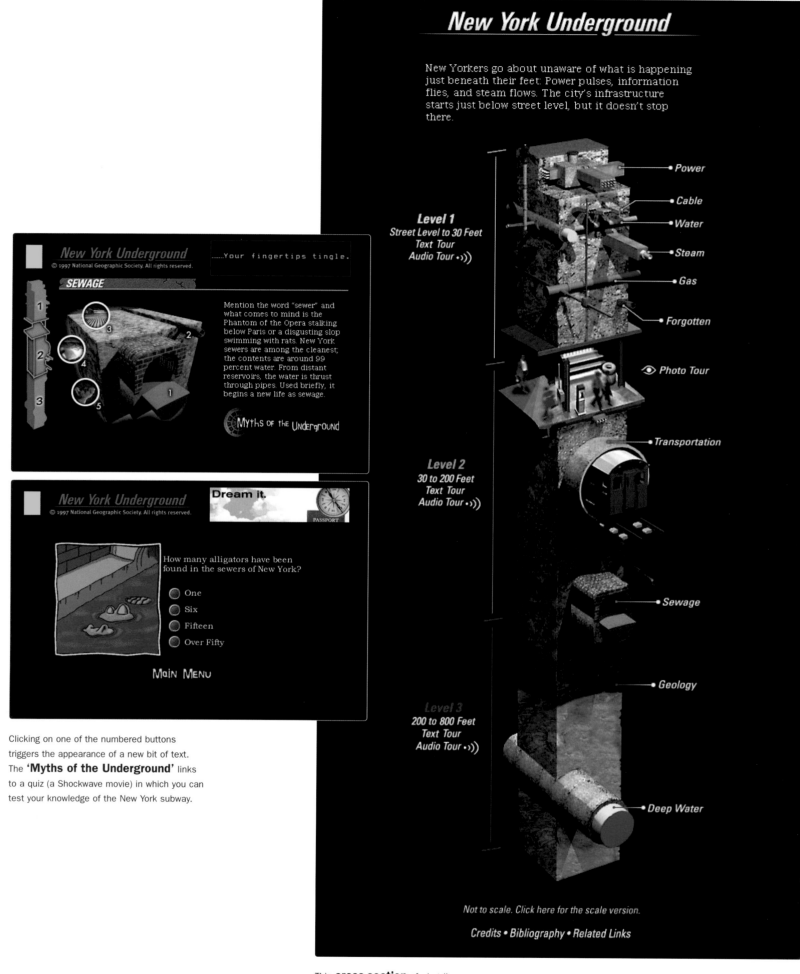

New York Underground

New Yorkers go about unaware of what is happening just beneath their feet: Power pulses, information flies, and steam flows. The city's infrastructure starts just below street level, but it doesn't stop there.

Power

Cable

Water

Steam

Gas

Forgotten

Photo Tour

Transportation

Sewage

Geology

Deep Water

Level 1
Street Level to 30 Feet
Text Tour
Audio Tour •))

Level 2
30 to 200 Feet
Text Tour
Audio Tour •))

Level 3
200 to 800 Feet
Text Tour
Audio Tour •))

Not to scale. Click here for the scale version.

Credits • Bibliography • Related Links

New York Underground

.......Your fingertips tingle.

SEWAGE

Mention the word "sewer" and what comes to mind is the Phantom of the Opera stalking below Paris or a disgusting slop swimming with rats. New York sewers are among the cleanest; the contents are around 99 percent water. From distant reservoirs, the water is thrust through pipes. Used briefly, it begins a new life as sewage.

Myths of the Underground

New York Underground

Dream it.

PASSPORT

How many alligators have been found in the sewers of New York?

- One
- Six
- Fifteen
- Over Fifty

Main Menu

Clicking on one of the numbered buttons triggers the appearance of a new bit of text. The **'Myths of the Underground'** links to a quiz (a Shockwave movie) in which you can test your knowledge of the New York subway.

This **cross-section** of what lies underneath New York is the starting point for exploration.

PLACE AND DATE OF DESIGN Midway / Tutankhamen: Washington D.C. | Alexandria LA. Underground: Washington DC | Marina del Ray CA. November 1996 - March 1997. Expeditions: Washington DC | Portland OR, 1998 ✈ **CLIENT** National Geographic Online / National Geographic Society

LANGUAGE English ✈ **COPYRIGHT OWNERS** National Geographic Online ✈ **PRODUCTION** Midway / Tutankhamen: Bart Marable, Raymond Simmons, Angela Nida Marable. Underground: Wide Interactive, Illustrator, National Geographic Interactive, Don Foley, Maria S. Bunai, Tim Stanton.

Xpeditions: Second Story (Brad Johnson, Julie Beeker), National Geographic Interactive (Curtis Hovey) ✈ **EDITORIAL** Midway / Tutankhamen: Michael Heasley. Underground: National Geographic, Don Foley, Wide Interactive. Xpeditions: M. Ford Cochran, Ted Chamberlain, Peter Winkler

CONTRIBUTORS Midway / Tutankhamen: Thomas B. Allen, Mark Thiessen, Valerie May, Peter Winkler, Linda Rinkinen, Paula Willard. Underground: Wide Interactive ✈ **SCREEN DESIGN** Midway / Tutankhamen: Bart Marable, Raymond Simmons, Michael Heasley. Underground: Trevor Elliott, Don

Foley. Xpeditions: Second Story (Brad Johnson, Julie Beeker) ✈ **INTERACTION DESIGN** Midway / Tutankhamen: Bart Marable, Raymond Simmons, Angela Nida Marable, Michael Heasley. Underground: Maria Bunai, Trevor Elliott, Don Foley, Tim Stanton, Mark Holmes. Xpeditions: Second Story

ANIMATION/GRAPHICS Midway / Tutankhamen: Bart Marable, Aleece Langford. Underground: Trevor Elliott, Don Foley. Xpeditions: Jim Ludtke ✈ **PLATFORM USED FOR DESIGNING THE SITE** Macintosh 50%, Wintel 50%

NATIONAL GEOGRAPHIC

http://www.nationalgeographic.com

Well-known around the world since 1889, a monthly magazine, a financier of geographical expeditions, maker of TV programmes about wildlife and nature, National Geographic has a reputation at stake. It has no choice but to make one of the best and most successful sites in the world. It is, after all, the largest non-profit scientific and educational institution in the world.

National Geographic's mission has always been to raise the level of geographical knowledge among 'the people', which now also means raising consciousness on ecological issues. The Web, as an interactive learning environment, a database of knowledge and a platform for discussion, fits their mission very well. So it is not surprising that National Geographic is serious about learning on the Web and learning through interactivity.

Behind the inconspicuous homepage lies a richness of single features about wildlife, polar expeditions, indigenous peoples and the like, coupled with a lot of encyclopaedic and cartographic information, additional links, forums for discussion. These features, which form the heart of the site, are composed by different designers. Every feature is a finished piece of work and has its own distinctive visual look. At first it seems that the site, risking visual chaos, is only held together by an ugly frame with the title of the feature, a yellow and black rectangle that links to the homepage, and the recurring use of advertisements. But when you spend more time on the site you become aware of a few conventions in the use of navigation and the distribution of content across frames and pages, conventions that return in almost every feature. It is these conventions that are also responsible for the site's feel.

Most features start with an intro before arriving at the actual content: text and images. Then the page is usually split into frames. Texts are kept short, and are distributed over several pages that are linked in a linear fashion. Every page contains general navigation for the feature as a whole, as well as navigation for the content. Another recurring trope is the use of separate windows for extra information or context.

The site's focus is obviously on interaction with content, with a didactic edge. The use of new techniques like dhtml and java is functional, aimed at transferring knowledge and involving the user in the experience of exploring a topic. The same holds for the use of RealAudio and the daily e-mail dispatches from journalists and explorers on a National Geographic-sponsored mission (at home you can follow their adventures almost live). This, together with the forums, makes it possible both to get connected and to feel a connection with the issues and expeditions.

It's a pity that the most well-designed features are often the ones that are the least interesting and important from an ecological and political perspective. There's also the danger that critical issues get frozen in beautiful pictures; in other words, all the criticisms that apply to National Geographic in general apply to the website as well. On the other hand, the geography teacher who's out of ideas for a lesson can turn to this website to find complete teaching programmes, including materials, questions to ask, and Web resources to make use of. There are printable maps (in easy-to-photocopy black and white) and other applications such as the World Viewer, where you can look at the world from different perspectives (e.g. political or cultural).

The children's features, already highly praised, are simple and colourful. Often a first person perspective is used in order to immerse you in the exploration of an issue and to let you find out for yourself, through trial and error, how the world is organised.

At the National Geographic website, you are an explorer of knowledge; you learn by surfing, reading encyclopaedic information or e-mail dispatches, looking at images, and playing with maps. It may well be that the Internet has made (factual) knowledge obsolete — what counts is how to use knowledge that anyone can find instantly. But really, not much can beat the good feeling of actually learning some facts, gathering insights and getting to know your geography. And that's just what National Geographic.com gives you.

by Arie Altena

How far will explorer Bob Ballard go to find
the lost carriers of the Battle of Midway?
Dive deep down to find out.

Ocean Surface

400 feet deep
(122 meters)
This was the depth to which
World War II U.S. and Japanese
submarines operated.

1,250 feet deep
(381 meters)
At this depth, the
Empire State Building
would be completely
under water.

1,600 feet deep
(488 meters)
Below this depth, sunlight
from the ocean surface
is not visible to
the human eye.

2,800 feet deep
(853 meters)
This is the depth of the ancient
Roman shipwreck Robert Ballard's
research team explored in the
Mediterranean Sea.

5,280 feet deep
(1,609 meters)
One mile.
Sperm whales often dive
this far in pursuit of
the giant squid.

6,600 feet deep
(2,012 meters)
Modern Russian nuclear-
propelled submarines can
reach this depth.

10,560 feet deep
(3.2 kilometers)
Two miles.

14,494 feet deep
(4,418 meters)
At this depth, Mount Whitney,
the highest peak in the
contiguous United States, would be
completely submerged.

15,617 feet deep
(4,763 meters)
The German warship Bismarck
sank to this depth in
the North Atlantic
on May 27, 1941.

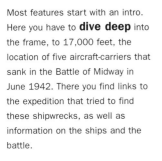

U.S.S. Yorktown
Height: 109 ft.

Depth 17,000 feet.

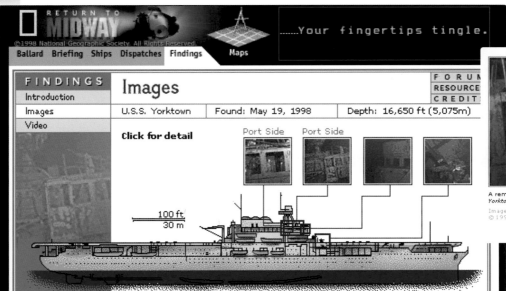

RETURN TO
MIDWAY

Ballard Briefing Ships Dispatches Findings   Maps

......Your fingertips tingle.

FINDINGS

Introduction
Images
Video

Images

FORUM
RESOURCE
CREDIT

U.S.S. Yorktown   Found: May 19, 1998   Depth: 16,650 ft (5,075m)

Click for detail

Port Side   Port Side

100 ft
30 m

A remotely controlled camera provides a glimpse in
Yorktown's aircraft control center.

close window

The feature about the **Battle of Midway**
has a distinctly graphical look.

Most features start with an intro.
Here you have to **dive deep** into
the frame, to 17,000 feet, the
location of five aircraft-carriers that
sank in the Battle of Midway in
June 1942. There you find links to
the expedition that tried to find
these shipwrecks, as well as
information on the ships and the
battle.

View source

In a site like National Geographic,
featuring as it does such an incredible
number of contributions from a variety
of writers and designers, it is of course
very important to develop a kind of
standard format. In this case the overall
layout is determined by an occasionally
complex set of frames. Usually,
one frame set designates the position
of the 'article' onscreen. This applies
particularly to the older pieces that
were designed for 640 x 480 screen
resolution, keeping them aligned centre-
screen in higher resolutions. Further
subdivided frame sets provide space for
advertisements, general site navigation
and, of course, the different elements
that make up the articles themselves.
Subdividing the information and
illustrations over frame sets definitely
makes these pieces more flexible and
interactive, and also makes the most
of the available space onscreen. More
recent contributions such as 'At the
Tomb of Tutankhamen' employ
advanced java scripting to keep
track of the user's whereabouts and
automatically update the appropriate
navigation menus.
     Of special interest is the use of
java applets, such as the one used
in the 'Xpeditions' section. This applet
provides a spatial menu for all of the
section's contributions. From an
interactive floor plan representing a
virtual Xpeditions Hall at the National
Geographic Society, the user can enter
a number of rooms which in turn give
access to the various contributions.
The applet highlights each room as it
is pointed to and lists its name and
contents below, thus providing the user
with the necessary information for
navigating this section.

This java applet first immerses the user
in a **virtual environment** that looks
suspiciously like an adventure game.
The idea is to activate a viewer to look at
different maps of the world. The diagram
at the right is used for navigating the
various rooms.

  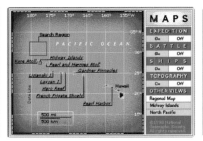 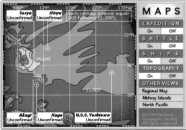

A map can sometimes tell more than a thousand words: here the user can call up **different layers of information** regarding a map of the North Pacific and Midway Islands.

The story about **the Tomb of Tutankhamen** is designed to look like a National Geographic issue from 1923. This feature is a good example of how this site's information is generally split up into sections, and how navigation is handled. The frame on the left contains the feature's general navigation, including credits, links and resources. In the yellow border you find links to the different parts of the subsection, in this case the actual story. Upon entering the tomb, the background colour changes to black. A picture of the tomb functions as an interface for further exploration.

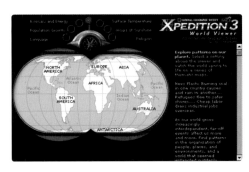 

The **World Viewer** gives access to different maps of the world. The switch on top toggles between topics such as population growth, language and religion. Clicking on a button at the right fills the empty map with information.

The handle on the left switches between three different projections, while the one on the right colours the map with either outlines, 'living earth', physical, or political information.

Look up 'calculator' in the index, and you'll be here in a click. Clicking on the telephone or Valentine typewriter will provide the viewer with a **close-up** of his or her choice.

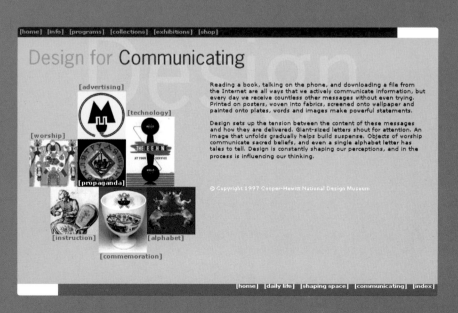

The opening page of the exhibit, showing the three main sections. In the top frame, the general navigation for the museum site always remains present.

This particular area offers an **array of atypical design notions**. An explanation of its relevance to the exhibition is necessary, and provided.

TITLE OF SITE Design for Life: A Centennial Celebration ❧ URL http:/www.si.edu/ndm/dfl/ ❧ PLACE AND DATE OF DESIGN New York, September 1997 ❧ CLIENT Cooper-Hewitt, National Design Museum, Smithsonian Institution ❧ LANGUAGE English

COPYRIGHT OWNERS Cooper-Hewitt, National Design Museum, Smithsonian Institution ❧ PRODUCTION Elisabeth Roxby, ROXX.COM ❧ EDITORIAL Website Editor: Julie Hathaway Keisman, Exhibition Co-Curators: Gillian Moss, Susan Yelavich, National Design Museum

CONTRIBUTORS National Design Museum Website Coordinator: Barbara Livenstein, Smithsonian Institution Webmaster: Peter House ❧ SCREEN DESIGN Elisabeth Roxby, ROXX.COM ❧ INTERACTION DESIGN Elisabeth Roxby, ROXX.COM

AWARDS Top Ten Websites, How Magazine - 10/98; High Five Award for Design Excellence - 11/19/97, Adobe Site Case Study - 3/98 ❧ PLATFORM USED FOR DESIGNING THE SITE 100% Macintosh ❧ APPLICATIONS USED Adobe Photoshop 4.0, Adobe Illustrator, Adobe Premiere, BBedit

DESIGN FOR LIFE:
A CENTENNIAL CELEBRATION

http://www.si.edu/ndm/dfl/

Elizabeth Roxby's Design for Life website supplements the centennial exhibit at the Cooper Hewitt Design Museum, celebrating 100 years of collecting. It constitutes one of several subsites within the museum's general website. The Design for Life site is structured to match the curatorial framework of the real-life exhibition. The website's uniqueness lies in its ability to present a plethora of material with simplicity, structure, technical virtuosity and a meticulous attention to detail.

The site begins with a homepage presenting three categories: 'Daily Life', 'Shaping Space' and 'Communication'. The notion of 'three' also sets the design context for the rest of the site. Compositionally, its frames follow the rule of thirds. Whatever margin the image offsets itself from, nothing hits the viewer dead centre. Compositional virtuosity is also clear in Roxby's choice of background colours. Olive drab, surgeon greyish-blue and mustard yellow backgrounds don't distract, but instead support the images that are either in front of or next to them, much in the way that the neutral colours of a museum wall do.

Roxby's site exemplifies classic html at its most articulate. Tables are used to collage images together and position the accompanying texts. Images fit together with jigsaw-puzzle congruency. Roxby has a great sense of positioning text on the page. Thanks to the use of Mathew Carter's Verdana font, which was designed especially for the screen, the text is always clear and readable. Most pages are contained within a single screen. Only a few pages require scrolling in order to experience the complete image or information. This single screen option is an aesthetic.

One can surf smoothly and quickly through the site. There are subcategories within the general topics. A Christian altar book can be found under the general topic of 'communication' and the specific subtopic of 'worship'. To find a Coca Cola storyboard, you have to go through 'communication' to get to 'advertising'. The homepage not only serves as a location reminder, but, upon returning to it, the viewer is also reminded of the context of the object within the exhibition.

The browsing process evokes the stroll you might take through an actual museum. The viewer is encouraged to skim before focusing on a particular item. Once an area of the site has been entered, a brief introduction explains the relevance of the particular subject before the actual exhibition items are viewed. You can wander, item by item, through the website as if it were a physical space. The options are continuous. Close-ups are provided wherever details matter. Explanations cut to the core, so that the surfer is never bludgeoned by info-overkill.

The site provides the opportunity to zoom in on details that you can only assume are Roxby's personal favourites. Her most extravagant re-creation is a page from an Alice in Wonderland pop-up book, in which the Cheshire Cat disappears and reappears. You could only experience this phenomenon more closely by interacting with the Cheshire Cat himself.

This site is, among other things, a research tool. With an itemised alphabetical index, designers, researchers, historians and collectors can find fabrics, fans and flashlights within clicks. It's unfortunate that such a valuable research resource contains no external hyperlinks. All links on the site are internal ones, connecting only to other areas of the Cooper Hewitt Museum's website. But even so, a researcher who finds it via a standard Internet search engine wouldn't necessarily need to look any further, let alone enter a real museum at all.

by Susanna Speier

Design for Daily Life

[dress]

"Nothing can be ascertained about Mrs. Brown, the owner of this magnificent shoe, except her name," records T. Watson Greig of Scotland. In 1885, seeing his outstanding collection of shoes age and crumble, he commissioned a book to document the lot, to which he added meticulous notes about the former occupants.

Ladies' Old Fashioned Shoes, Plate IX

T. Watson Greig Edinburgh; David Douglas, 1885

[flip through the whole book]

[women]

[open the book]

© Copyright 1997 Cooper-Hewitt National Design Museum

[next plate]

© Copyright 1997 Cooper-Hewitt National Design Museum

A shoe historian's dream — if there is such a thing. Anyway, here's the option of browsing through a 19th-century shoe collection, if you've ever wondered whether there were feet under those long Victorian skirts.

View source

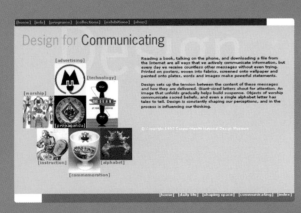

The computer within the computer. You get here through the communicating/technology geek link, of course.

*The first thing that strikes you in this site is its **clear-cut design**. In these days of absolute positioning through dhtml, it's wonderful to see this example of **classic html** layout. With the help of tables and the proper alignment, this can go a long way. Roxby has put together a clever combination of **background images** (the colour bars) and overlying **table structures** to make a layout collage, disrupting its rigidity by creating overlaps. The irregular shapes of her illustrations hide smart table constructions and transparent spaces in her images. It takes some confidence to split up a text element across multiple images (such as the images that describe the main sections on the homepage) and then paste them together by means of a table, especially considering that they have to be displayed in **exact alignment** with the colour bars in the background. Since tables don't behave very dependably across different browsers, this is very tricky indeed.*

Design for Daily Life

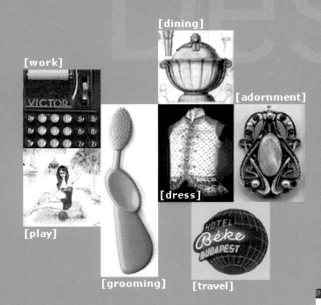

[work] [dining] [adornment] [dress] [play] [grooming] [travel]

We live our lives surrounded by objects, some hardly noticed, others cherished. Whether purely functional or beautiful to look at, the success of an object depends on the effectiveness of its design.

The objects we choose reflect our personal preferences. To one person a well-designed cup is one with a sturdy handle that is easy to grip. To another, a delicate teacup of fragile elegance is much more appealing.

These small, private decisions quickly become public statements of our personalities, backgrounds, and place in society. From the cut of our clothes to the tools of our trade, design declares our identity and lends meaning to the routines and rituals of our daily lives.

© Copyright 1997 Cooper-Hewitt National Design Museum

[next]

© Copyright 1997 Cooper-Hewitt National Design Museum

Design for Daily Life [play]

[games] [for your listening pleasure] [cocktails] [relaxing]

Both children and adults devise endless ways to have a good time. This gives the designer great opportunities to add wit, style, and charm to every variety of fun.

[home] [daily life] [shaping space] [communicating] [index]

This early version of a bartending course is a link from **'Daily Life'**.

Design for Communicating [advertising]

The most successful advertisements subtly, but constantly, maintain a presence in the consumer's mind.

[home] [daily life] [shaping space] [communicating] [index]

Design for Communicating [advertising]

M&Co. created these story boards to illustrate their concept for a television commercial for Coca Cola. Musicians and dancers transform the iconic bottle and can into musical instruments, playing on the function of the beverage containers.

Story boards
Designer: Tibor Kalman,
(b. Hungary 1949; active USA)
Renderer: Michael Wodkowski
Producer: M&Co. Labs
New York, 1992

Gift of Tibor Kalman, 1993-151-1

Watch the full storyboard in action
[quicktime, 1.1MB] [avi, 1.1MB]
[mpeg, 472K]

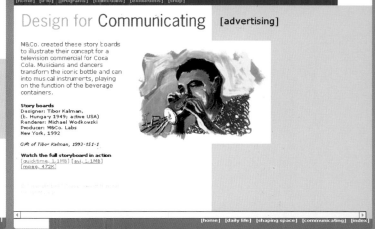

[home] [daily life] [shaping space] [communicating] [index]

It's hard to escape Coca Cola ads, even at museum exhibits. A **storyboard** shows how these things are dreamed up. The storyboards can be viewed in different formats.

WEDNESDAY
16th December 1998

BBC ONLINE

BBC Education

Online

BBC Homepage
BBC Site Map
Search

BBC Education

Homepage
Copyright
Help

Windrush

About this site
What is Windrush?
BBC Windrush Files
Windrush Community
Windrush Site Map
Coming Soon
Feedback
Credits
Home

Welcome to the Windrush Files

About this site
What is Windrush ?
BBC Windrush Files
Windrush Community
Windrush Site Map

Whats New   Coming soon

Welcome aboard the "Empire Windrush", this ticket is issued to those who wish to embark on a voyage of
discovery around "Black Britannia".

We hope that each port of call will enlighten, entertain and inform you.

Thank you for choosing the Windrush web site, and here's hoping you have a pleasant voyage.

TITLE OF THE SITE BBC Windrush ➤ OFFICIAL URL http://www.bbc.co.uk/education/windrush/ ➤ PLACE AND DATE OF DESIGN London, May 1998 ➤ CLIENT BBC Education Digital Media ➤ LANGUAGE English

COPYRIGHT OWNERS BBC Education. The Crown copyright passenger list for Empire Windrush (BT 26/1237) in the Public Record Office is reproduced by permission of the Controller of Her Majesty's Stationery Office

PRODUCTION Michael Bedward ➤ EDITORIAL Michael Bedward ➤ CONTRIBUTORS Arthur Torrington (Windrush Foundation), Stephen Bourne, HOP Ltd & Helen Denniston Associates ➤ PICTURE CREDITS Savana Picture Library Hulton Getty

SCREEN DESIGN Paul Mitchell ➤ INTERACTION DESIGN Paul Mitchell ➤ SOUND DESIGN Michael Bedward ➤ ANIMATION/GRAPHICS Paul Mitchell ➤ PLATFORM USED FOR DESIGNING THE SITE Macintosh 100%

APPLICATIONS USED Photoshop version 4, After Effects version 3, Freehand 7

BBC WINDRUSH

http://www.bbc.co.uk/education/windrush/

When the Empire Windrush docked in London in June 1948, it began Black people's mass migration to Britain. The Windrush website is a celebration of that transatlantic journey; it focuses on the African-Caribbean contribution to the formation of contemporary British citizenship and national identity. As part of the BBC's educational website, the site aims to 'enlighten, entertain and inform you about the achievements of African-Caribbeans over the past 50 years'. It also attempts to celebrate positively cultural differences, promoting an understanding of a general, shared, multicultural heritage at the same time as providing an opportunity for communication with the African diaspora living within the culturally diverse communities of Europe, the US, the Caribbean and Africa.

It is always a mistake, I think, to imagine that the new media replace older forms of media. Instead, the older forms of media become reconfigured as we view them from the standpoint of newer technologies, such as the Web. Windrush manages to show how new media and older forms of media begin to live together, cross-pollinating and forming new syntheses whereby one enriches the other. In this case, the BBC have used the Windrush website to enlarge the context and audience of the television show. The online aspect works in some respects as a variation on printed books and pamphlets that often accompany television shows of this nature, yet in this sense the network technology improves the ability to permeate the audience/producer barrier, and in so doing promotes a much more active, dialogic relationship between the two. Net users can help build the site by adding artefacts or sharing experiences and emotions, while the international aspect of the Web allows people from other countries (which may or may not broadcast the BBC) to join in discussions and give personal experiences of their lives in their respective countries. In the message board area, there are many messages from outside the UK, and what comes across from the comments is how touched people are by the site, and the way it has recalled memories and experiences for them. And this often applies to those who have never even seen the television programmes!

What impresses about the Windrush site is the depth of its content and its attention to detail, which shows a level of thought and consideration for the audience which is often lacking in sites that use more 'bells and whistles' to attract attention. There is, of course, material taken directly from the television programmes, but there are also sections that review relevant literature from well-known Black authors, specially commissioned poetry and book reviews, and a 'community' section which is in effect the 'engine-room' of the site, driving the main interaction with the Web audience: it contains a page for sending postcards, a contributory photo section, the message board, information on community centres and learning centres which arrange events in the UK, and links to every conceivable relevant organisation.

The BBC is in a unique position to use its substantial archives to enrich the content of a site such as this. This potential is perhaps best shown in the 'timeline' sections featuring radio and television programmes from different eras that are relevant to the audience and subject matter. 'Mouth' icons can be clicked to hear dialogue from some of the recordings, and it is easy to imagine (where bandwidth or developments in digital television allow) how archives like the BBC's could become more 'hypertextual' in nature, linking to specific subjects and 'given' contexts, created as much by 'the viewers' as by the production team. As such, in this site we may well be seeing a stepping-stone on the way to a redefinition of what the space between television and the Web is, and the possibility for an altered, more progressive relationship between producer and audience, audience and producer.

by Noel Douglas

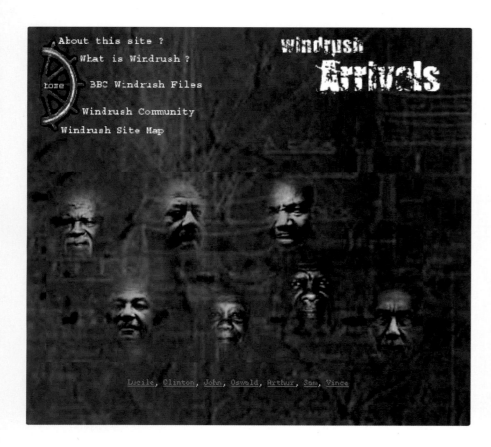

Lucile, Clinton, John, Oswald, Arthur, Sam, Vince

Being part of the BBC, the site's design is always considerate of the needs of users: here the producer responds to the complaint, posted as part of the message in the **message board**, about the slow downloading speed of the site's graphics, and promises to reduce their size.

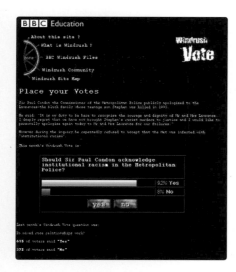

The site has a **monthly vote on issues** directly affecting the Black community in the UK. Here the issue of racism in the police force draws a strong response.

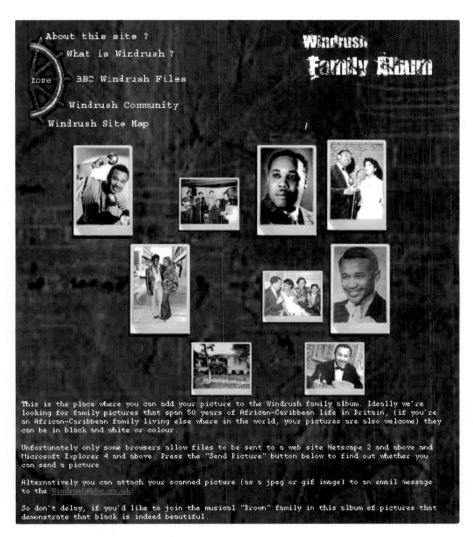

This is the place where you can add your picture to the Windrush family album. Ideally we're looking for family pictures that span 50 years of African-Caribbean life in Britain, (if you're an African-Caribbean family living else where in the world, your pictures are also welcome) they can be in black and white or colour.

Unfortunately only some browsers allow files to be sent to a web site Netscape 2 and above and Microsoft Explorer 4 and above. Press the "Send Picture" button below to find out whether you can send a picture.

Alternatively you can attach your scanned picture (as a jpeg or gif image) to an email message to the Windrush@bbc.co.uk

So don't delay, if you'd like to join the musical "Brown" family in this album of pictures that demonstrate that black is indeed beautiful.

Here users can share their **personal memories** of growing up in the UK by posting pictures of themselves and their families to the site, a nice reversal of the standard 'broadcast' model of the television programme.

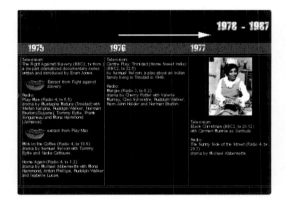

View source

*One consideration when designing a website is how to deal with media such as **video** and **sound**, especially since a large part of your audience might be viewing at home where downloading large files can take a long time; this can undermine the enjoyment of a particular site. To get around this problem, the **RealPlayer** plug-in has been used. It 'streams' the computer data 'live' from the server and, curiously enough (at least in regard to this site), it does so in a similar way to radio or TV broadcasts, meaning that the clip can be played as it is downloaded. In certain cases, the sound (or video stream) is actually live (as with some radio stations which also 'broadcast' on the Web) but in other cases it is pre-recorded (so that a clip is available on demand whenever people request it).*

RealPlayer works by adjusting the quality of the sound or video according to the speed of your Internet connection at that time. If the Internet becomes very busy for a moment, the quality will decrease slightly but will increase again when the load on the Internet has been reduced. To help with this process, RealPlayer builds up a small store of sound or video on your computer (known as a 'buffer') before it starts to play, thus enabling large computer files to run over slow Web connections.

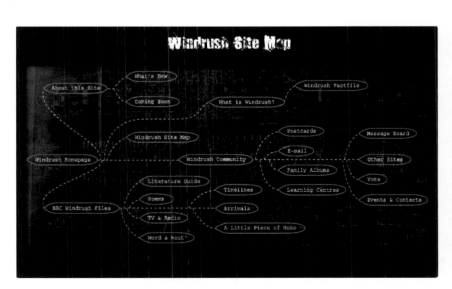

Often overlooked in the design of websites is the use of overviews such as this **site map**, useful if you're using a low-bandwidth connection or know exactly what you want to go to, as it's also a clickable map.

About this site ?
What is Windrush ?
Home — BBC Windrush Files
Windrush Community
Windrush Site Map

Windrush Arrivals

Ration books to-day

To-day officials of the Food and Labour Ministries will go down the Clapham shelter to issue identity cards, and ration books. It should have been done yesterday, but reception plans made by the Colonial Office went badly awry. After the Jamaicans disembarked at Tilbury, there was no one to direct them into the waiting buses. After about an hour a Government Press Officer had to do the job.

Daily Graphic
June 23, 1948

Back

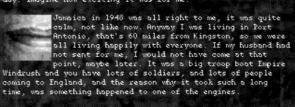

About this site ?
What is Windrush ?
Home — BBC Windrush Files
Windrush Community
Windrush Site Map

Lucile Harris

I come here in 1948 my husband sent for me. He and his brother came up a year before. I reached here the 22nd June, it was a lovely day, beautiful, and they were all at the dock waiting for me. I think it was Tilbury, I was very excited. The journey took 22 days, and that was a very long time. We enjoyed the journey, I was coming up to meet my husband, I was very anxious to come and meet him, because when he left we were just married, we got married and he left the following day. Imagine how exciting it was for me.

Jamaica in 1948 was all right to me, it was quite calm, not like now. Anyway I was living in Port Antonio, that's 60 miles from Kingston, so we were all living happily with everyone. If my husband had not sent for me, I would not have come at that point, maybe later. It was a big troop boat Empire Windrush and you have lots of soldiers, and lots of people coming to England, and the reason why it took such a long time, was something happened to one of the engines.

They went to Tampico and spent about 3 or 4 days there and after that we pass by Havana but we didn't dock. Then on to Bermuda and we spend another 4 days there, where we did land and the people there were very nice, they received us and they had a party and took us places. There were lots of men, more men than women, what I can remember now, there was a woman that stowed away on the boat, a woman you know, they found her and, she got VIP treatment, I saw her and spoke to her. She went to Birmingham.

When I come to England I live in Brixton, near the market. I tell you when I come here there were hardly any buildings standing and far as you can look it bomb and burn outright through and through. My husband sorted out a place to live, before he sent for me.

About this site ?
What is Windrush ?
Home — BBC Windrush Files
Windrush Community
Windrush Site Map

Windrush Arrivals

Stowaways section of the "Empire Windrush" passenger list highlighting Evelyn Wauchape a 39 year old dressmaker from Kingston, Jamaica.

© Crown Copyright: Public Record Office.
This document may be copied and downloaded for personal and research use only.
You must apply to the Public Record Office for permission for any other use

Stowaway Avrll got £50

Most popular girl aboard the Windrush was 25-year-old Avril Wauchope, pretty and dusky Kingston dressmaker. She was a stowaway.

Evening Standard,
Tuesday, June 22 1948

Back

Linking personal experience to the wider events of history could be said to be this site's 'theme'. Here some of the original passengers of the Windrush relate their stories, which are often linked to actual historical documents such as ship's logs and press cuttings from the era's papers.

Essential Books

The Essential Books of black British writing are the books which shook British culture. They introduced radical new voices and agenda, produced new movements and approaches to literature and raised profound questions about issues such as identity, gender, history, race, class, sexuality, and the role of the artist. They are also beautifully written texts, which capture the experience of a generation. Cultural critics and prominent literary personalities review them.

A House For Mr Biswas
Review by Kwame Dawes

To Sir, With Love
Review by Yasmin Alibhai-Brown

Second Class Citizen
Review by Leone Ross

The Buddah Of Suburbia
Review by Ann Ogidi

The Satanic Verses
Review by Pervaiz Khan

Yardie
Review by Tony Sewell

In The Castle Of My Skin
Review by Jacob Ross

Dread Beat & Blood
Review by Kwame Dawes

The Famished Road
Review by Jane Bryce

I Is A Long Memoried Woman
Review by Merle Collins

The Lonely Londoners
Review by Onyekachi Wambu

Staying Power
Review by Bernardine Evaristo

Particularly useful to the younger users of the Web are the resources that link to the history of the Black experience both inside and outside the UK. Here, significant **books by Black writers** are reviewed by various guest reviewers.

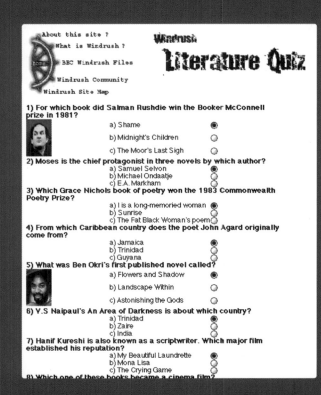

About this site ?

What is Windrush ?

BBC Windrush Files

Windrush Community

Windrush Site Map

Windrush
Literature Quiz

1) For which book did Salman Rushdie win the Booker McConnell prize in 1981?
- a) Shame
- b) Midnight's Children
- c) The Moor's Last Sigh

2) Moses is the chief protagonist in three novels by which author?
- a) Samuel Selvon
- b) Michael Ondaatje
- c) E.A. Markham

3) Which Grace Nichols book of poetry won the 1983 Commonwealth Poetry Prize?
- a) I is a long-memoried woman
- b) Sunrise
- c) The Fat Black Woman's poem

4) From which Caribbean country does the poet John Agard originally come from?
- a) Jamaica
- b) Trinidad
- c) Guyana

5) What was Ben Okri's first published novel called?
- a) Flowers and Shadow
- b) Landscape Within
- c) Astonishing the Gods

6) V.S Naipaul's An Area of Darkness is about which country?
- a) Trinidad
- b) Zaire
- c) India

7) Hanif Kureshi is also known as a scriptwriter. Which major film established his reputation?
- a) My Beautiful Laundrette
- b) Mona Lisa
- c) The Crying Game

8) Which one of these books became a cinema film?

About this site ?

What is Windrush ?

BBC Windrush Files

Windrush Community

Windrush Site Map

Word a mout'

Arrival

Help with Real Audio

Connie Mark (Former Auxiliary Territorial Service (ATS) Corporal)
"...they begged people. Come and fight for your motherland.."

Arthur Curling (Windrush Passenger)
"...I came to England in the airforce when I was sixteen..."

Luton Christian (Windrush Passenger)
"...this Empire Windrush they send it to Jamaica..."

RealAudio is used throughout the site for the reading of poetry, segments of radio shows, and for testimonies from some of the first immigrants to come to the UK.

Writers Biographies

Buchi Emecheta

Ben Okri

CLR James

Caryl Phillips

George Lamming

Joan Riley

Linton Kwesi Johnson

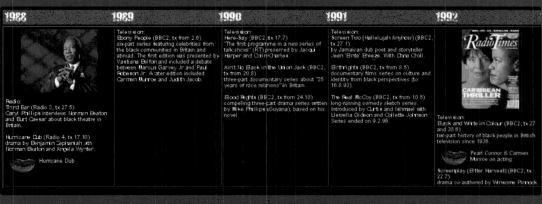

1988	1989	1990	1991	1992
Radio: Third Ear (Radio 3, tx 27.5) Caryl Phillips interviews Norman Beaton and Burt Caesar about black theatre in Britain. Hurricane Dub (Radio 4, tx 17.10) drama by Benjamin Zephaniah with Norman Beaton and Angela Wynter. — Hurricane Dub	Television: Ebony People (BBC2, tx from 2.6) six-part series featuring celebrities from the black communities in Britain and abroad. The first edition was presented by Vastiana Belfon and included a debate between Marcus Garvey Jr and Paul Robeson Jr. A later edition included Carmen Munroe and Judith Jacob.	Television: Here-Say (BBC2, tx 17.7) 'The first programme in a new series of talk shows" (RT) presented by Jacqui Harpier and Colin Charles. Ain't No Black in the Union Jack (BBC2, tx from 20.8) three-part documentary series about "25 years of race relations" in Britain. Blood Rights (BBC2, tx from 24.10) compelling three-part drama series written by Mike Phillips (Guyana), based on his novel.	Television: Screen Two (Hallelujah Anyhow) (BBC2, tx 27.1) by Jamaican dub poet and storyteller Jean 'Binta' Breeze. With Dona Croll. Birthrights (BBC2, tx from 8.5) documentary films series on culture and identity from black perspectives (to 16.8.93). The Real McCoy (BBC2, tx from 10.5) long-running comedy sketch series. Introduced by Curtis and Ishmael with Llewella Gideon and Collette Johnson. Series ended on 9.2.96.	Television: Black and White in Colour (BBC2, tx 27 and 30.6) two-part history of black people in British television since 1936. Pearl Connor & Carmen Munroe on acting. Screenplay (Bitter Harvest) (BBC2, tx 22.7) drama co-authored by Winsome Pinnock.

The educational nature of the site means that many of the documents available in the site are also duplicated in print, and although these features can be technologically 'hidden' in the formatting of the html, the design decision of making it an explicit link shows that all levels of users are considered, and not just the most net-savvy.

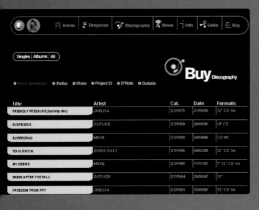

Selecting items from the discography, puts them into a **virtual 'bag'** which records choices that then reappear when the 'buy' section is chosen.

Chosen items which reappear in the 'buy' section can then be edited (by changing the format, for example) before being purchased or deleted.

Icons from **the main menu** at the top appear to the left of the main text signifying a link to the links page, plus individual tracks are highlighted in colour in the body of the text which link directly to the discography.

DORADO.NET

http://www.dorado.net

Dorado.net is the home of Dorado and Filter records, based in the famous square mile of London's Soho. The labels specialise in a crossover of rap, soul, jazz, rock and funk-flavoured music from artists such as D-Note, Jhelisa and Moke, and claim to aim at making records with 'passion and attention to detail'. Dorado.net is the creation of freelance designers Fabian Sasson and Tom Hingston, who translate the labels' aims into a clean, thoughtful and well-designed website which gives the impression of labels that take themselves, their artists and their customers seriously.

The homepage offers the choice of either a standard or an enhanced site. Although the design translates well in both versions, the enhanced site, as one would presume, contains a richer mixture of Web techniques. Clicking the enhanced version option launches this area of the site in a fixed-size window, a device that helps to maintain the design integrity of the user's viewing area. This is then cut up into three frames, the first being a menu bar which, as you would expect, links directly to all the main areas. A similar sized panel containing a Flash animation with the name of the particular section being viewed then appears, fading in with the look and feel of television graphics. This is a clever device, as placing the Flash within a frame means that the site can benefit from the quality of Flash's 'RAM-happy' animation techniques, but can still utilise html and java in other frames. And lastly there is the bottom frame, which holds the main content, be it more Flash (as in the illustrated story of the label) or more standard html tables (as in the discographies). Navigation is not restricted to direction buttons or the menu bar: colour-coding and icons are used throughout to provide a subtler, more intuitive blend. When looking at an overview of an artist's recordings, for instance, yellow 'tabs' containing the song titles lead to a yellow frame containing more detailed information, such as RealAudio samples of that particular track. Alternatively, icons will be used to cross-reference frames that are related in terms of content, as this gives the navigation a far more transparent quality.

As well as acting as a general promotional tool for the label and the artist's work, the site has a secure ordering system with some programmed intelligence. For instance, if you browse the site and choose to order certain tracks but then change your mind, your order remains active for one day, so that you can go to and from the site, adding items at will before purchasing. Ordered items can also be 'edited' before purchase, for example to change the format from CD to vinyl, or to alter the quantity.

Any record label worth its salt takes its listeners seriously, but on Dorado.net this is more than mere rhetoric: the site's users can mail their comments, subscribe to the Dorado.net e-mail bulletin, chat to each other within the designated chat room, and even add their own reviews of an artist's music or gigs! This is interesting, since what is so often forgotten by Web designers and their clients is that the Web always works best when two-way dialogues can be initiated. By giving the site and company this openness (everyone in the company can be contacted directly from the site via e-mail), the designers have shown that they understand what differentiates the Web from other media. Dorado.net, then, addresses the main concerns of a user interested in the label by means of artist and label biographies, press statements, track samples and mail ordering. It includes an attempt to foster a sense of label 'community' and mixes it with a tasteful, intelligent blend of Web techniques, all of which add up to a powerful example of the possibilities of contemporary promotional Web design.

by Noel Douglas

TITLE OF THE SITE Dorado.net ❧ **OFFICIAL URL** http://www.dorado.net ❧ **PLACE AND DATE OF DESIGN** London, October 1997 ❧ **CLIENT** Dorado Records Ltd ❧ **COPYRIGHT OWNERS** Dorado Records Ltd ❧ **LANGUAGE** English ❧ **CONTRIBUTORS** Ollie Buckwell, Roisin Duffy, Sam Sandell, Marc Waxman, Sasha Nixon ❧ **EDITORIAL** Ollie Buckwell ❧ **PRODUCTION** Fabian Sasson, Tom Hingston ❧ **AWARDS** Winner for Best Web Site Design, CAD (Creative and Design Awards) 1998 sponsored by Music Week, Macromedia Shock Site of the Day (SSOD) ❧ **SITE DESIGN & PROGRAMMING** Fabian Sasson, Tom Hingston ❧ **GRAPHICS & DESIGN** Tom Hingston ❧ **HOSTING & CONSULTATION** London Web Communications ❧ **APPLICATIONS USED** Macintosh: Adobe Photoshop, Macromedia Freehand, Macromedia Flash. Wintel: Adobe Photoshop, Macromedia Flash, Microsoft Office, Syntrillium Cool Edit, Allaire Cold Fusion Studio, O'Reilly Web Site, Real Networks Real Audio Client & Server ❧ **PLATFORM USED FOR DESIGNING THE SITE** Windows NT, Windows 95, Macintosh 30% Wintel 70% ❧ Freehand, Macromedia Flash, Macromedia Flash, Adobe Photoshop, Macromedia Flash, Macromedia Shock Site of the Day (SSOD)

Have your say! Perhaps the most interesting aspect of the site is the **response section**. In this screen, the labels' fans can publish their own reviews of an artist's work.

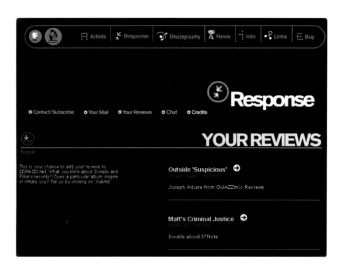

The response section also allows **a closer relationship between the label and its customers**. Here, label manager Sam Sandell directly answers an e-mail query from a fan.

View source

*The title page allows us to see how the splitting of the browser window into three frames creates a dynamic, **'cinematic' entrance** to the main sections of the site. The main graphic in the bottom frame appears first, with the label name, situated in the middle frame, following closely behind. As these become clearer, the menu bar finally appears in the top frame; this then becomes the only element that remains constant when you jump to other sections. Once the page has finished loading (which, with a fast connection, only takes a matter of seconds), the main graphic actually becomes a set of **roll-over buttons** which offer alternative navigation routes to the other sections. The overall effect is an excellent example of the dynamism of Web media, and cutting up the screen in this subtle, unobtrusive way means that, regardless of whether the technological content of the frame is Flash, java script or more standard html formats, the whole screen is neither too unwieldy in terms of its file size nor static in content.*

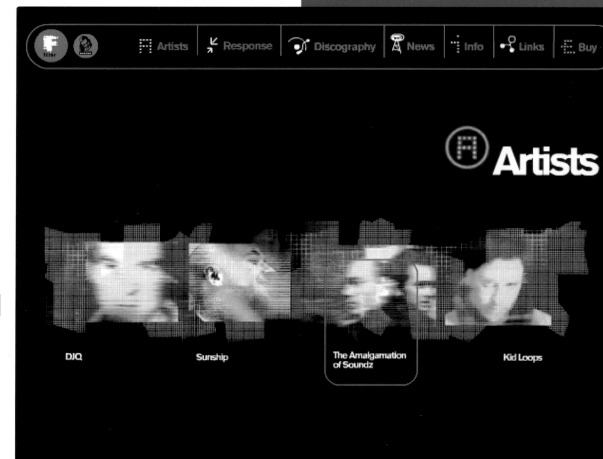

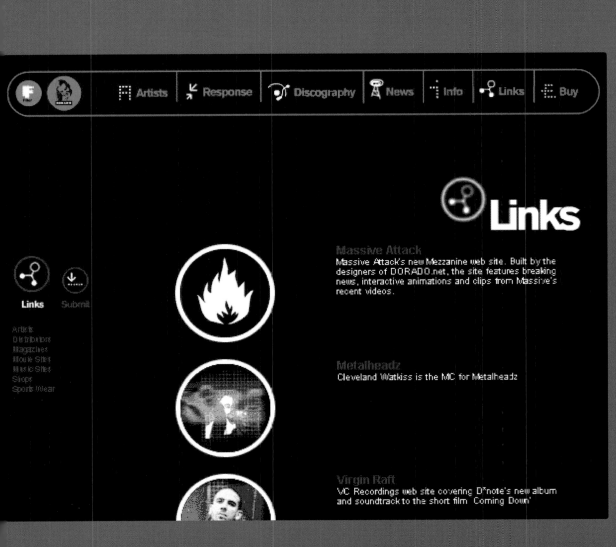

Artists | Response | Discography | News | Info | Links | Buy

Links

Links   Submit

Artists
Distributors
Magazines
Movie Sites
Music Sites
Shops
Sports Wear

Massive Attack
Massive Attack's new Mezzanine web site. Built by the designers of DORADO.net, the site features breaking news, interactive animations and clips from Massive's recent videos.

Metalheadz
Cleveland Watkiss is the MC for Metalheadz

Virgin Raft
VC Recordings web site covering D*note's new album and soundtrack to the short film 'Coming Down'

Unsurprisingly for a company that spends so much of its money on promotion, **artwork from the advertising campaigns** features heavily in the main European site.

This is the **site map**. As well as letting you know where you've been, it also includes the interesting addition of a search function.

PLACE AND DATE OF DESIGN Designed by Lateral, London. Both White Tab 'On the Highway' and Red Tab 'Tremor' campaigns, October 1997 - February 1998 ➤ **CLIENT** Levi Strauss Europe Middle East & South Africa ➤ **LANGUAGE** White Tab 'On the Highway': English, French, Italian, Spanish, Portuguese, German. Red Tab 'Tremor': English only ➤ **COPYRIGHT OWNERS** Levi Strauss & Co ➤ **PRODUCER** Lateral ➤ **PRODUCTION** Lateral ➤ **RED TAB** Creative Director: David Jones ➤ **EDITORIAL** Content on both White Tab & Red Tab: David Jones, Robbie Tingey, Valerio Martinez. Red Tab: David Jones ➤ **CONTRIBUTORS** Video in Red Tab: The Exploding Cinema ➤ **SCREEN DESIGN** White Tab: Robbie Tingey, Valerio Martinez. Red Tab: Henry Newton-Dunne, James 'Bigson' Gibson ➤ **INTERACTION DESIGN** White Tab: David Jones, Robbie Tingey, Valerio Martinez. Red Tab: Robbie Tingey, Henry Newton-Dunne, James 'Bigson' Gibson ➤ **SOUND DESIGN** White Tab: Robbie Tingey, Valerio Martinez, David Jones. Red Tab: Henry Newton-Dunne ➤ **ANIMATION/GRAPHICS** Illustration on White Tab: Peter Fowler. Flash Animation: Valerio Martinez, Robbie Tingey. Illustration on Red Tab: Thomas Barwick. Animation: James 'Bigson' Gibson, London Web Communications ➤ **AWARDS** White Tab 'On the Highway': Finalist in Consumer Goods category of 1998 London International Advertising Awards. Red Tab 'Tremor': Finalist in Special Award for Innovation category of 1998 New Media Age Effectiveness Awards, UK ➤ **APPLICATIONS USED** Director, Flash Shockwave, Photoshop, BBEdit. Red Tab: Hand coded dhtml! ➤ **PLATFORM USED FOR DESIGNING THE SITE** Macintosh 100%

Homepage

LEVI STRAUSS & CO. EUROPE

http://www.eu.levi.com

In 1997, Levi Strauss & Co. Europe asked the London-based design agency Lateral to revise Levi's presence on the World Wide Web. This complete project resulted in three sites: a general site (Levi's Europe) and two sites coupled to particular clothing lines, the well-known White Tab and Red Tab.

Entertainment conspicuously forms the main part of all three sites, with product information actually only claiming second place. This isn't unusual in itself, considering that everyone already knows what Levi's sells; after all, Levi's has been synonymous with jeans for several generations now. These aren't promotional sites, then, but rather sites that rejuvenate and reinforce Levi Strauss's image. Yet the three sites are considerably different in terms of atmosphere. The White Tab site, for instance, employs a cartoon style that recalls the hippie mood of the '60s. The Red Tab site hacks (wink wink) its way into computer game interfaces. The central site of Levi's Europe can best be compared with an art collection: the playful element is indeed present but is much more neutrally presented.

This latter site begins with two warnings: 'To start navigating, click ONLY ONE word or image' and 'Things Are Not Always What They Seem...'. Both of these instructions immediately arouse curiosity. Clicking further opens up a new window containing the site's main interface, which functionally most closely resembles that of a jackpot. It consists of two sets of four text buttons and four small icons which generate combinations of concepts such as 'style-info-advert'. Via this interface (which Lateral dubs a 'concept browser'), the $4 \times 4 \times 4 = 64$ combinations of concepts grant access to an equal number of small collages and movies. Several of the combinations — with 'info' being their central concept — load a short text and image into the main frame which have to do with a chapter from Levi's history. There's also a lot of interactive fun to be had at the site, thanks to Shockwave. In 'original-sounds-style', for example, you can use the cursor to direct a school of fish in a child's drawing, and also control the sound. Alternatively, you can download advertising spots from the site, etc. Eventually it becomes difficult to remember if you've already seen all the various bits, at which point it's wise to consult the site map. This can be accessed via the start window ('wild-info-time'). The site map doesn't provide an overview of the entire site, but rather keeps track of which bits you've already visited by means of whiting them out. Via the empty boxes, the unvisited features become directly accessible.

All in all, the site is a collection of various presentations and experiments, and thus the obligatory interface element, which here is a stable factor that always remains visible, is hardly a superfluous luxury. Yet the design of the symbols in the navigation icons also provides unity amidst the diversity. These symbols pop up on various pages, sometimes unexpectedly. A simple example is the bed with question marks you can find in the 'Help' function page. The 'Help' function, by the way, is unfortunately a bit concise. It's also a shame that the names of the makers of the site's mini-artworks are nowhere to be found.

Finally, the site does indeed contain a product information section, which is certainly worth checking out. Using the 'Fit Guide', for example, you can see the fit of the various models of jeans, a section which includes the use of Quicktime movies. The only thing still missing is the virtual fitting-room.

by Harry Roumen

These are some examples of the many Shockwave **games** available at the **White Tab site**, all complete with a 'groovy' illustrative graphic style. Clicking on the icons in the bottom part of the screen changes the game in the top half.

Ah yes, here it is... the postcard...

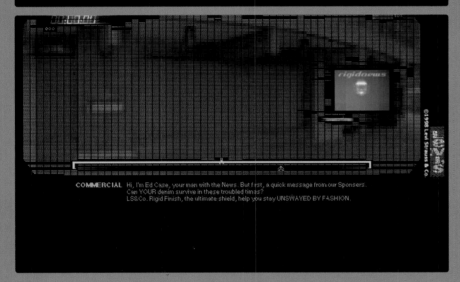

Tremor is the first **dhtml** experiment which Levi's
implemented. These screens show the view through the
'head-mounted display' supposedly being worn by the
user. Movement is accomplished by moving the mouse left
and right. In some parts, the 'transmission' button starts
to flash when clicked. It then reveals a small video screen
showing all manner of weird creatures about to descend
on the unsuspecting user if he or she doesn't act quickly.

Take a trip with the White Tab crew
across Europe in this Flash movie
extravaganza!

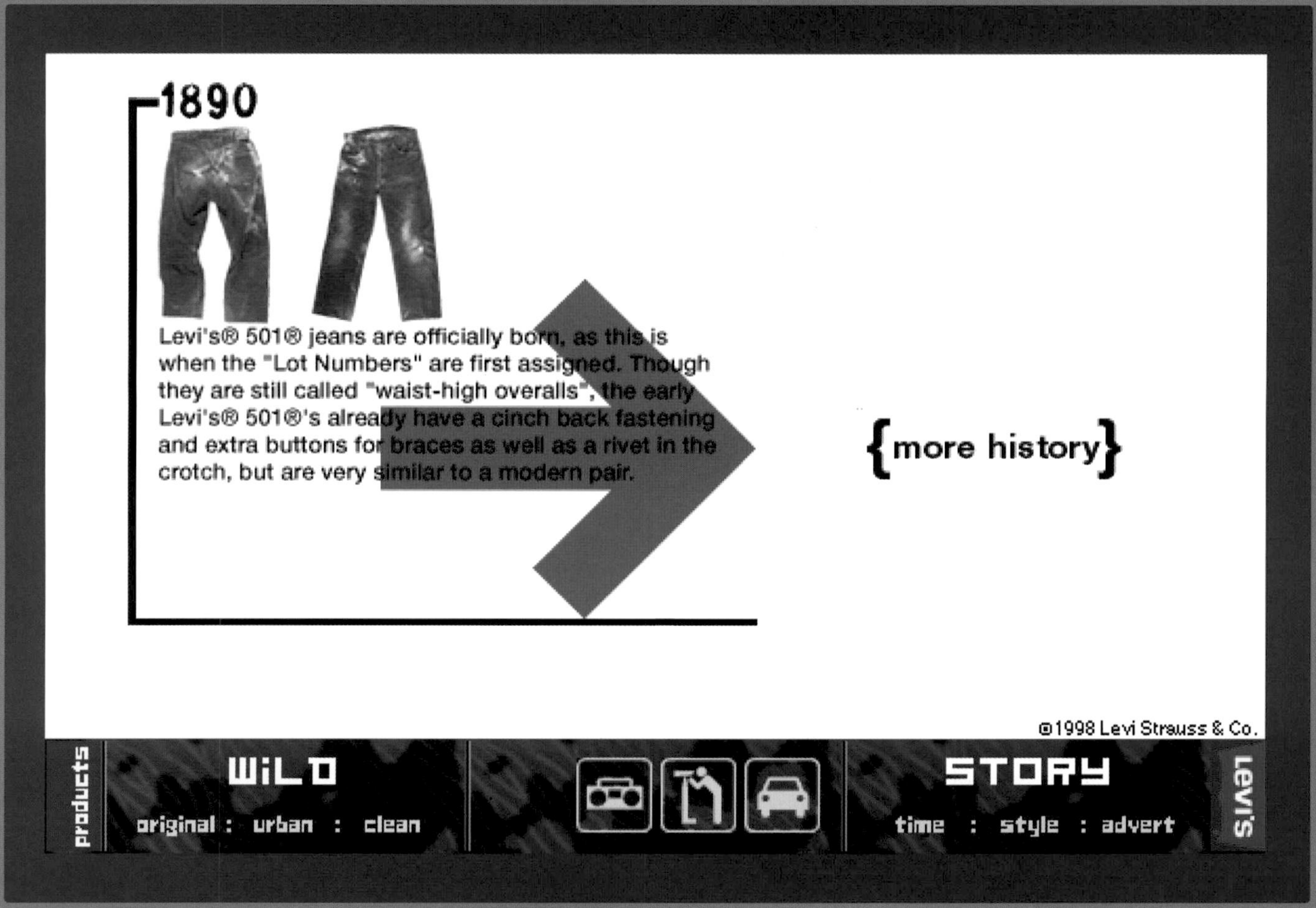

1890

Levi's® 501® jeans are officially born, as this is when the "Lot Numbers" are first assigned. Though they are still called "waist-high overalls", the early Levi's® 501®'s already have a cinch back fastening and extra buttons for braces as well as a rivet in the crotch, but are very similar to a modern pair.

{more history}

products

WiLD

original : urban : clean

STORY

time : style : advert

LEVi'S

The Levi's site uses many techniques to sell both itself and its jeans. One of the most interesting techniques is the use of Apple's **Quicktime VR technology** to view 360° images of the various cuts of their jeans. The browser treats the Quicktime VR movie like any other Quicktime movie, but what distinguishes a Quicktime VR movie is its ability to show what appear to be panoramas, or complete rotations, of scenes or objects, and to let the user control the movement in or around the movie. Yet the movies aren't really three-dimensional; in fact, the software cleverly processes and stitches together a series of still images taken from different angles to make them appear as a homogenous space in which you can move around. Not many sites have used this tool as anything more than a gimmick, but here Lateral have utilised it in a way that makes sense, adding to the site's usefulness for the user.

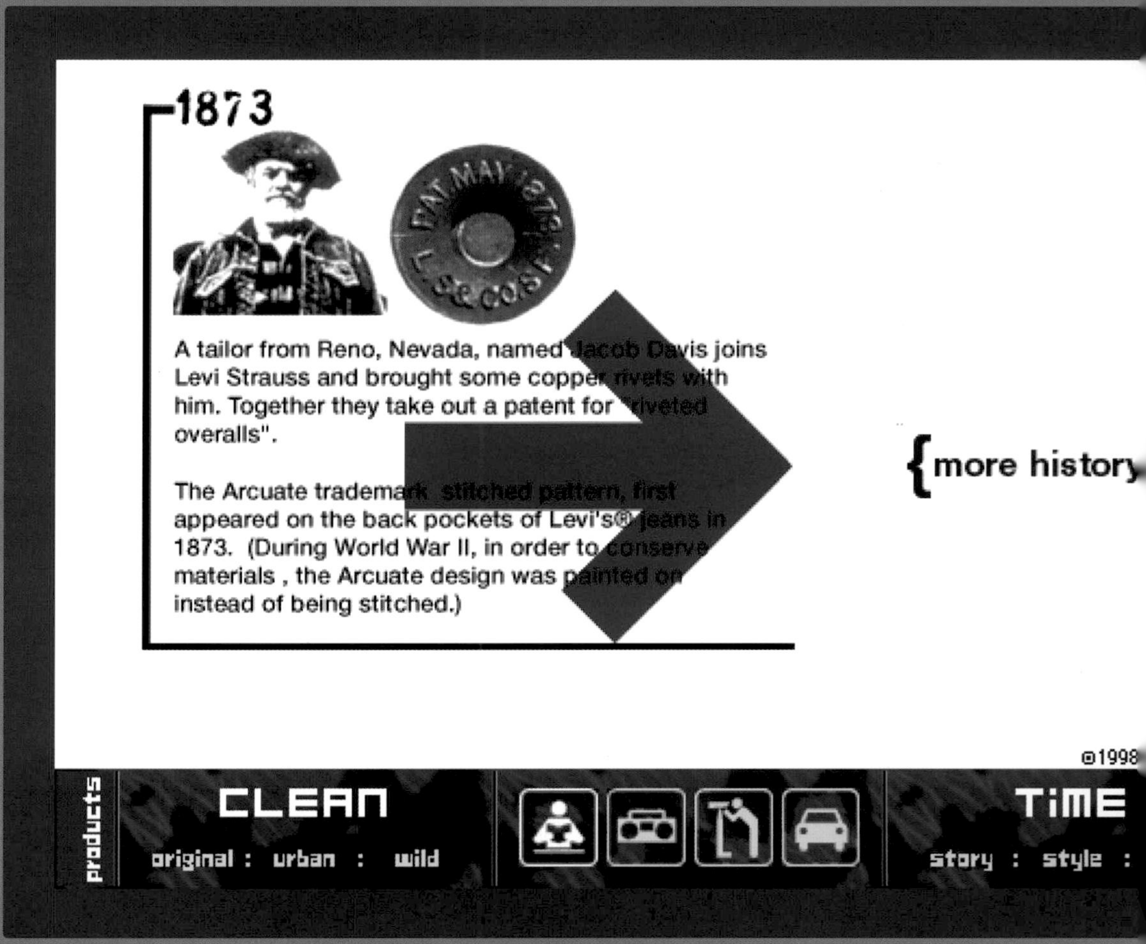

1873

A tailor from Reno, Nevada, named Jacob Davis joins Levi Strauss and brought some copper rivets with him. Together they take out a patent for "riveted overalls".

The Arcuate trademark stitched pattern, first appeared on the back pockets of Levi's® jeans in 1873. (During World War II, in order to conserve materials , the Arcuate design was painted on instead of being stitched.)

products

CLEAN

original : urban : wild

TiME

story : style :

Want to know when Levi's started?
This and other assorted trivia from
Levi's past is revealed in the
'History' section's timelines.

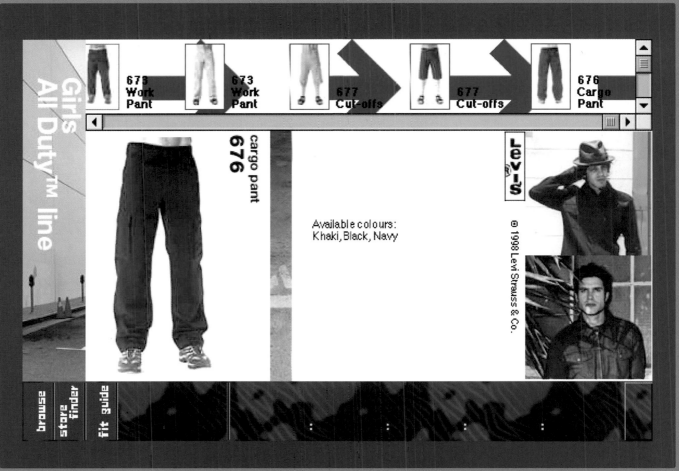

It's not all fun and games: Levi's makes jeans, too! Here you can view all of **the different fits** with the help of Apple's Quicktime VR software, which allows you a 360-degree view of the clothes.

Roll-overs activate the buttons and turn them into **expanding menus**. The menu expands forward in the direction of your movement, branching off into submenus.

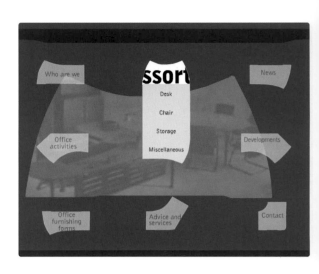

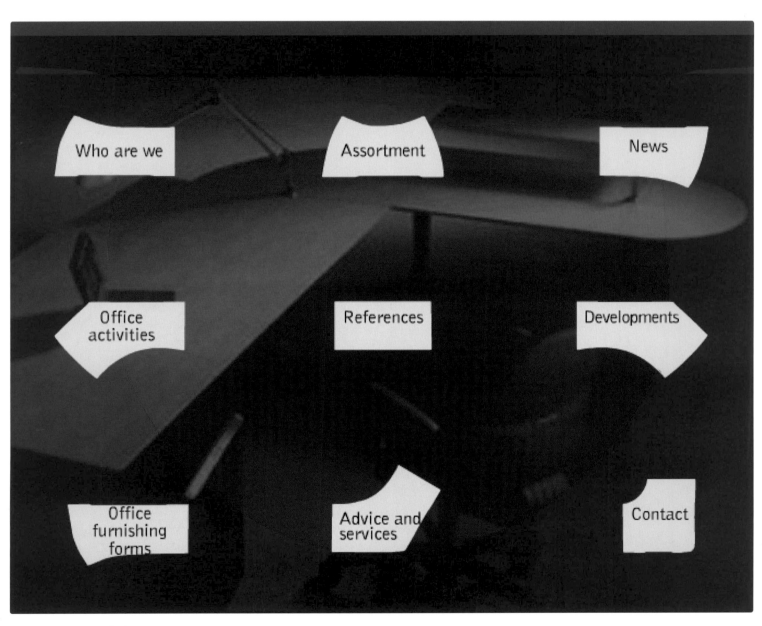

The Gispen site's **opening screen**. Arranged like an office layout, buttons shaped like desktops designate the various sections. In the background, composed of transparent layers of different colours, an example of Gispen office furnishings can be seen.

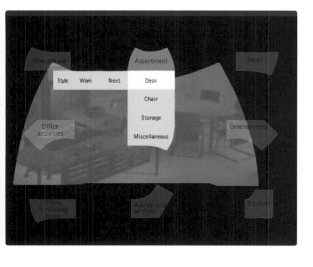
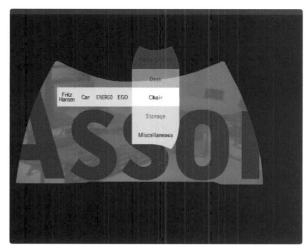

GISPEN

http://www.gispen.com

Innovations in information technology change the way people work as well as the environments they work in: this remarkably accurate observation can be found within the website of one of the leading Dutch industrial design companies. Ever since founding father Willem Hendrik Gispen made a name for himself as an industrial designer, his company has risen to national and international fame for its office furniture and design. Its ability to adapt to new demands and new situations has supplanted Gispen's long-standing sense of tradition and replaced it with an open mind towards technical and ergonomic innovation.

Pitching for a state-of-the-art Web presence, Gispen sought out the help of Web designer Sander Kessels, one of the prime Flash experts in the Dutch design community. Developing the site for Gispen, Kessels fostered the idea of creating the first completely click-free and scroll-free website. No more RSI injuries through an ergonomically designed site, one which is completely in line with Gispen's design philosophy. Although still far from perfect, the site is well worth a look, or should I say a feel.

After loading the first part of this Flash-based site, a menu screen unfolds, consisting of nine main sections. Realising that these sections are represented by icons modelled after Gispen's office desktops, it suddenly dawns on you that you're looking at a spatial arrangement for an office layout. Short textual animations, that run through these desktop shapes, indicate section headings like 'Who We Are', 'Developments' or 'Office Furnishing Forms'. Being lured into action by these animated icons, the user will start by pointing the mouse at one of the icons, preparing to click his first button. Yet upon rolling-over one of the 'desktops', it will immediately expand in different directions, offering a number of possible routes to follow. The next surprise comes when you realise that the menu will keep expanding, rolling ahead of your mouse and fading where you've just left. This interaction scheme, which ultimately branches off to display the actual information in image and text, relies heavily upon a sense of tactility. The user's inclination to point and click is replaced by the notion of feeling one's way around the site. 'Walking' across these buttons is like running your hand across the smooth surface of a Gispen desktop.

Generally, the site's design is dominated by a continuous play between transparency and opacity in layers of colour, image and text. This applies both to the way unused options from the menu fade until recalled, and to the dynamic presentation of the actual information on Gispen's mission, office furnishing forms, design strategy, etc. Throughout the site slightly blurred images taken from the Gispen archives serve as background illustrations. Information requested from the menus is collaged transparently over these background images, supplemented by sequenced slide-shows of illustrations showing off older as well as new designs. Once you've entered a section, what follows is a carefully timed event, from the line-by-line fade-in of text to the moment when an illustration slides in. Timing is everything here, as it sets the tone of the site as much as the restrained graphics do. The site simply unfolds, without ever pushing or urging the user along.

To be honest, by the look of its screen design, you'd never expect this to be a website. A multimedia presentation on CD-Rom would probably be your first guess. Whether Flash will dominate the future of Web design remains to be seen, but Sander Kessels has definitely made a commendable attempt to set a new standard.

by Geert J. Strengholt

TITLE OF THE SITE Gispen ➤ **OFFICIAL URL** http://www.gispen.com ➤ **PLACE AND DATE OF DESIGN** Amsterdam, October 1998 ➤ **CLIENT** Gispen ➤ **LANGUAGE** Dutch/English

COPYRIGHT OWNERS Gispen / Kessels Vormgeving ➤ **SITE DESIGN & GRAPHICS** Sander Kessels ➤ **PRODUCTION** Sander Kessels ➤ **EDITORIAL** Mark van Leeuwen

PLATFORM USED FOR DESIGNING THE SITE Macintosh 100% ➤ **APPLICATIONS USED** Adobe Photoshop, Macromedia Flash3, Pagespinner

Gispen STyle: stylish

Enterprises wishing to show their (strong) identity indoors, often choose for Gispen STyle. STyle creates tranquility and space. Creating an ambiance that incites to work, to reflection. STyle gives structure to a furnishing - well-considered and in a grand manner. Unlike many furniture programs, STyle complies with all offfice forms: from the traditional group office to the contemporary activity-related office.

Style   Work

Fritz Hansen   www.fritzhansen.com

Fritz Hansen   Car

For those wishing both a functional and a pretty office environment, there is the Fritz Hansen collection. A carefully composed assortment of chairs, characterized by a feeling for design and a high degree of quality.

Fritz Hansen makes use of international designers and architects, who employ in their designs the same starting-points : form, function and quality . In her production process she applies quality materials, that, combined with the craftmenship employed, guarantee high end results and long term of life.

In short: Fritz Hansen stands for design and quality
It goes without saying, that you will find this collection at Gispen.

Two pages from **the 'Collection' section**, where Gispen furniture designs, such as chairs, couches and desks, are presented. The images on the right automatically scroll from bottom to top, but this movement can be halted for a closer look.

View source

*The complete site for Gispen was created using Macromedia's **Flash**. One of the advantages of using Flash is that it uses vector-based graphics, which means that a Flash document's data size remains relatively small. The download size of the initial part of the site (i.e. the general interface including background images and sounds) is only 119 K. The document is loaded in a 'streaming' fashion, which means that, using a 28.8 K connection, you'll have complete control over the site within a few seconds.*

*Flash allows for very subtle interaction and feedback. The interaction of Gispen's expanding menus is based on the use of **roll-overs**, the **fading** of **buttons** and subtle **audio** feedback. Roll-overs on the main buttons trigger the appearance of new options, while simultaneously fading previous buttons by 33%. Going one step further in the menu will once more fade previous buttons by another 33%, the ones before that by 66%, etc. The result of this is that only the options which are more or less relevant to the user remain visible. A small clicking sound replaces the sensation of clicking onto the next option.*

In the Gispen site, Kessels has made clever use of the possibility of using imported images in a variety of ways. One photograph included in a Flash animation can be changed at will (colours, transparency, etc.) and used in multiple ways without any consequences for the file size of the Flash document.

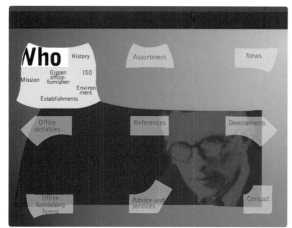

A bit of company information, including some historical background on founding father Gispen. In these screens, you can clearly see the continuous **play of transparency** and opacity of layered shapes and images.

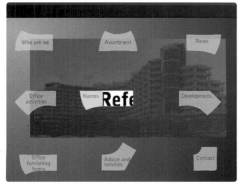

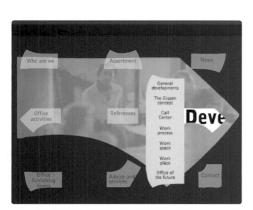

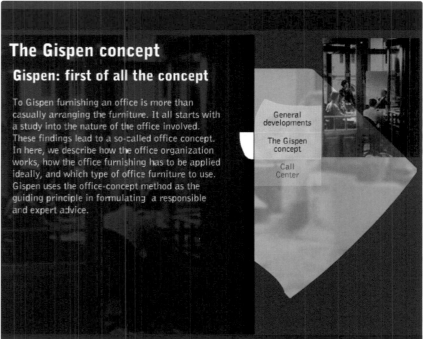

The Gispen concept. Text and images gently fade in, either across or through colourful backgrounds, based on a carefully planned timeline.

The **intro window** of the G-Shock site. In the uppermost frame, a slide-show is presented with photos, symbols and drawings. The Flash-generated navigation is located on the bottom left-hand side. Of note is the page division which results from the frame borders.

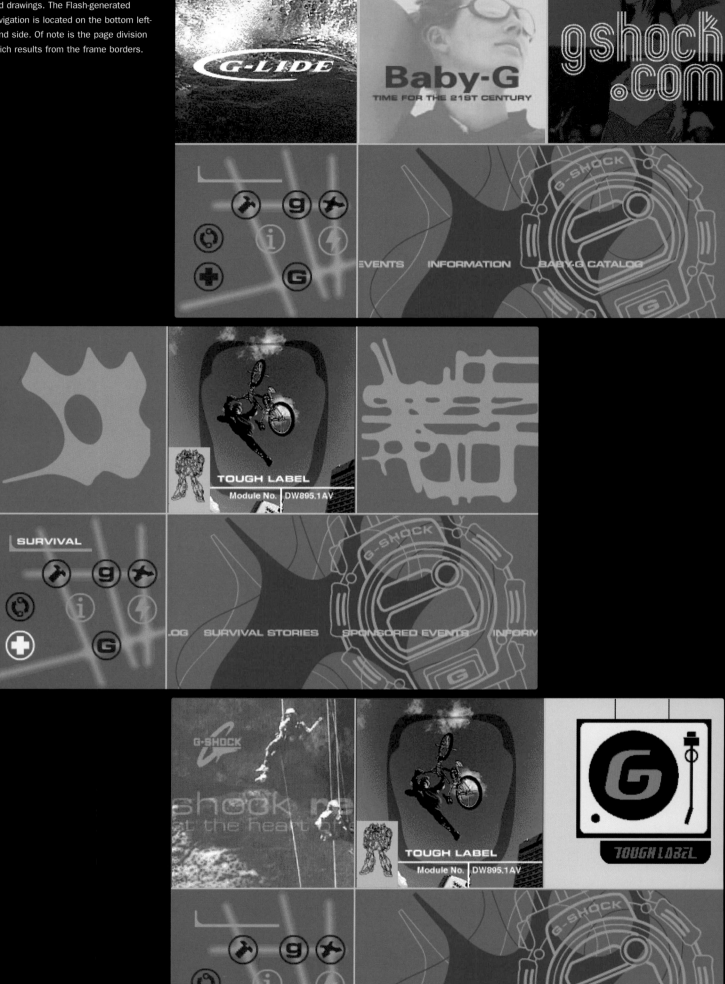

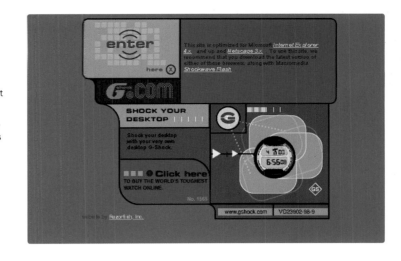

Arriving at the **G-Shock splash page**, a java script identifies the browser version and checks for the presence of the proper plug-in. For the layout, optimal use is made of a table combined with transparent GIFs. No common colour-palette is used throughout (to avoid dithering), but there are some common colours used as a basis.

TITLE OF THE SITE G-shock.com: Time for the 21st Century ❧ **OFFICIAL URL** http://www.gshock.com ❧ **PLACE AND DATE OF DESIGN** Razorfish Inc. New York. Launch Date: April 17, 1998 ❧ **CLIENT** Casio ❧ **LANGUAGE** English

COPYRIGHT OWNERS Casio, and Razorfish Inc. ❧ **EDITORIAL** Louise Zonis, Producer. Kevin Cancienne, Senior Developer. Shin Ogino, Programmer. Louise Zonis, Producer. Leen Al Bassam, Production Artist

CONTRIBUTORS Peter Seidler, Chief Creative Officer. David Warner, Design Director. Sean Nassy, Senior Designer. Henry Min, Designer. Matt Hanlon, Developer. Kevin Cancienne, Senior Developer

SCREEN DESIGN David Warner, Design Director. Sean Nassy, Senior Designer. Henry Min, Designer. Matt Hanlon, Developer. Kevin Cancienne, Senior Developer

ANIMATION/GRAPHICS David Warner, Design Director. Sean Nassy, Senior Designer. Henry Min, Designer ❧ **PLATFORM USED FOR DESIGNING THE SITE** Macintosh: 75%, Wintel: 25% ❧ **APPLICATIONS USED** Adobe Illustrator, Adobe Photoshop, Macromedia Flash ❧ **INTERACTION DESIGN** David Warner, Design Director. Sean Nassy, Senior Designer. Henry Min, Designer ❧ **PRODUCTION** Matt Hanlon, Developer. Shin Ogino, Programmer. Kevin Cancienne, Senior Developer. Henry Min, Designer. Matt Hanlon, Developer. Leen Al-Bassam, Production Artist

G-SHOCK.COM: TIME FOR THE 21ST CENTURY

http://www.gshock.com

A good watch is contemporary, keeps you on the ball under any conditions and during any activities, and is millennium-proof to boot. According to Casio, however, the most important thing a timepiece can be is shockproof, and this quality was the starting-point for the development of the G-Shock at the beginning of the '80s. Casio takes the principle of 'shockproof' to its ultimate limit by claiming that the watch even has to be able to survive a fall from the top floor of an apartment building; thus there's a reason why the 'G' stands for 'gravity'. After a difficult start, the G-Shock has been experiencing a strong comeback in the '90s, its target group being skaters, surfers, snowboarders, downhillers, etc. In short, they form a dynamic, sporty and streetwise group who can definitely use a watch that can withstand rough treatment.

The watch was made popular by a TV ad in which hockey players bashed around a puck with a G-Shock attached to it. The site that Razorfish Inc. has designed for Casio is a bit more subtle than that. But the dynamic image is still clearly recognisable, and the site meshes perfectly with the target group's lifestyle. The dynamism is achieved by a slick use of java script and Flash, as well as graphics which have been appropriated from skate culture.

After the splash page, the site shifts to a new window comprising multiple frames. The conspicuously visible borders emphasise the individual screens, a design which makes it possible to present diverse topics and forms together in a coherent way. An example is the intro window, in which the G-Shock image is called up via a sequence of high-tech ray tracings and dynamic action photos. Instead of immediately clicking past this, it's worth your while to take the time to look at all the illustrations and combinations. This also holds true for almost all of the site's sections.

The main navigation runs via a Flash-generated menu from which you can find out everything you might want to know as a (future) G-Shock owner. For example, under 'Support' you'll find the answers to FAQ's such as, 'My watch came with a Japanese manual — is an English one available as well?' To comply with the demand for sales addresses, the 'Locator' was created (limited to addresses within the US), which allows you to get a complete list of local addresses by filling in your postal code or state. Unfortunately, the searcher that moves across a map of the US isn't connected to the search function, and thus it's merely decorative. In the 'Survival' section, you can find stories from G-Shock owners who have survived an accident with their G-Shocks in tow. No, there's no one who's fallen from the top floor of an apartment building, but titles such as '16,000 Volts' indicate that this isn't kids' stuff here. Of course there's a comprehensive catalogue where you can see and compare the various models (such as G-Cool, G-Lide and Baby-G).

All in all, this is a site with a comprehensive content, and one in which the section navigation and the co-ordination between frames runs very well. Unfortunately, the site's dynamics (the changing images and frames) sometimes suffer from the speed limitations of Internet connections. Audio is conspicuously absent, but at least a desktop G-Shock is available for virtual surfers.

Just how much atmosphere this site exudes becomes clear when you decide to take a look at Casio's online shop, which is so average and mainstream that you immediately ask yourself if you've arrived at the right company's site.

by Harry Roumen

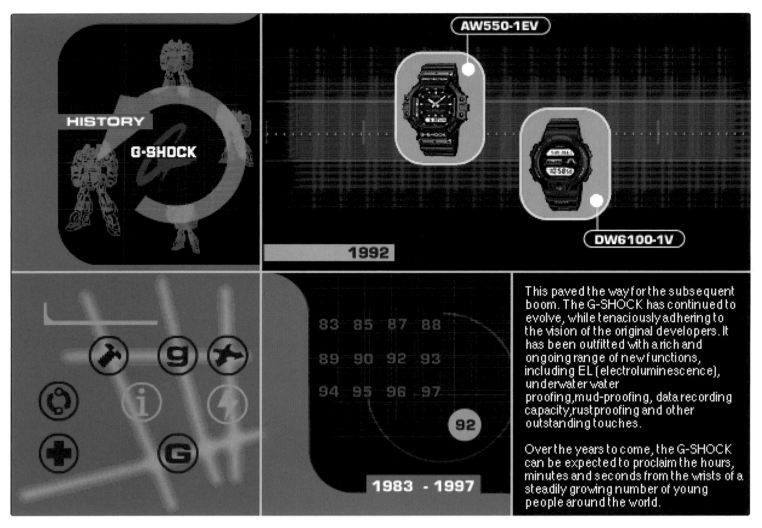

In the **catalogue section**, information can be found about the history of the watch and the development of the models. This is visualised by a timeline that be called up on a year-by-year basis. The 'calendar' in the middle of the bottom part of the screen is the subnavigation; the years are highlighted via mouse-over. The fluid lines that seem to connect the frames are interrupted by frame borders.

View source

*The G-Shock site uses a mixture of Web techniques, old and new, to achieve its dynamic impact, using **frames** to create a basic layout of the constrained window. Despite first impressions, it then only takes a simple **java script** continuously to load new arrangements of its funky imagery across different frames. This java script simply sets a **time-out** for each image page, which then in time moves on to the next page. The use of frames also makes it easy to add Flash animations (such as the main menu) and other animated parts (such as the locator for North America) to the overall layout.*

By connecting page layouts across separate frames, the designers play around with hiding and revealing the frames' layout (for instance in the timelines and the model presentations). Generally, keeping track of what to load, where and when, is the main difficulty with these kinds of complex frame sets. The way Razorfish has taken control of this makes it seem like a piece of cake.

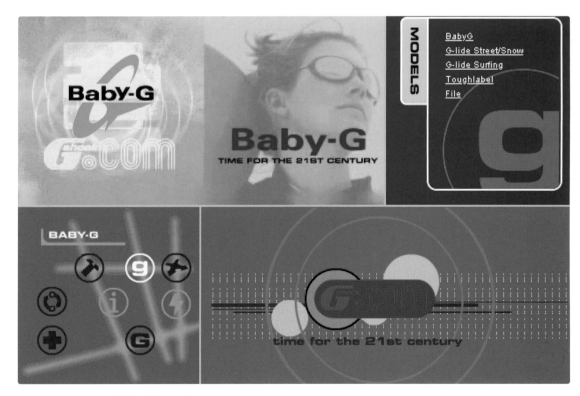

Flash animations in the **Baby-G section**.

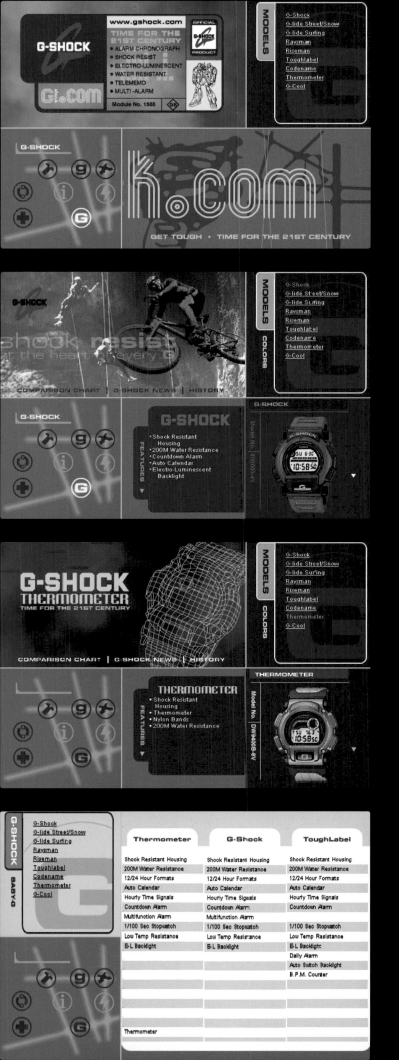

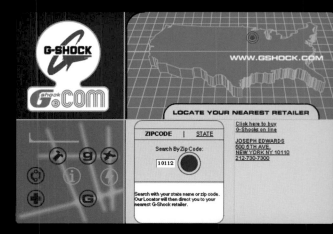

The **'Locator'** makes it possible to find a retailer by inputting a postal code or state. In the box on the bottom right, an address list appears.

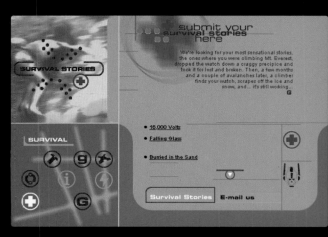

Submit your **survival stories** here. Particularly conspicuous in this screen is the fact that the visible frame borders are not always a fortunate choice in every window. Here we see frames that together form one unit, which makes the border become intrusive.

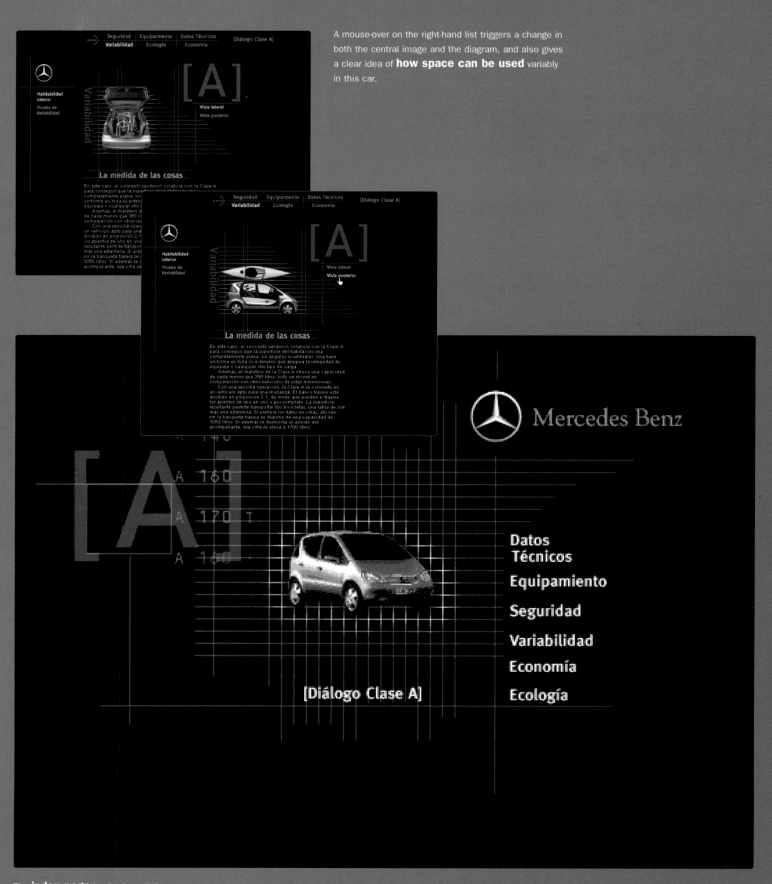

A mouse-over on the right-hand list triggers a change in both the central image and the diagram, and also gives a clear idea of **how space can be used** variably in this car.

The **index page** is simple and clear. The Mercedes logo links to the general Mercedes site.

By simply loading two pages in a frame set, you can easily **compare the technical data** of the four different Mercedes in the A-class.

Every page has the same structure:

general navigation on top, a central image on a grid, subnavigation on the left, extra information on the right and text that can be accessed by scrolling.

MERCEDES-BENZ A-CLASS

http://www.clase-a.com

Colloquially known as the Baby-Benz, the Mercedes A-Class is a smaller car that should give the German industrial concern more credibility in a market that's slowly becoming environmentally conscious. The Spanish website that promotes this next generation Mercedes tries to foreground the ecological aspects of the A-Class, but doesn't really succeed: using a picture of the car coupled with a beautiful butterfly doesn't quite do the trick. After all, there's not much that's ecologically friendly about a petrol-driven car. But the site is much more successful when it comes to other aspects such as security, the variable use of space and this car's more characteristic accessories. They also provide more possibilities for creating web-specific solutions for communicating the message, which is, of course, that the A-Class is a 'car of the future', suitable for a whole range of uses.

This promotion site, designed by Icon MediaLab, is straightforward and simple, and delivers the user the most important information about the A-Class in what seems to be an objective way, refraining from too much marketing language. A typographical grid forms the basis for all subsequent pages. An image, superimposed upon this grid, forms the centre, around which all other elements are clustered: the general navigation on the top, subnavigation on the left, extra navigation on the right and text below. The general navigation is used for reaching the six different content sections; the subnavigation is used for getting to the different pages within a given section. The extra navigation usually triggers the appearance of an extra window or a change in the image. Overall, this gives the site's content a very well-structured 'feel'. The pages themselves look nice and compact. The predominantly black background goes very well with the metallic feel of the colours used in the images and the greys of some of the text. The grid keeps the five elements of a page together, and fits beautifully into the lines that indicate where pictures will eventually appear (when the site happens to be loading slowly). Good use is made of simple dynamic features like the highlighting of links, or images which change via mouse-over. Animations are only used when they can tell more than a still image, for example with the virtual crash test. Here lies the main advantage of a promotional brochure on the Web compared to one made of paper (it's a pity, though, that no use is made of style sheets for the text layout).

What does seem somewhat strange is that very little use is made of the interactive possibilities that the Web offers: no feedback, no links to dealers, no comparisons to other cars, no information about where to book a test ride. On the other hand, this just might be the site's strong point. It's honest about what it is: a promotional product 'brochure', and, with its clear structuring and strong dynamic graphics, it's a particularly good example at that.

by Arie Altena

TITLE OF THE SITE Mercedes-Benz A-class **OFFICIAL URL** http://www.clase-a.com **PLACE AND DATE OF DESIGN** Madrid (Spain), August/September 1997 **CLIENT** Mercedes-Benz España **LANGUAGE** Spanish

COPYRIGHT OWNERS Icon Medialab España **PRODUCTION** Johan Thorngreen, Mans Shapshak, Juan Mantilla **SCREEN DESIGN** Andreas Gronqvist (concept), Juan Mantilla (art direction)

INTERACTION DESIGN Juan Mantilla (interface design), Johan Thorngreen (java script development), Mans Shapshak (active-x programming) **ANIMATION/GRAPHICS** Juan Mantilla

AWARDS Eye candy awards of excellence design, Anuncios, best spanish commercial web **PLATFORM USED FOR DESIGNING THE SITE** Macintosh 80%, Sgi 5%, Wintel 15%

APPLICATIONS USED Macintosh: FreeHand 8, Photoshop 4.0, BBEdit, Gifbuilder, AfterEffects. Wintel: HomeSite, Photoshop 4.0

Clicking on the **interior** or the **exterior** generates a large image of the car, on which important details are highlighted.

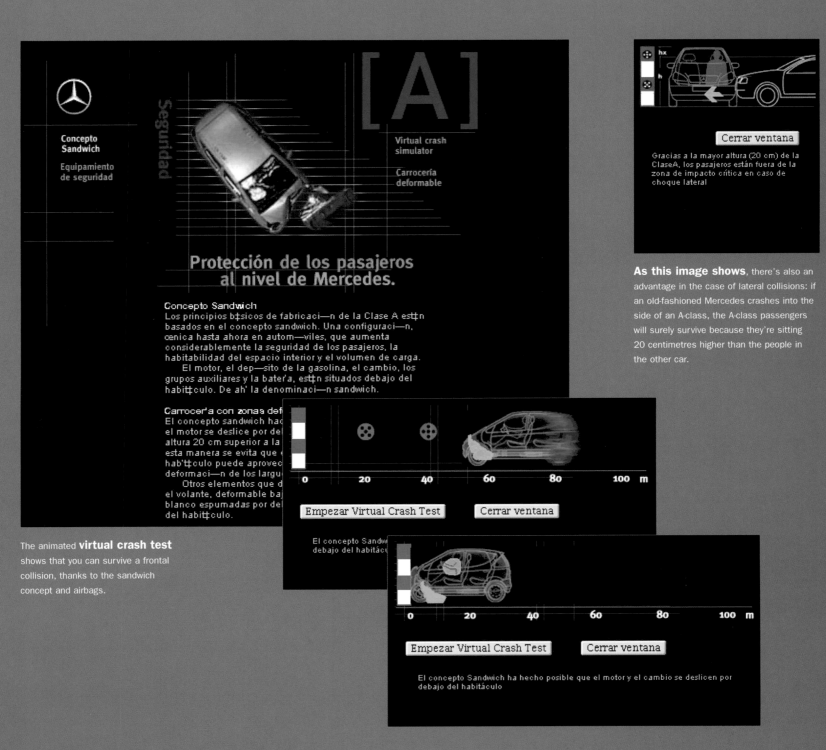

As this image shows, there's also an advantage in the case of lateral collisions: if an old-fashioned Mercedes crashes into the side of an A-class, the A-class passengers will surely survive because they're sitting 20 centimetres higher than the people in the other car.

The animated **virtual crash test** shows that you can survive a frontal collision, thanks to the sandwich concept and airbags.

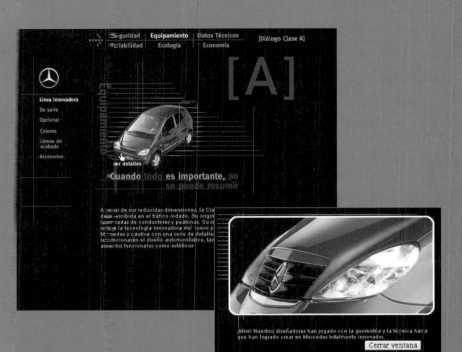

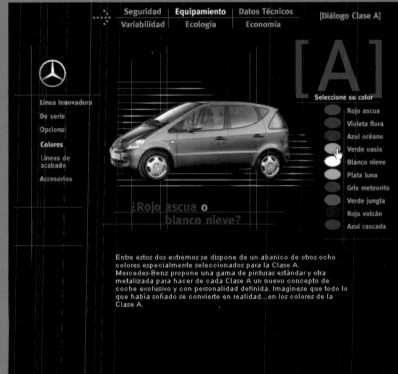

Choose your favourite colour and
see what the car will look like.

The designers of the A-class have certainly looked into **the ecological aspects** of the car, so it's possible to install a bike-rack on the roof. Mouse-overs trigger images of the other accessories that appear in the centre.

customer care | help and information | pay and mail | call back | travel agents and ticket sales retailers | main

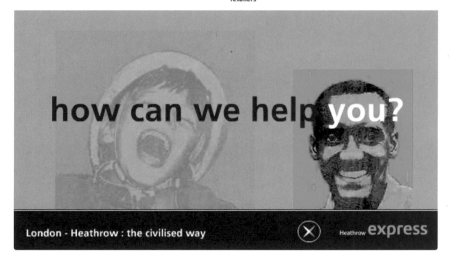

how can we help you?

London - Heathrow : the civilised way   Heathrow **express**

BAA ◢ | about Heathrow Express | buying a ticket | express yourself | where to find us | customer care | flight arrivals & bookings | what's new | travel trade talk | faqs

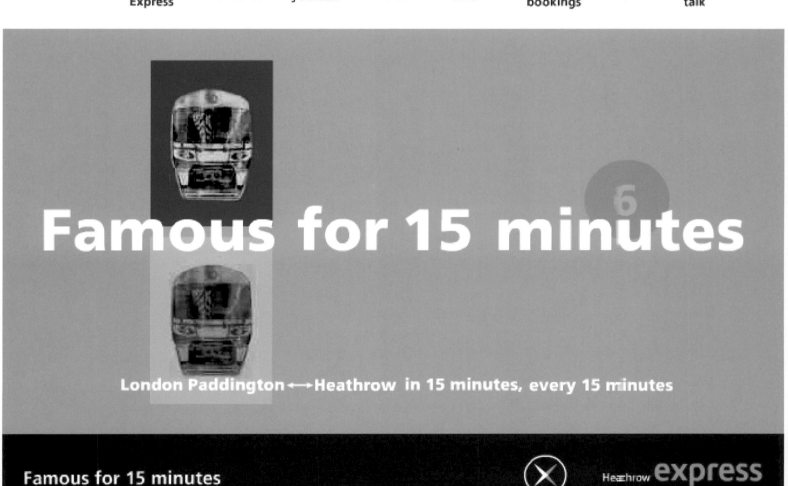

Famous for 15 minutes

6

London Paddington ←→ Heathrow in 15 minutes, every 15 minutes

Famous for 15 minutes   Heathrow **express**

Famous for 15 minutes: Andy Warhol's dictum gets a twist when used as a statement about the short amount of time it takes to travel from Heathrow to Paddington.

Information is given in a straightforward way, and can be picked up at a glance.

All the information pages have **the same look**: a navigation bar and a general bar frame the actual info. The text is short and to the point, while the images to the left are more or less the same size on any page.

HEATHROW EXPRESS:
FAMOUS FOR 15 MINUTES

http://www.heathrowexpress.co.uk

TITLE OF THE SITE Heathrow Express: Famous for 15 minutes ➤ OFFICIAL URL http://www.heathrowexpress.co.uk ➤ PLACE AND DATE OF DESIGN Crown Digital, London, June 98 ➤ CLIENT Heathrow Express ➤ LANGUAGE English

COPYRIGHT OWNERS Heathrow Express ➤ PRODUCTION Alex Parkinson, Jeremy Gaywood, Charles Paintain, Scott Ewings ➤ EDITORIAL Sam Owens (Crown), Sue Reeve (Heathrow Express) ➤ CONTRIBUTORS Heathrow Express

SCREEN DESIGN Jo O'Driscoll, Sue Reeve (Heathrow Express), Scott Ewings, Charles Paintin (Crown) ➤ INTERACTION DESIGN Charles Paintin, Alex parkinson (Crown) ➤ ANIMATION/GRAPHICS Charles Paintin, Scott Ewings (Crown)

AWARDS Macromedia Site of the day, 23 June 98, London International Advertising Awards, 1998 ➤ PLATFORM USED FOR DESIGNING THE SITE Macintosh 5%, Wintel 95%

APPLICATIONS USED Macintosh: Flash 3.0. Wintel: Flash 3.0, Flash generator, Photoshop 4.01, Illustrator 7.01, Visual Inter-Dev, SQL Server, Dreamweaver

Heathrow Express is the commercial train service that takes 15 minutes to travel from Heathrow Airport to Paddington in the centre of London. It has a website that functions both as a promotion for the train service and as an information desk where you can find timetables, competition information and special offers. It's also an online counter where you can even buy tickets for the train. There are a lot of websites that give the user these different opportunities, but not many of them have a characteristic design; BAA's Heathrow Express site does.

In addition to timetables and the like, the site hosts diagrams of the platforms and animations of the route you have to follow. A lot of background on the history and technological aspects of the train service is provided, as is some tourist information; of course, the environmental aspects are covered as well (at present, no corporate website can do without this aspect). It even furnishes a number of links to other websites, which open in a new window; only two clicks away, for instance, you can book a flight directly at the British Airways website. The goal of the site is to aid the customer effectively and to arouse positive feelings about the train by showing how safe and fast it is, and by placing it within the context of an overall London experience. This site is built with Flash — there is no classic html around on these pages (or should one say movies?) — and because it is Flash only, the site comes across as extremely fluid. Every new 'page' loads quickly and seamlessly. Some dynamic elements are used throughout: texts and images fly and circle around before finding their proper spot on the screen. This gives a feeling of movement that fits well with the subject matter. Employing Flash-only screens means that all the texts are actually pictures. The danger in this is that the letters can blur onscreen and become unreadable; this problem is tackled by use of a rather large sans serif font.

The size of the info on screen is fixed, and scrolling is never necessary. The navigation method is rather conventional: a navigation bar with links to the site's various sections is in the upper part of the screen. Whenever a section divides again into subsections, a new navigation bar, with links to the subsections, replaces the general one. A simple 'back' links to the intro screen of the section with the general navigation bar. It is easy to use, and all information can be found quickly. Some screens that fit in different sections, such as the timetable, are actually present in the different sections: a user-friendly and functional redundancy. Even less-experienced Web users will find their way easily here. Much feedback is given, with words growing larger or darker via a mouse-over, and there's always a clear mention of a page's location within the hierarchy. Generally, you are taken by the hand and lead through the site; some interactive sections are even explained in text. This is a superfluous but helpful element on a site where the typical user will not be willing to spend a minute or so on figuring out how the interface works. Two critical remarks: after a while, you get weary of the way a new screen is loaded — every other time, the letters come flying in and then settle at the right place (but in all likelihood, a typical user wouldn't spend enough time at the site to be irritated by this). Furthermore, some images seem to be of substandard quality. Nevertheless, Heathrow Express's website is a good example of a promotion and transaction site which takes a different route than standard html transaction sites, and which can be accessed equally well as a stand-alone kiosk, from the office desktop computer, or from home.

by Arie Altena

View source

In order to convey the image of the relentless, and yet effortless, traffic back and forth between London and Heathrow, the designers of the Heathrow Express site opted for the animation qualities of **Flash 3**. *Even though both navigation bars (on top and below) are also done in Flash, the main statement is made in the middle section, where Flash animations continuously push forth new images, headlines and statements. Hardly any information is presented in a neutral, static way without at least having been introduced by a cinematic fade-in. Once*

again, it is Flash's illustrative qualities, more than its potential as an interactive element, that are explored here.

Apart from the clear-cut typography, the designers clearly chose to use a mix of smooth vector graphics (generally associated with Flash) with almost painterly graphics in bitmap format. The fact that **Flash supports and deals with bitmapped images just as easily as it does with vector-based imagery** *is one of Flash's lesser-known qualities.*

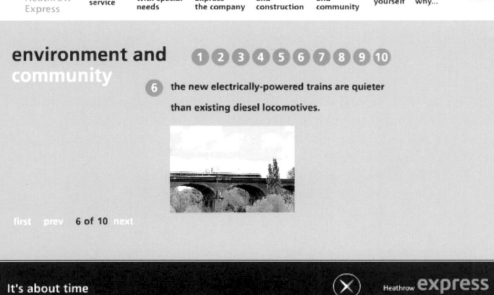

When there's more to tell, the subject is split up into sections that can be accessed by clicking on either a number or on 'next'. Clear feedback is given regarding where you are.

On some pages, **mouse-overs** are used: moving over the pictures of the trains triggers the appearance of a piece of textual information.

The possibility of making **fluid animations** with Flash is exploited in this slowly building diagram of Paddington's relative location.

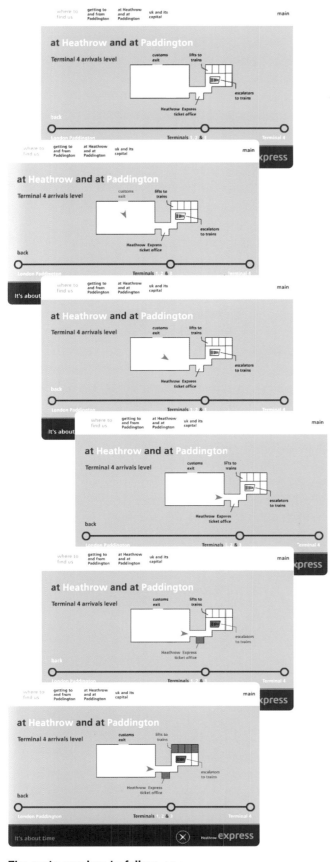

The route one has to follow at the terminals to find the train is indicated by a small animated arrow that travels over the screen.

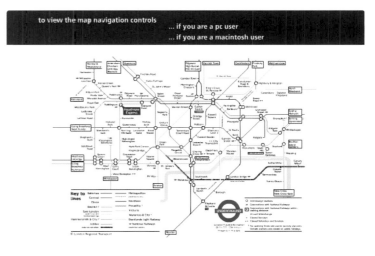

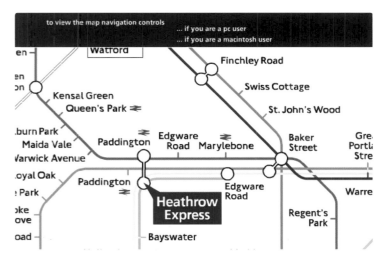

Anyone who has checked out this site at home before travelling to London will have no problems finding a connection to the Underground: this great service allows you to **zoom in on the map** of the London tube.

On roll-over, the constantly present navigation bar on the right-hand side elaborates subgroups. When clicked, animated transitions will load, displaying an unfolding architectonic dynamic.

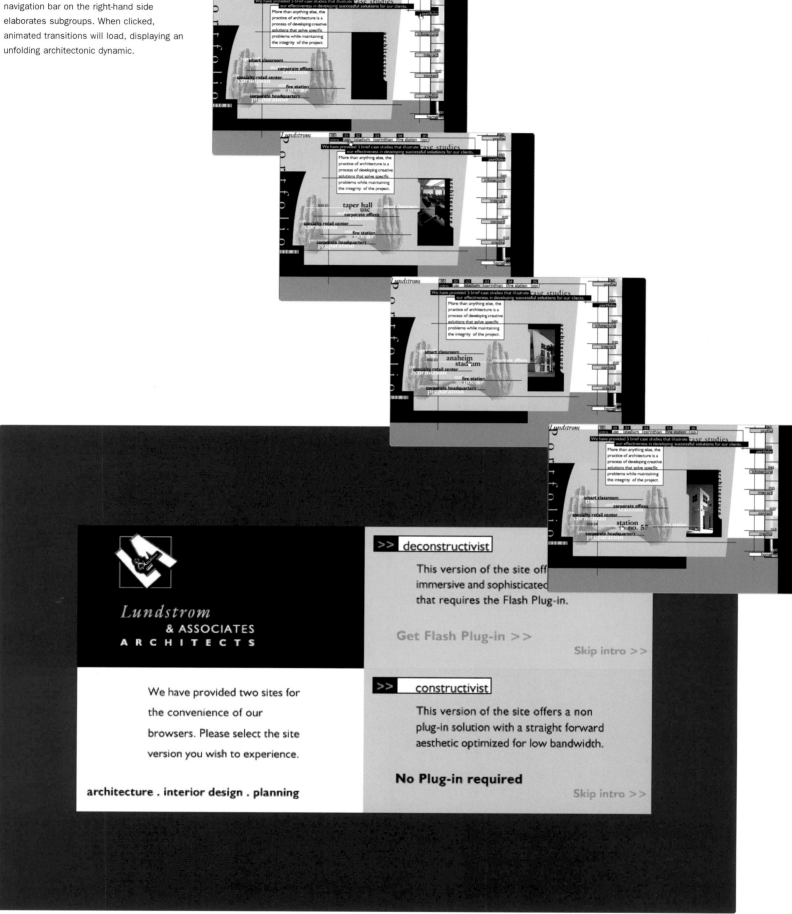

Constructivist: low-bandwidth, low-tech version for the non-plug-in operator (text-based).
Deconstructivist: offers, we are informed, 'a highly immersive and sophisticated experience'. (Macromedia Flash Plug-In Required).

LUNDSTROMARCH.COM

http://www.LundstromARCH.com

TITLE OF THE SITE LundstromARCH.com ➤ **OFFICIAL URL** http://www.LundstromARCH.com ➤ **PLACE AND DATE OF DESIGN** Irvine CA, Jan. 1998 ➤ **CLIENT** Lundstrom & Associates Architects ➤ **LANGUAGE** English ➤ **COPYRIGHT OWNERS** Juxt Interactive,

Images: Larry Falkie and Photodisc ➤ **PRODUCTION** Todd Purgason, Shaun Hervey ➤ **EDITORIAL** Todd Purgason, Shaun Hervey ➤ **SCREEN DESIGN** Todd Purgason ➤ **INTERACTION DESIGN** Todd Purgason, Shaun Hervey

ANIMATION/GRAPHICS Todd Purgason ➤ **AWARDS** High Five, Communication Arts Site of the Week, eMarketer Top Ten Business Sites, Macromedia, Inc. Shocked Site Of the Day, Archinect Site of the Month ➤ **PLATFORM USE FOR DESIGNING THE SITE**

Macintosh 99%, Wintel 1% ➤ **APPLICATIONS USED** Macintosh: Macromedia: Freehand, Flash, Dreamweaver. Adobe: Photoshop, Premier, BBedit. Wintel: Cold Fusion

The craft of architecture has good reason to feel at home on the Web, and if you weren't aware of this yet, then the Californian practice of Lundstrom Associates will show you. As builders of real spaces, they have the expertise needed to tame the virtual realm, and what's even better is that they can make the two become one. Integrating the real and the virtual is one of Lundstrom Associates' architectural fortes, and serves as the underlying theme of their website. The site also invokes postmodern theory: its jargon is used for general symbolic resonance, as a glue that helps to turn architecture and new media into a continuum. On arrival, the visitor is prompted to choose between a deconstructivist and a constructivist version of the website. The latter option offers a low-tech, text-based pathway for the non-plug-in operator. Siding with the deconstructivists is rewarded with a savvy showcase of animations and transitions. It engages the visitor primarily on a visual level, for which Flash provides the tool. You simply sit back and enjoy the meal.

Opting for 'deconstructivism', the visitor is welcomed by an animated introduction to the virtual/real architect. A narrative of emerging and overlaying textual plays sets off the mind: 'What is an architect? A designer? An artist? A technologist? A co-ordinator? A manager? No! An architect is a translator.' This, then, is a highly polished linear experience: you witness a simulation of construction in which the elemental visual styling (drawn from what looks like an architectural CAD package) blends in and out. It sets the tone of the site's strong focus on presentation: the unfolding of image/text constructions begins anew with every page. Navigation is kept simple. A limited number of undifferentiated options respond to cursor proximity with a standard roll-over.

The simple navigation and rolling animations have a relaxing effect, allowing for a concentration of details on the pages themselves. This is pushed furthest in the portfolio section: in one dense 640 x 480 knot, you're offered images, text, Quicktime and QTVR. What could conceivably have been a pigsty of information is presented with frank clarity. This is achieved by means of the intelligent exploitation of roll-overs and animated layers, unveiling information on demand over the existing layout. The portfolio can thus be recognised as the heart of the site, without any other emphasis. What is palpably absent is sound. A missed opportunity, perhaps? It's certainly one of Flash's key features. And the Lundstrom smart classroom (a lecture hall which assists in multimedia-enhanced education) in the 'infotechture' section makes one expect that they'd exploit the sensory spectrum to the fullest.

An 'interact' section is added to the site as a side dish to the main course of projects on display. There's an easily digestible multiple-choice quiz, with juicy architectural questions sent in by site visitors: 'Which architect is buried in one of his client's projects? a) Frank Lloyd Wright, b) Carlo Scarpa, c) Imhotep, d) Eric Mendelsohn.' Like the quiz, the site as a whole seems to be best appreciated as an attractive general feature, as intelligent candy. In fact, if it is addressing an audience with a professional interest, then it's not only Lundstrom's future customers, but design pro's as well. The second half of the 'interact' section is taken up by a leave-your-opinion corner, which counts more compliments for the site itself than it does comments on architecture.

Lundstrom's site is branded, with the brand referring not to the architecture it presents, but rather to the site's design. Very postmodern indeed! A list of website awards which pops up on the homepage, as well as a garish thumbs-up logo which appears later in the site, puts the craftsmanship of the Juxt designer collective in the spotlight. Its marking of the site also catches the visitor's eye: colourful geometries unfold with the loading of each new page. Thus, it's the site's sophisticated spatial organisation that makes LundstromARCH.com worth a visit. And, regardless of whether the space is virtual or real, isn't that what an architectural office is supposed to be good at?

by Noortje Marres and Alex Wilkie

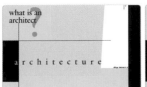

View source

The 'Deconstructivist' branch of the Lundstrom site was produced using Macromedia's Flash. Flash's facility for using fully **anti-aliased graphics and typography** in motion sequences is pushed to the extreme in these animated 'pages'. As if following the detailed blueprints of an architectural design, textual statements, images and elaborate typographic elements slide, twist, turn and fade into position. Witnessing the **gradual, carefully timed build-up of information**, you're guided through a series of statements which ultimately focus your attention on the main message. Roll-overs are kept to a minimum, giving only subtle feedback on navigational options here or switching an image there. Small animated sequences, like the one running through the letters that spell out L-U-N-D-S-T-R-O-M, continue unobtrusively on the side.

Despite the use of Flash, the Lundstrom site is not wildly interactive. Ultimately it was for the animated sequences (the flow and build-up of information) rather than for the interaction that Flash was employed here.

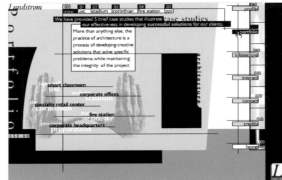

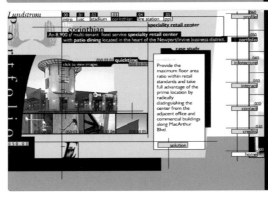

The auto-racing company interior **QTVR and the QuickTime Movies** of the Mall 'Corinthian' are cross-positioned within the portfolio alongside images and text.

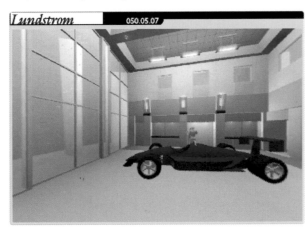

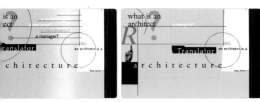
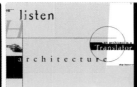

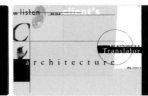

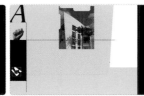

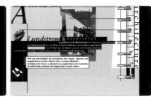
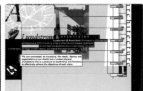

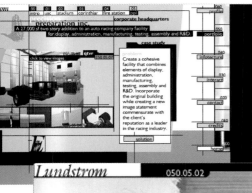

Thumbs up to Juxt! A showy animated GIF displays the Web designer's name and a pixelated hand in a pop-up window, emphasising their branding of the s te.

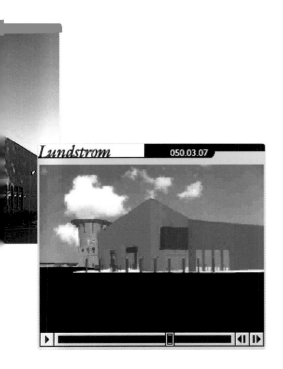

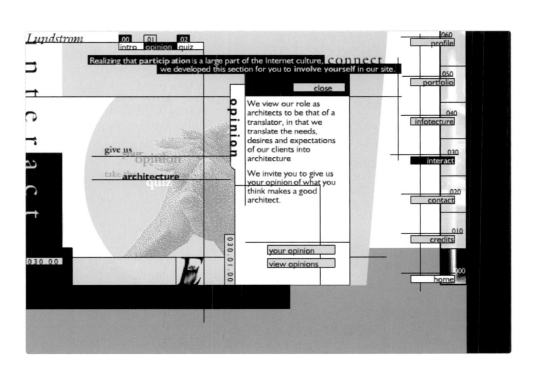

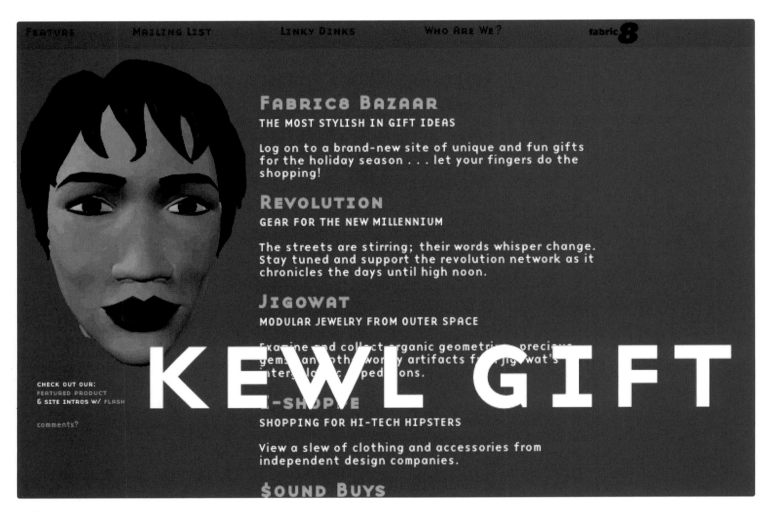

The **homepage** for the Fabric8 website features an artificial host welcoming you to the site. Created in dhtml the guide will spit out descriptions of the various boutiques in the site in response to roll-overs.

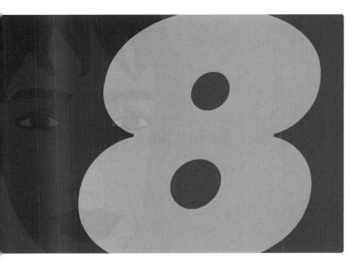

As interludes, or bumpers, between the different shops or sections in the Fabric8 site, these Flash animations serve as **'in-yer-face' ads** for Fabric8. Ooh lala lalalalalala...!

TITLE OF THE SITE Fabric8 ➦ **OFFICIAL URL** http://www.fabric8.com ➦ **PLACE AND DATE OF DESIGN** San Francisco, summer 1998 ➦ **CLIENT** (in-house) ➦ **LANGUAGE** English ➦ **COPYRIGHT OWNERS** Fabric8

PRODUCTION Fabric8 ➦ **EDITORIAL** Olivia Ongpin ➦ **CONTRIBUTORS** Fabric8 ➦ **SCREEN DESIGN** Olivia Ongpin/Antony Quintal ➦ **INTERACTION DESIGN** Olivia Ongpin/Antony Quintal ➦ **SOUND DESIGN** Antony quintal

ANIMATION/GRAPHICS Fabric8 ➦ **AWARDS** Project Cool Sighting of the Day, DHTML Zone Spotlight, Macromedia's Dreamweaver Site Gallery, Macromedia's Shocked Site of the Day, Web Magazine's Editor's Choice

Award for Arts, Netscape 1st Annual Developer's Conference, Netscape Shopping Destination ➦ **PLATFORM USED FOR DESIGNING THE SITE** Macintosh 40%, Wintel 40%, Other (Linux) 20%

FABRIC8

*http://*www.fabric8.com

When you set your mind to it, you can buy just about anything you want to by hooking up to the Net. From your favourite books at Amazon to your daily pizza, it's all just a few clicks away. So if the Web is such a viable medium for marketing a wide range of mass-produced goods, why not try and set up a website that fosters the unique talent of young fashion designers, musicians and artists instead? To quote Olivia Ongpin and Anthony Quintal, who launched the Fabric8 website in 1996: 'Up-to-date global communication is available now at relatively low cost, so an independent designer no longer has to rely on appealing to a majority in a limited geographical space — success can be achieved by appealing to a minority all over the world.' In an attempt to realise this potential of the Web, Fabric8 set up a site that promotes and sells unique products from a variety of San Franciscan designers and artists.

The Fabric8 website consists of a collection of online boutiques, presenting independent designers with the opportunity of setting up shop and selling their one-offs on the Web. Along the way, it presents a variety of showcases that demonstrate the rich palette of Web design techniques which Fabric8 has mastered as a design company. In a rich San Franciscan street style which employs everything from Flash and dynamic html to serious java scripting, Fabric8 is trying to create unique shopping experiences. Customisation is the key word, in more ways than one.

Each boutique, gallery or designer outlet in the Fabric8 site has its own look and feel, ranging from the '70s-warped-into-'90s look of gender-blending fashion designer Paul Gallo's hang-out, to the hi-tech display of Jigowat's intergalactic jewellery. The latter site is characterised by an intuitive understanding of the nature of these jewellery designs. Jigowat considers his ring designs to be kinds of artificial life-forms which undergo an evolutionary process. The rings are modular, and can be adapted to the client's wishes. Fabric8 created a fitting display for this new species of jewellery by allowing the client to explore its characteristic features in an artificial VRML environment. Sui Generis, a clothing line by Nancy Eastep, was the first to set up shop with Fabric8 (then still called Check-it.com). With its clear layout of the collection, this online catalogue almost understates its potential. Its fitting-room, for instance, masks a complex system of order forms which makes sure that the client is provided with made-to-measure pieces.

One of their latest additions is the 'Shopping Bazaar', featuring holiday shopping for hi-tech hipsters. As a user, you can adjust the handy list of gift suggestions to have them presented by company, category or price. A little inserted window in the main screen (created in Flash) displays a continuous flow of gift previews, and provides the opportunity to go immediately to the product info when something comes along that catches your fancy.

Since many of the items on sale in Fabric8 are unique, handcrafted creations, the site demands a careful and complex arrangement for processing orders. Not only do the transaction forms need to provide a way of dealing with custom measurements, but they also have to allow for any other customisations the client may wish for. Through some pretty state-of-the-art java scripting, Fabric8 has been able to deal with most of these requirements. Thus, based on their extensive offerings, Fabric8 has been extremely successful at doing business online, with clients ranging from their next-door neighbours to young Japanese hipsters across the ocean.

by Geert J. Strengholt

Two screens from the latest addition to the site, the **'Shopping Bazaar'** for speciality holiday gifts. The 'Shopping Bazaar' allows you to arrange your list by company, category and, of course, price.

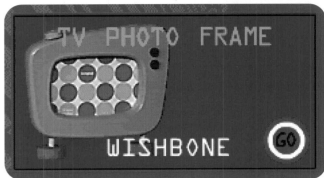

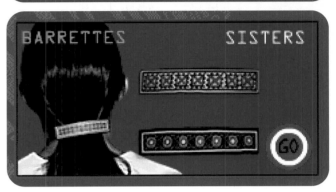

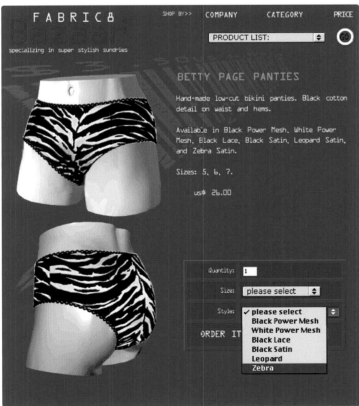

Lodged within the **'Shopping Bazaar'** page is a Flash movie presenting a continuous flow of graphic gift suggestions. Clicking the bulls-eye will take you to more information about that particular gift and ... an order form.

sui generis

HOME | **FITTING ROOM** | **SHIRTS** | **JACKETS** | **PANTS** | **SUITS**

Sui Generis creates high quality clothing for men and women. Our collection of jackets, shirts, and pants are good looking, well-fitting, great feeling, and long-lasting.

Each of our garments is hand-made in our San Francisco warehouse. From wool crepe trousers to a silk-linen dress shirt, we have a good fit and attitude for every moment.

A Brief History of Sui Generis

It was in 1849 that Sui Generis was established. Learn about how it was started in a San Francisco warehouse by two can-can girls and one cowboy, then progressed into what it is today.

Design

What it is that makes us stitch

Upcoming Events

Wear your SG clothes to these upcoming parties.

Join the Sui Generis mailing list!

---

sui generis

HOME | **FITTING ROOM** | **SHIRTS** | **JACKETS** | **PANTS** | **SUITS**

The Fitting Room

Sui Generis methods for fitting Shirts and Jackets.

Our techniques for fitting Pants.

Stand up straight before the mirror in your best fitting clothing. If you would like to save yourself the following effort, just measure a shirt/jacket or a pair of pants that you like the length of. Or have a friend do it. Or your parents.

Let's fit you for a shirt or jacket.

For shirts and jackets, we need your **chest size** only. Measure the circumference of your chest, looking in the mirror to make sure that the tape runs around the fullest part of your chest (do not stretch or pull tightly), and stays parallel to the floor. Remember to stand up straight!

Chest

32" / 81.5cm
33" / 84cm
34" / 86.5cm
35" / 89cm
36" / 91.5cm
37" / 94cm
38" / 96.5cm
✓ 39" / 99cm
40" / 101.5cm
41" / 104cm
42" / 106.5cm
43" / 109cm
44" / 112cm
45" / 114.5cm

(please check your measurement)

Submit ... cket Size

Two pages from the **'Sui Generis' collection** show a display of designs and a fitting-room where you can enter your measurements. A java script will do the calculations for you, making sure the clothes you order are made to measure.

Suits @ Sui Generis

Our suits are individually hand-tailored to ensure a perfect fit for you. We have several jacket styles to accommodate the leisure to business spectrum of suit-wearing. Like all of our styles, SG suits are available for men and women.

The Partisan

Cut slim and simple, our suits are available in wool crepe, flannel, gabardine, and novelty woven fabrics for a clean look and a comfortable feel. The jackets are fully lined and include an inside zipper pocket (aka passport pocket).

The Emissary

The Partisan

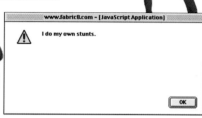

The Partisan is a standard three-button suit. The jacket is fully-lined and has a Western lapel and two patch pockets. The trousers (aka SG Ds) feature side seam pockets, back darts, one back welt pocket, and straight-cut legs.

It is nothing but comfortable, and ideal for business or traditional suit events. It's even gotten a few people jobs!

---

www.fabric8.com – [JavaScript Application]

⚠ I do my own stunts.

[OK]

Rebecca M, marketing rep for **Respect Jewelry**, is like a diamond in the rough. If you give her her props, she'll treat you real nice. If you do her wrong, we're talking fire and brimstone, baby.

Rebecca M in SGChs without pockets.

SG Ch - Order Form

Size Waist (Hips)	Inseam Length	Fabric
○ 30" (35")	○ 29"	○ Caramel Cotton Twill
○ 32" (37")	○ 30"	○ Chocolate Brown Cotton Twill
○ 34" (39")	○ 31"	○ Blue-green Cotton Twill
○ 36" (41")	○ 32"	○ Deep Sea Green Cotton Twill
	○ 33"	○ Black Cotton Twill
		○ Black Wool/Polyester

Fabric Swatches

Quantity: 1

[order it] [checkout]

View source

This piece of source code shows that, like everything else in the Fabric8 website, all **dhtml coding, java scripting** and **Flash animations** were handcrafted by Fabric8.

hand made by elves

dec/4/98 06:24:52

san francisco time

limited technical support on these scriptz w/ every fabric8 purchase (please support us :)

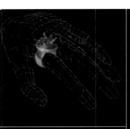

Displayed herein are jewelry specimens collected by noted ringologist Jigowat. This fearless explorer travels the ends of the universe to uncover genera of rings never before seen by the human eye.

home

Introduction

Evolution

VRML

A Love Story

Mailing List

Each ring in this lovely collection is a one-of-a-kind, hand-made artifact, and is fully modular: just one sterling silver band (with a screw) can be used for all of these rare species!

News Flash: Jigowat stows away on spacecraft Cassini for the first leg of his newest intergalactic excursion. Join our mailing list to find out about the species he discovers en route to Saturn.

fabric8

copyright © fabric8
website by fabric8 productions

home   styles

sizing   order

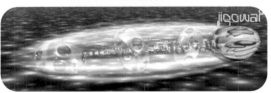

The display of **Jigowat's jewellery** is supported by VRML, allowing the client to examine these 'artificial creatures' from any possible angle. The graphics attempt to support the appropriate 'off this planet' experience.

Spikus domububblicious

The "shiny cactus" habitate in desert regions. Their bubble-like bases are filled with nutrients which allow the spikes to emerge. This species flourish during the dryest seasons and often uproot and float away during desert storms.

- **SIZE** 20mm wide, 15mm tall

- **HABITAT** Ideal on the index, middle, or ring finger

- **COMMENTS** Its dome, bubbles, and spikes are formed from the same metal; however, this species has been seen in several different types of metal (thick silver band ordered separately).

Price: $68
$93 w/ band

To view this species in 3D, click on **vrml mode** in the top left window.

Spikus domububblicious - Order Form

Size (jigos)	Silver Band	Metal
select ▼	● None	● Shiny Brass
	● Shiny	● Matte Brass
Your ring size	● Matte	● Shiny Copper
		● Matte Copper
		● Shiny Silver
		● Matte Silver
Quantity: 1		**View Metals**

order it   checkout

Note: This site uses JavaScript to process your transactions. If you prefer to place your order using a different method, feel free to either **email us** with your order, or send us your **order form** via fax, email, or snail mail.

fabric8

1.888.554.4321
copyright © fabric8
website by fabric8 productions

Enter Your Name And Password

Enter username for film at cinema.vpro.nl:

Name : Peter Gorgels

Password : ●●●

Cancel   OK

24h

Om uw voorkeuren te verwerken en u via email van advies te dienen heeft de 24h Cinema Service uw emailadres en een unieke gebruikersnaam nodig. Deze informatie wordt uitsluitend voor die doeleinden gebruikt.

Uw persoonlijke wachtwoord wordt binnen vijf minuten naar het door u ingevulde emailadres gestuurd. Met dat wachtwoord heeft u direkt toegang tot de 24h Cinema Service.

meld aan   log in

Cinemien   Internationaal Film Festival Rotterdam   Nederlands Film Festival   Nederlands Filmmuseum   Schokkend Nieuws   Skrien   VPRO

The **opening screen** to the 24h Cinema Service. Here you can sign up as a member, log in, or request information about the interactive film guide. The animation which displays the name of this database and the legendary film stills within the characteristic five-pointed star add a dynamic element to the otherwise stark screen design.

U heeft een wachtwoord nodig, zodat de 24h Cinema Service u een persoonlijk advies kan geven.

EEN NIEUW ACCOUNT   OPNIEUW
AANVRAGEN   INLOGGEN

meld aan   log in

TITLE OF THE SITE 24h Cinema Service ❧ OFFICIAL URL http://cinema.vpro.nl ❧ PLACE AND DATE OF DESIGN Hilversum, January 1998 ❧ CLIENT VPRO ❧ LANGUAGE Dutch ❧ COPYRIGHT OWNERS System and design: VPRO Digitaal. Content: copyrights remain with the institutions/people who put the information at the disposal of the Cinema Service ❧ PRODUCTION Petra Schrevelius ❧ EDITORIAL Bruno Felix, Carine Jamin, Dick Rijken, Femke Wolting ❧ CONTRIBUTORS System: Mosion, CIBIT, VPRO. Content: Nederlands Film Museum, Skrien, Nederlands Film Festival, Internationaal Film Festival Rotterdam, Schokkend Nieuws, Cinemien, VPRO ❧ SCREEN DESIGN Robin Verdegaal, Mieke Gerritzen ❧ INTERACTION DESIGN Robin Verdegaal ❧ SYSTEM DESIGN Rico Jansen, Daniel Ockeloen ❧ APPLICATIONS USED Macintosh: Pagespinner PhotoShop. Other: VI, Informix Dynamic Server 9.X, JDK (Sunsoft Java 1.1.6) ❧ ANIMATION/GRAPHICS Paul Mitchell ❧ PLATFORM USED FOR DESIGNING THE SITE Macintosh 40%, Other 60% (Solaris)

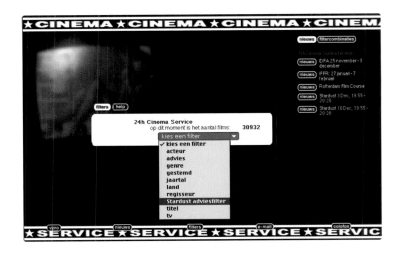

The main interface to the 24h Cinema Service. In the large frame on the left you can make a selection from the films in the database based on the available filters. From the frame on the right, you can access the news page.

24H CINEMA SERVICE

http://cinema.vpro.nl

Aside from music, one of the most popular topics of conversation is probably film and television. It usually provides enough common ground between people to keep a hearty discussion going for hours. This communal interest provides the basis for this online database service created by the experimental department of VPRO, one of the Netherlands' main independent broadcasting organisations.

Analogous to FireFly's experiments with music databases, VPRO has developed a searchable film database/archive that is connected to an individual rating system. Logging on to the VPRO's 24h Cinema Service, users are provided with a set of tools: namely, filters that allow them to customise and personalise their interaction with the database. Searching the Cinema Service database is facilitated by a clear interface, consisting of a number of filters. The user can select films based on filters such as 'actor', 'director', 'title', 'genre', 'year' and 'country', or any combination thereof; each selection can then be saved and stored. Yet this alone wouldn't distinguish the experience from any other database.

What does make the Cinema Service special is the added value of filters such as 'voted', 'advice' and 'TV'. Each user can give ratings to films in the database, ranging from one to six stars. These films are then stored in the user's personalised filter, labelled as 'voted'. Cross-matching the user's personal ratings with the collective ratings of all the users, the Cinema Service can then recommend new films to the user. These are stored in the personal filter called 'advice'. Ultimately, the 'TV' filter will present only those recommended films that will be shown on TV within the next four days.

Apart from a film database, the Cinema Service also serves as an interactive TV guide. It regularly informs the film fan about when a film that matches his or her 'taste' will be shown on TV. When film fans combine the 'TV' filter with their selections, the Cinema Service will inform them by e-mail when a film that might interest them will be featured on TV. One of the World Wide Web's most important design principles is 'proximity'. By means of hyperlinks, information that is physically distant, yet conceptually related, can be connected. Good navigation will take you on a tour along information that has a meaningful relationship. This is one of the Web's greatest strengths.

In the VPRO's Cinema Service, proximity plays an important role in a variety of ways. Obviously it is an important navigation feature, but this also applies to the inner workings of the database itself. Films with similar ratings will be connected, thereby creating a web of 'taste patterns' that can be of use to the film fan. Furthermore, there is also the proximity of time and space. Twice a week, information is sent out via e-mail. Much like a roadside billboard that informs those who pass it every day, the Cinema Service's e-mail keeps modern film fans informed as they rush along the digital highways.

Since the Cinema Service is a database-driven site, most pages are generated by pre-designed templates, illustrated by randomly assigned images. The general feel of these templates resembles film reels as well as the film timetables commonly found in Dutch cinemas. This screen design in the Cinema Service, dominated by a series of five-pointed stars, elegantly supports both content and functionality. In rating the films, one of the site's main features, appreciation, is expressed by these starry icons. The fact that they play such a prominent role in the overall style is no surprise once you realise that this is actually what the site is all about: rating films, movie stars, etc. Even the VPRO's own film magazine is called Stardust. But the nicest thing about VPRO's Cinema Service is that, in the end, everybody is a star: not just for 15 minutes, but for the full 24 hours.

By Peter Gorgels

In **the right frame**, you can request the filter combinations you've previously saved and named. For each selection, you can turn the e-mail service on or off.

After selecting a filter, the user gets a short explanation. This page displays the filter of Stardust, the VPRO's film programme. Here you can choose from your **favourite critics' recommendations**.

View source

It may be clear that although the user is looking at a number of webpages, this site is actually based on a growing **database** of information. The advantage of running a website from a database is that you'll be storing information, text, images, and maybe even sounds, that can be used for multiple purposes and be presented in various ways. Everything depends on what you want to present to whom, which command you use and how you want to display it. Customisation is at your fingertips.

First and foremost, VPRO's Cinema Service stores its users' suggestions and ratings, and responds to their requests. This means that the first design challenge to be met was **the interface** which people would be using **to interact with the database**. This interface consists of a number of fixed webpages and menus which get your communication with the system going, provide you with search and filter options, etc. Most of the remaining pages, i.e. your search results, rating-lists and even the requested articles, are constructed on the fly. In response to your interaction, the database will generate html pages based on a number of templates. These templates, which are **pre-designed and tagged html documents**, make sure that the retrieved data is properly displayed in the right format. In the Cinema Service these templates are supplemented with a designated or randomly assigned illustration, as these images are already available in the database.

The combination 'komnoordamerikoptv' shows all of the **comedies from North America** that will be shown on TV within the next four days.

In the **'country' filter**, you can select films by continent or country. In the background, legendary film stills from the database appear at random.

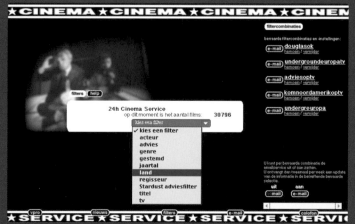

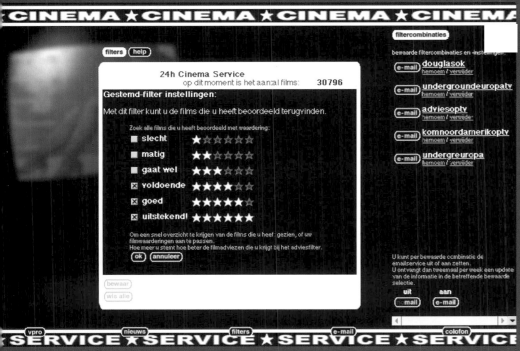

By clicking on the number of **remaining films** (in this case '17') within the search screen, all remaining films appear in the frame on the right, along with their ratings.

In the **'voted' filter**, you can recall films which you've already rated. It allows you to indicate that only highly rated films should be saved. This way you create a selection which, in combination with other filters, becomes a powerful selection tool.

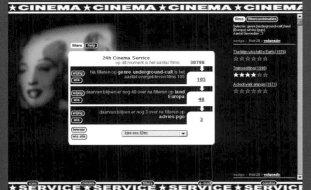

You can make optimal use of the Cinema Service's power by combining your favourite film selection with the **'advice' filter**.

Along with the credits for each film, you also get **extra information** from film magazine articles selected by the VPRO, as well as a series of related films recommended by the film database.

Rabobank

| Particulier | Bedrijven |

Op vakantie gaan

Lenen
- korte lening/
- overbruggingslening
- middellange lening
- langlopende lening

Kredieten
- Krediet in Rekening Courant
- Rekening Courant Krediet

Bankgaranties
- betalingsgarantie
- biedingsgarantie
- uitvoeringsgarantie
- vooruitbetalingsgarantie
- kredietgarantie
- onderhoudsgarantie
- garantie wegens ontbrekend
  connossement

Leasing
- financiële lease
- operationele lease
- wat kan ik leasen?

zoek op trefwoord:

[   ] Zoek

Op vakantie gaan

Betaalgemak op vakantie
Hoe betaalt u in het buitenland? Bekijk hier de mogelijkheden. »

Verzekeren
Verzekeringen voor op reis: een kortlopende of doorlopende reisverzekering en Rabo Interhelp Extra. »

Checklist
Heeft u overal aan gedacht voordat u vertrekt? Doorloop de checklist. »

Het Reisbureau
Wordt het een weekje Terschelling of een cruise rond de wereld? Maak een keuze uit ons reisaanbod. »

Financieren

Lenen
U wilt voor een korte of lange termijn geld beschikbaar hebben om te investeren. »

Kredieten
Tijdelijk extra ruimte op uw rekening. »

Bankgaranties
De zekerheid voor uw leverancier of opdrachtgever, dat u uw verplichtingen nakomt. »

Leasing
U wilt bepaalde objecten wel gebruiken, maar ze niet zelf kopen. »

Trade Finance
Zekerheid over de betalingen van uw debiteuren. »

Groenfinanciering
Regelingen van de overheid die bepaalde milieuvriendelijke investeringen fiscaal extra aantrekkelijk maken. »

Onderwerpen   Nieuws   Betaalgemak op vakantie   Verzekeren   Checklist   Het Reisbureau   Service

De bank van:
Anna Benckert

Instellingen

Bookmarks
Betalen
Rabo internet bankieren
Rabobank direct betalen
I-pay
Financiëren
langlopende rekening
Externe bookmarks
www.postbank.nl
www.mediamatic.nl
www.yahoo.se

[   ] Zoek

Uw lokale bank
Rabobank Amsterdam,
Nieuwmarkt 20

Vorige bezoek:
28 december 1998

Colofon

Particulier

Op vakantie gaan

Betaalgemak op vakantie
Hoe betaalt u in het buitenland? Bekijk hier de mogelijkheden. »

Verzekeren
Verzekeringen voor op reis: een kortlopende of doorlopende reisverzekering en Rabo Interhelp Extra. »

Checklist
Heeft u overal aan gedacht voordat u vertrekt? Doorloop de checklist. »

Het Reisbureau
Wordt het een weekje Terschelling of een cruise rond de wereld? Maak een keuze uit ons reisaanbod. »

Screens respectively from the general Rabobank and the personalised site. In the first site, which provides information for the occasional visitor, further navigation is presented on the left. From its menu above, you can access the special site which power users can utilise to create their own personal sites. The larger screen is an example of such a personal site, with the personal navigation menu on the left. As you can see, content (in this case information about holidays and financing) is shared between the two sites. Yet the fact that the context in which this information is presented is a personal one makes all the difference. Note that the navigation bar above has adapted to the topic which is presented on screen.

Welkom op mijn.rabobank.nl
U heeft op uw eigen financiele site meer ruimte op uw scherm om uw bankzaken te regelen. Alle informatie is direct toegankelijk in het onderwerpenmenu. Bovendien kunt u de site aanpassen aan uw eigen voorkeuren, door te klikken op ⊕.

» Ik wil nu mijn eigen financiele site maken. Aanmaken
» Ik wil eerst een rondleiding door mijn.rabobank.nl Tour
» Ik wil zelf rondkijken op mijn.rabobank.nl Rondkijken
» Ik heb al een eigen financiele site, en wil me aanmelden:

gebruikersnaam:
wachtwoord:
          Ga verder

» Ik wil terug naar de Rabobanksite. www.rabobank.nl

TITLE OF THE SITE Rabobank Internetbankieren ⟩⟩ **OFFICIAL URL** http://www.rabobank.nl ⟩⟩ **PLACE AND DATE OF DESIGN** Amsterdam, August 1998 / February 1999 ⟩⟩ **CLIENT** Edwin Rietkerk, Rabobank Nederland ⟩⟩ **LANGUAGE** English

COPYRIGHT OWNERS Mediamatic Interactive Publishing ⟩⟩ **PRODUCTION** Info NL, Gerlach Velthoven, Denise Kuipers ⟩⟩ **EDITORIAL** Rabobank ⟩⟩ **SCREEN DESIGN** Anna Benckert, Liesbeth den Boer, Jeroen Janssen, Willem Velthoven, Yoe Han Oei

INTERACTION DESIGN Liesbeth den Boer, Jeroen Janssen, Willem Velthoven ⟩⟩ **ANIMATION/GRAPHICS** Diederik van Huijstee, Yoe Han Oei ⟩⟩ **PLATFORM USED FOR DESIGNING THE SITE** Macintosh 95%, Other 5%

APPLICATIONS USED Photoshop, Illustrator, Dreamweaver, BBEdit

RABOBANK INTERNETBANKIEREN

http://www.rabobank.nl

Programmers and software developers alike are going out of their way to make the conducting of financial transactions via the Web as secure as moving gold through Fort Knox. Small wonder, then, that banks in particular are keen to explore the possibilities of dealing with their clients by means of their websites. In the Netherlands, the Rabobank holds a very special position. Originally a series of small community-based banks, the present-day Rabobank is still an organised collective rather than a centralised company. This means that the individual Rabobanks are still very much oriented towards maintaining a personal relationship with the local community. But how can you have a personal relationship when you're communicating with your bank online?

In developing the Rabobank's general online presence as well as the facilities for online banking, a personalised way of dealing with clients has been of core interest. In the preliminary stages Mediamatic generated scenarios for future methods of using the Web in a customised way. These were of key importance to the general development of the Rabobank site. Thus one of the aims was to create, or rather to allow clients to construct, personalised environments where they could perform their online banking transactions and get an overview of their financial affairs. In these personal spaces, clients would also be able to receive and gather customised information concerning their personal interests and their relationship to the bank in a more general sense.

After a few conceptual experiments, Mediamatic was asked to design the look and feel of the site as a whole, as well as the visual side of the personalised client/server interaction. Yet in this third version of the Rabobank site, the total number of features became so extensive that it was decided to split the site into two different sections. One site now focuses on the occasional visitor, while the other caters to the needs of the heavy user who wants the full functionality of a personalised site. This decision has allowed the designers to employ browser 4.x technology in the latter version. Within this dynamic site, you, the client, can create a personal profile (by specifying your personal, professional or business interests) which will determine both the look and the content of your personal site. Your personal site allows you to set a general atmosphere, add bookmarks (even to other banks), or modify topics for regular news updates. This profile remains completely modifiable, even during a banking session. You can perform these modifications either ad hoc or by reviewing a complete list of your current profile. And whenever you wish to carry out some banking business, you can simply log on to your private page, which is your personal niche or node in the Rabobank network.

A clever combination of java-scripted menus and style sheets keeps this information-heavy site manageable for its users. Note the economically adaptive menus that change in accordance with your current information and activities, much like the menu of an operating system. Pop-up menus, which allow you to revise your personal page, also let you create shortcuts to sections concerning investments and online banking, or link to the special sites and services that the Rabobank has to offer. Obviously, the general look of both sites is in keeping with the Rabobank's house style. By using a palette of predominantly blue and orange as basic colours and, more recently, applying Arial and Times as base fonts throughout the style sheets, the site looks tight. The restrained use of images and decorative elements (which are used mainly in the faded backgrounds and subtle animations) breaks up the layout without being obtrusive.

The present Rabobank site is in a new phase of development, as Mediamatic is planning to explore even further the personalisation and customisation of content and services. In the meantime, Mediamatic's clear, crisp and functional design for this technically advanced Rabobank site has already set a standard for transaction websites.

by Geert J. Strengholt

To set the desired tone for your **personal site**, you can choose from a number of designs for your personal menu. The menu contains your bookmarks for parts of the Rabobank site and its services, but also for external sites (such as those of other banks) whose services you use. The menu can be modified at any time simply by clicking the 'hand' (see detail), which then folds away when the arrow is clicked.

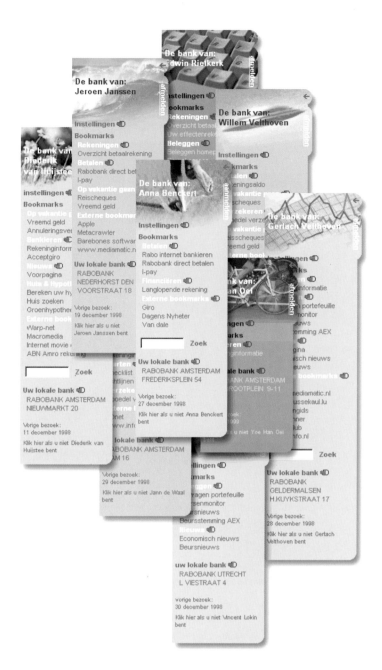

View source

The 1999 edition of the personalised Rabobank site was created in **dynamic html**, using style sheets to control the overall design. It is especially the use of **layers** and java script that has improved control over both navigation menus and the interactive modification of the personalised client pages. The condensed and adaptive navigation menu simply expands into more detailed submenus which roll down on mouse-overs. The **pop-up menus**, necessary to customise personal pages and profiles, are kept hidden in layers but can be called to the surface at all times. Thus it only takes a few clicks to alter a page dynamically. Hiding parts of the navigation menu and some of the pop-up menus, and offering the possibility of folding the personal menu away, not only creates excellent functionality but also produces a very open and clear screen design.

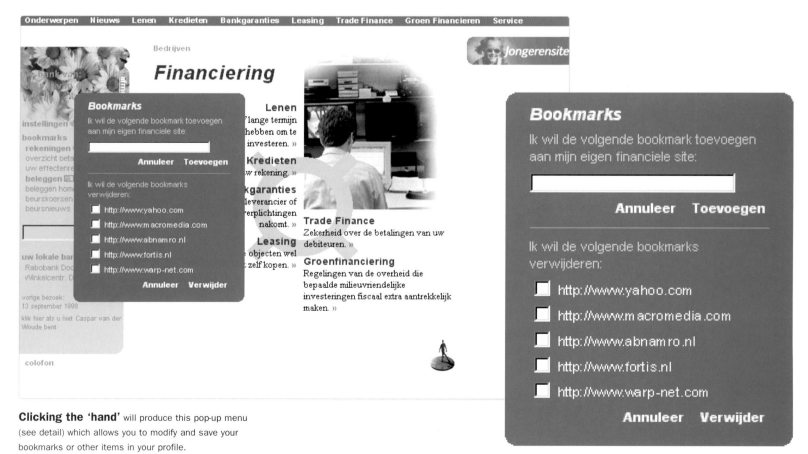

Clicking the 'hand' will produce this pop-up menu (see detail) which allows you to modify and save your bookmarks or other items in your profile.

These **site maps** (one showing the general Rabobank site and the other showing the personalised site) reflect and clarify the navigation menus which guide you on your way. The site map for the personalised site is actually a collection of dynamic menu bars, and shows how the top menus adapt to the context you're currently in. Much like the menu of an Operating System, it only presents options which are relevant to the current context. Further options simply roll down from the menu bar via mouse-overs.

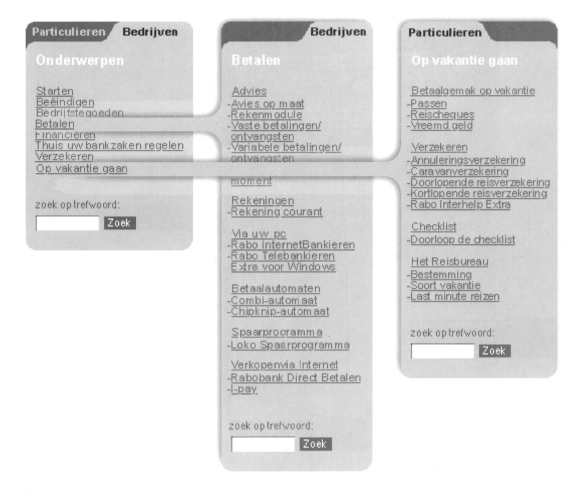

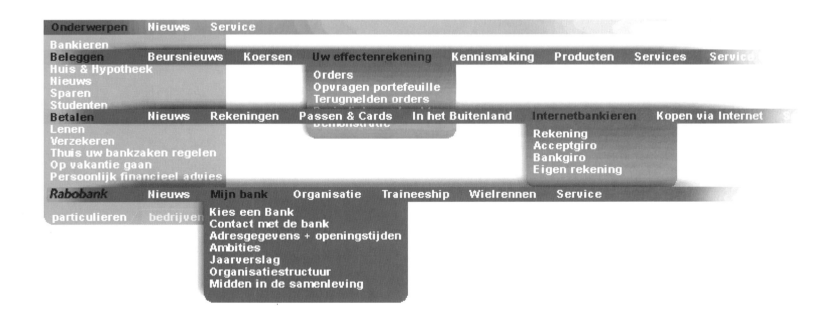

In your personal site, you can use the fully functional **on-line banking facilities**. After logging-in to your account and making the necessary payments, you can check your accounts and have a look at your current financial situation.

Particulier | Beleggen | Koersen

Jongerensite

Koersenmonitor

**Koersen van de AEX- en Dow Jones indices en van de hoofdfondsen van de Amsterdamse Effectenbeurs.
De koersen van de hoofdfondsen worden doorgegeven met een vertraging van 15 minuten.**

↑ Stijging t.o.v. slotkoers   ↓ Daling t.o.v. slotkoers

Fonds		Recent	Openingskoers	Slotkoers	Delta	%	Cum-vol	hoog	laag	Tijd
AEX INDEX	↑	1172.38	1152.73	1155.35	17.03	1.47		1174.85	1152.49	10:57:00
DOW JONES INDEX				9044.46						
ABN AMRO HOLDING	↑	39.7	38.8	38.9	0.8	2.06	1838551	39.8	38.8	10:41:34
AEGON	↑	226.7	223.1	223.6	3.1	1.39	647163	228	222.2	10:41:27
AHOLD KON	↑	69.9	69.1	69.2	0.7	1.01	838414	69.9	69.1	10:41:38
AKZO NOBEL	↑	81.4	79.1	80	1.4	1.75	365175	81.6	79.1	10:41:24
ASM LITHOGRAPHY HOLDING	↓	56.3	56.1	56.4	-0.1	-0.18	102587	56.6	56	10:37:12
BAAN COMPANY	↑	19.3	19.2	19.3	0.1	0.61	538477	19.5	19.1	10:41:37
BOLSWESSANEN KON CTA		23.2	23.2	23.2	0	0				
BUHRMANN NV	↑	32.8	32.8	32.1	0.7	2.18				
CSM CTA	↓	102.4	102.5	103	-0.6	-0.58				
DORDTSCHE PETR IND MIJ	↓	81.5	80.9	82	-0.5	-0.61				
DSM	↑	175.4	174.1	174.5	0.9	0.52				
ELSEVIER	↑	26.6	26.5	26.5	0.1	0.38				
FORTIS AMEV CTA	↑	150.6	149	150.2	0.4	0.27				
GETRONICS	↓	89.2	90.8	90	-0.8	-0.89				

Beursnieuws voorkeuren

heel belar

Beursstemming internationaal ◯

Beursstemming AEX ◯

Internationaal ◯

Marktcommentaar ◯

Tips ◯

These pages show **world news and information from the international stock exchanges**, continuously brought to you on the basis of your personal preferences. You can modify your profile via pop-up menus (see detail), but you can also modify them via individual items. Note how the personal menu folds away and effectively creates the maximum screen space for the desired information.

De bank van:
Willem Velthoven

Instellingen
Bookmarks
Betalen
Rekeningsaldo
Acceptgiro
Op vakantie gaan
Reischeques
Verzekeren
Inboedel verzekering
Op vakantie gaan
Reischeques
Vreemd geld
Externe bookmarks
www.mediamatic.nl
www.abnamro.nl
www.firstvirtual.com
Uw lokale bank
Rabobank Nederhorst Den
Berg, Voorstraat 18

Vorige bezoek:

Particulier | Betalen en Sparen

Bankgiro

Over te schrijven
ƒ 5,00

Uitvoerdatum
23-12-98

Van rekening
3938.80.966 - Betaalrekening - W. Velthoven

Naar rekening
3938.03.813

Toevoegen aan
adresboek ☐

Kies uit adresboek
Mediamatic Ip

Ten name van
Mediamatic Interactive

Omschrijving
Reiskosten

Plaats
Amsterdam

Spoed ☐   Periodiek ☐   Termijn

Aantal
99=onbeperkt

OK   Annuleren

OK + acceptgiro   OK + bankgiro   OK + eigen rekening   OK + verzenden

---

Onderwerpen   Nieuws   Uitleg Rabo Internetbankieren   Betalen & Sparen   Beleggen   Vragenlijst Rabo Internetbankieren   Service

De bank van:
Willem Velthoven

Instellingen
Bookmarks
Betalen
Rekeningsaldo
Acceptgiro
Op vakantie gaan
Reischeques
Verzekeren
Inboedel verzekering
Op vakantie gaan
Reischeques
Vreemd geld
Externe bookmarks
www.mediamatic.nl
www.abnamro.nl
www.firstvirtual.com
Uw lokale bank
Rabobank Nederhorst Den
Berg, Voorstraat 18

Vorige bezoek:

Colofon

Particulier | Betalen en Sparen

Rekeningoverzicht

23 december 1998

Rekening	Rekeningtype	Ten name van		Saldo
3034.11.414	Rekening-courant	Mediamatic Interactive	ƒ	-0,69
3938.03.813	Rekening-courant	Mediamatic Interactive	ƒ	165.441,17
3938.72.513	Rekening-courant	Mediamatic Netles Bv.	ƒ	45.515,40
3938.72.564	Rekening-courant	Velthoven Beheer Bv. Io.	ƒ	100,88
3938.80.966	Betaalrekening	W. Velthoven	ƒ	-459,04
3135.133.907	Telespaarrekening	W. Velthoven	ƒ	0,00
3135.859.584	Bedrijfsplusrekening	Mediamatic Interactive	ƒ	0,00
3135.883.809	Bedrijfsplusrekening	Mediamatic Interactive	ƒ	0,00

Hier kunt u een selectie uit uw transactieoverzicht maken.
3034.11.414 - Rekening-courant - Mediamatic Interactive
Kies een periode:
Begindatum   Einddatum   Toon lijst

Onderwerpen   Nieuws   Service

Nieuws

Nieuwsinstellingen

Voorpagina Beursnieuws Economisch Nieuws Financieel Nieuws Internetnieuws Rabobanknieuws Archief

29 december 1998 Laatste wijziging om 11:57

Stemming Azie: indices Tokio en Hongkong hoger de dag uit
Beursmedia/Betten, 29/12/1998

De toonaangevende aandelenindices van Azie-Pacific zijn dinsdag licht hoger de dag uitgegaan. De beursindices van Tokio en Hongkong wonnen respectievelijk 1% en 0,55%. De All Ordinaries-index in Sydney liet een kleine plus van 0,16% op 2768,40 zien. Lees verder...

Dagbladenoverzicht 29 december 1998
Beursmedia/Betten, 29/12/1998

De groep onbekende investeerders die het afgelopen jaar textielgroep Twenthe heeft overgenomen, wordt genoemd als tweede bieder op het beursfonds Koninklijke Ten Cate. (Het Financieele Dagblad) Lees verder...

Nikkei sluit 137,84 punten hoger in 13.846.90
Beursmedia/Betten, 29/12/1998

Op de effectenbeurs van Tokio is de Nikkei-index dinsdag 137,84 punten (1,01%) hoger gesloten dan het slot van afgelopen maandag. De index eindigde op 13.846,90. Lees verder...

Wall Street: Dow Jones wint 0,1% na rustige sessie
Beursmedia/Betten, 29/12/1998

De Dow Jones-index op Wall Street is maandag na een rustige sessie met een lichte plus gesloten. De toonaangevende Amerikaanse index won 8,76 punten op 9226,75, een winst van 0,1%. Gedurende bijna de hele sessie noteerde de index ongeveer 30 punten hoger. In het laatste uur deek de Dow Jones-index in een lichte min, om uiteindelijk toch nog iets hoger te sluiten. Lees verder...

Shell wil bouwstop botlekspoortunnel
Beursmedia/Betten, 29/12/1998

Koninklijke Olie/Shell Groep heeft de rechtbank in Rotterdam gevraagd de bouwvergunning voor de Botlekspoortunnel te schorsen. Dat meldt het dagblad Cobouw dinsdag. Lees verder...

Schuttersveld koopt Robert Schmidt (DLD)
Beursmedia/Betten, 29/12/1998

Schuttersveld heeft alle aandelen verworven in de Duitse producent van kunststoffen Robert Schmidt. Dat heeft de onderneming - een verzameling van toeleveringsbedrijven op het gebied van kunststof en metaal - dinsdag voorbeurs bekendgemaakt. Lees verder...

Hang Seng sluit 55,83 punten hoger op 10.225,997
Beursmedia/Betten, 29/12/1998

Op de effectenbeurs van Hongkong is de Hang Seng-index dinsdag 55,83 punten (0,55%) hoger gesloten dan het slot van afgelopen maandag. De index eindigde op 10.225,97. Lees verder...

Veel valse merkartikelen in beslag genomen in 1998
ANP, 29/12/1998
Lees verder...

Veemarkt Leiden 29 december
Beursmedia/Betten, 29/12/1998
Lees verder...

Veemarkt Leeuwarden 29 december 1998
Beursmedia/Betten, 29/12/1998
Lees verder...

Twentsche Kabel neemt Duitse Ernst & Engbring over
Beursmedia/Betten, 28/12/1998
Lees verder...

AEX zet openingsverlies om in kleine plus
Beursmedia/Betten, 29/12/1998

Op Beursplein 5 is de AEX-index dinsdag licht lager van start gegaan. De index opende 5,50 lager op 1186,89 en noteerde rond 10.30 uur rond de slotkoers van maandag op 1193,19, een plus van 0,80. Lees verder...

KPN aast op belangen in telecombedrijven Oost-Europa--media
Beursmedia/Betten, 29/12/1998

KPN aast op belangen in telecombedrijven in Slowakije, Slovenie en Polen. Dit bericht Het Financieele dagblad dinsdag op basis van uitspraken van directeur P. Martens, bij KPN verantwoordelijk voor de telecomactiviteiten in Oost-Europa. Lees verder...

Ministerie van Justitie: meer criminaliteit op het werk
Beursmedia/Betten, 29/12/1998

Werknemers maken zich steeds vaker schuldig aan diefstal, fraude en andere criminele handelingen op hun werk. Dat blijkt uit een onderzoek van het ministerie van Justitie. Dit meldt De Volkskrant. Lees verder...

Nederlanders gaan met plezier naar hun werk
Beursmedia/Betten, 29/12/1998

Van de werkende Nederlanders gaat bijna 90 procent met plezier naar het werk. Bovendien gaan vrouwen nog liever naar hun werk dan mannen. Dat blijkt uit de resultaten van een werkbelevingsonderzoek van het FNV in Groningen. Lees verder...

Stemming Europa: Frankfurt en Parijs licht hoger bij dunne handel
Beursmedia/Betten, 28/12/1998
Lees verder...

'ABN AMRO, ING bieden op Tsjechische bank CSOB'
Beursmedia/Betten, 28/12/1998
Lees verder...

Ten Cate: RvC wil opsplitsen noch verkopen
Beursmedia/Betten, 28/12/1998
Lees verder...

Japan: verkopen grote detailhandel november -1,5%
Beursmedia/Betten, 28/12/1998
Lees verder...

ngrijk minder belangrijk

○ ○
○ ○
○ ○
○ ○
○ ○

Bewaar

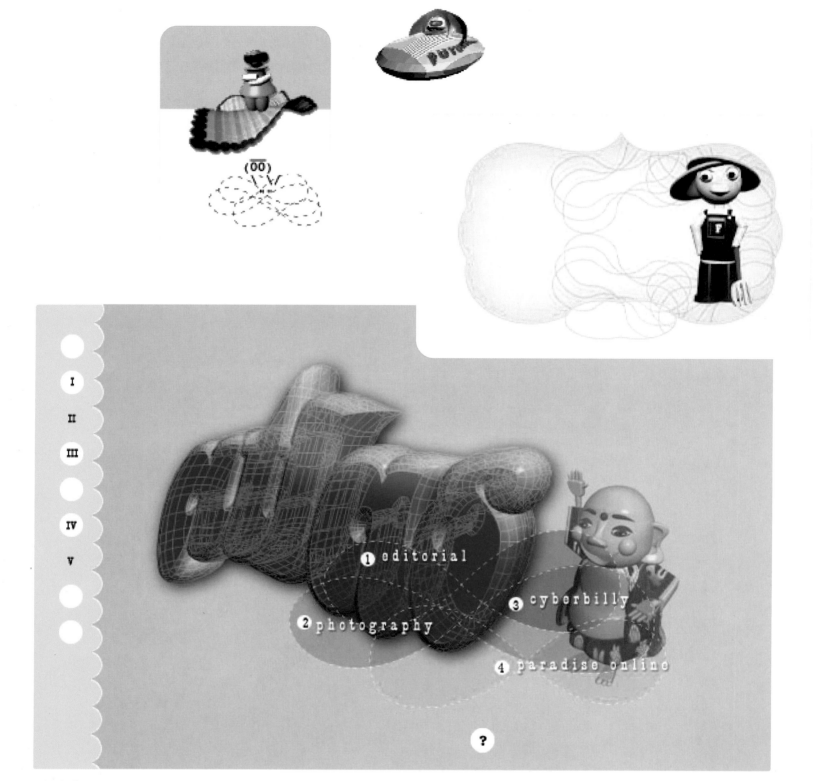

The Atlas **homepage** combines delicate animation with a clear layout of the content.

paradise online :

What's eating **Adam McCauley?** Find out in Fast food part II (265K).

TITLE OF THE SITE Atlas magazine ☙ OFFICIAL URL http://www.atlasmagazine.com ☙ LANGUAGE English ☙ COPYRIGHT OWNERS Amy Franceschini, Olivier Laude, Michael Macrone

PRODUCTION Atlas Web Design ☙ EDITORIAL Olivier Laude ☙ CONTRIBUTORS Multimedia: Terbo Ted. Web design (winter 96): David Karam. Sound mix (summer 96): Tom Bland. Copy supervision: Ken Coupland. Additional coding: Jean-Paul Guadagnin. Technical consulting: Paul Rauschelbach

SCREEN DESIGN Amy Franceschini ☙ INTERACTION DESIGN Amy Franceschini ☙ SOUND DESIGN Terbo Ted Airking ☙ ANIMATION/GRAPHICS Amy Franceschini ☙ AWARDS First website to become part of permanent collection of the San Francisco Museum of Modern Art. Webby Award for

art & design in both 1997 and 1998. (the Internet's Oscars). Winner of Communication Arts Digital annual two years in a row (1996, 1997). Winner of the 1997 New York Art directors club Digital Show Annual. Atlas is also included in mixing messages, a multimedia exhibit at the Cooper-Hewitt

National Design Museum ☙ PLATFORM USED FOR DESIGNING THE SITE Macintosh 99%, Other 1% ☙ APPLICATIONS USED Photoshop, Illustrator, Director, Shockwave, Dreamweaver, BBEdit, Infini-d, Gifbuilder, Gif Animation

PLACE AND DATE OF DESIGN San Francisco, 1995-present ☙ CLIENT Atlas Magazine

ATLAS MAGAZINE

http://www.atlasmagazine.com

In the preamble to Atlas 6, the editors talk of the lure of dynamic html that bought them back to their screens after a summer vacation away. In turn, dynamic html, java, roll-overs, midi and all manner of other modern Web 'bells and whistles' draw the audience back to this site as well. The pull is all the more magnetic since these elements are rather nattily held together in a webmagazine of some content, with masses of style.

From the delicately animated homepage, you scroll down, both literally and visually, through this issue's layout. Atlas currently boasts four real sections plus some extra 'stuff': 'Cyberbilly' (with the fun 'Buddha's Digitoscope Ant Farm'), followed by the editorial, featuring Pulitzer Prizewinner Stanley Karnow, Ken Coupland's online multimedia novel and a weekly 'Best Use of the Web'. There are also photography sections and 'Paradise online' (with a warning note about its 256k size, implying that this is fun Web stuff not meant for those impatient with 'content' downloads). For first-time users it may seem quite hard to get the measure of each section, but regular readers will be more familiar with the flavour each area has developed. Despite hours of Web browsing, I still occasionally crave the Web equivalent of a magazine rack 'quick flick', and the intro page doesn't give me quite enough of this. But you can use the extremely stylish animated site menu to get at least an overview of where you've been and the kind of breadth on offer. Even though you don't get a feel for each section, the animated roll-overs are nice enough to keep you playing through the issues, watching the shifts in content.

The section I actually responded to best was the photography area, perhaps since it seemed to mix good design with more substantial content, or perhaps because I'm always in admiration of a well-handled attempt to deal with a Web gallery! Included in this section are Adam Kufeld's images from Cuba, Bob Sacha's 'Under New York', Catherine Karnow's 'Bombay Bazaar' and Olivier Laude's 'Photographs of Chinese Rural Architecture'. Although in general the bright characters and slightly 'frothy' Atlas style is wonderful, I did wonder if it was at times a bit overwhelming, or at least less than complementary to the actual photographs, which were, on the whole, serious collections. Yet in Oliver Laude's section, for example, any intrusion from the floaty intro page is balanced out by the actual delight of using the interactive animated side bar in order to navigate through the photo journey. The images in this piece are also strong enough to withstand this type of framing.

Some of the other 'stuff' to be found within Atlas is probably the most fun, and I expect it draws the biggest crowds of devoted surfers/designers. As their slightly ostentatious list of Web awards testifies, Atlas is obviously a popular drop-off for those in search of the latest Web gizmo rendered with some panache. The Atlas gallery is great for these viewers — here you see the 'backstage' of all the html or java script additions they've tried, some of which make it to the magazine proper, some of which don't. For some inexplicable reason, I really delighted in 'Plug-in Array', which draws up a list of all the plug-ins currently 'attached' to your browser — sad, I know, but good fun!

The Atlas team produce a webmagazine that combines good content and delightful graphic design with a confident dose of solid interaction design — the small joys of mouse interaction do not pass unnoticed here.

by Nina Pope

‘**Paradise online**’ is certainly sunnier as it includes some fun animation, with a fast connection.

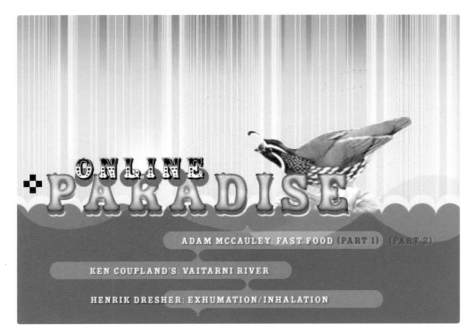

ADAM MCCAULEY: FAST FOOD (PART I) (PART 2)

KEN COUPLAND'S: VAITARNI RIVER

HENRIK DRESHER: EXHUMATION/INHALATION

Ken Coupland's dyspeptic online **multimedia novel** is featured in the editorial section.

The mystery guest knew he would have to work fast. He was waiting for someone to mention dinner. "I could go with you," he said.

And that was when the mystery guest made his mistake. When they all got where they were going there was a line to wait, and the mystery guest really needed a cup of coffee. When he came back, they were all gone.

The mystery guest was used to that too. He went back out on the street. How far could they go? The pink pastry sat there in his hand. It was going to be back to the roller rink again tonight, he knew.

The mystery guest pulled himself together. Whatever happened, this was not going to turn out like the potluck he'd found an invitation to on the bulletin board at the laundromat. The mystery guest noticed a restaurant next door where another line was starting to form. He made a mental note to return to the neighborhood. "Excuse me, there's someone waiting for me inside," the mystery guest said hopefully. The line parted and he walked in and went unnerringly towards the stairs to the mezzanine.

Mystery gu >

View source

One look at the source code for the Atlas homepage reveals an enormous **dynamic html** document. Version 4.x browsers allow for the animation of sprites like the small space-buggy that sometimes appears on the homepage, and also for the way in which the menu-circles on the left-hand side of the screen move up and down. Part of the html shows tell-tale signs of having been made using Macromedia's Dream-weaver software. Dreamweaver uses an interface, similar to Director's, to create **timelines** for the **animation paths of sprites** on the screen. The code which is generated creates a series of numbers in arrays, which in turn refer to the position of the sprite on the screen both vertically and horizontally.

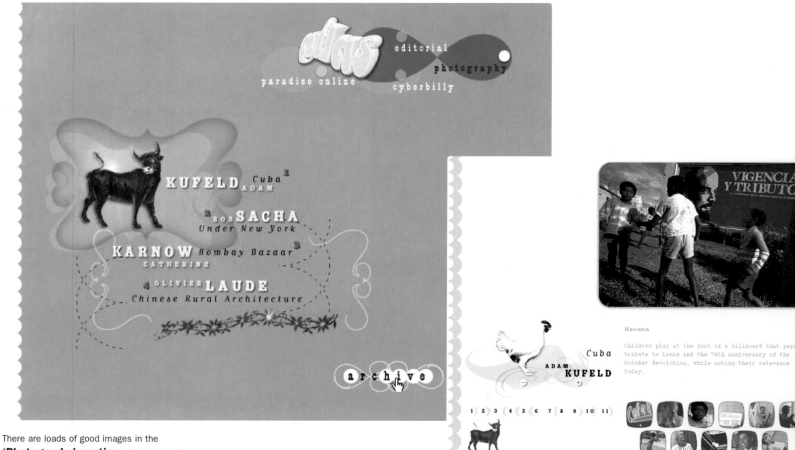

There are loads of good images in the
'Photography' section, where a lot of
effort has gone into display techniques.

Havana

Children play at the foot of a billboard that pays
tribute to Lenin and the 74th anniversary of the
October Revolution, while noting their relevance
today.

Further chapters of Cuba:
images 12 · 22

**Each artist has his or her own
section**, where you can click through a large
selection of available images as black and white
thumbnails. These flick over to colour as you
select them, when they then pop up in the main
viewing area of the page.

" Indians are supposedly shy
about being physically
aggressive ... "

Cricket Players

Practicing on the Oval Maidan. An Australian cricket
coach was brought over to train the boys, especially
to be more aggressive, as Indians are supposedly shy
about being physically aggressive towards each other.

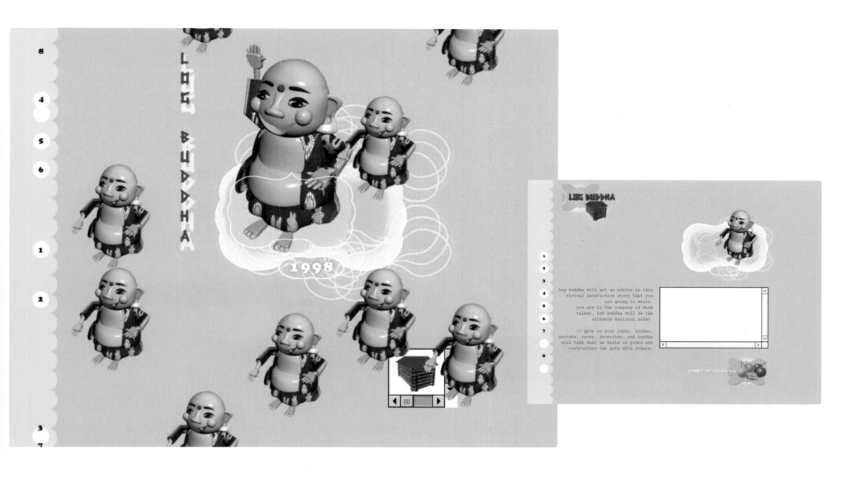

The animated route choices through **Olivier Laude's photo journey** looking at Chinese rural architecture are particularly elegant.

The **site map** is a great example of the elegant interaction design which is employed throughout the site. It may not give much detail, but the roll-overs are delightful.

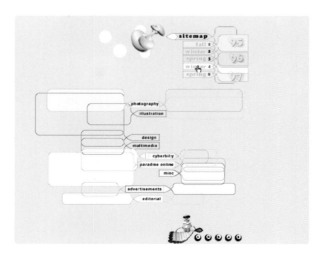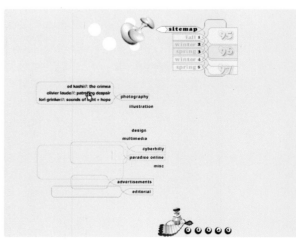

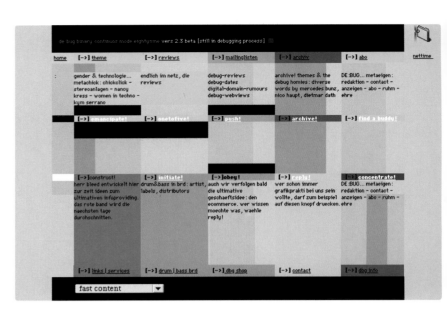

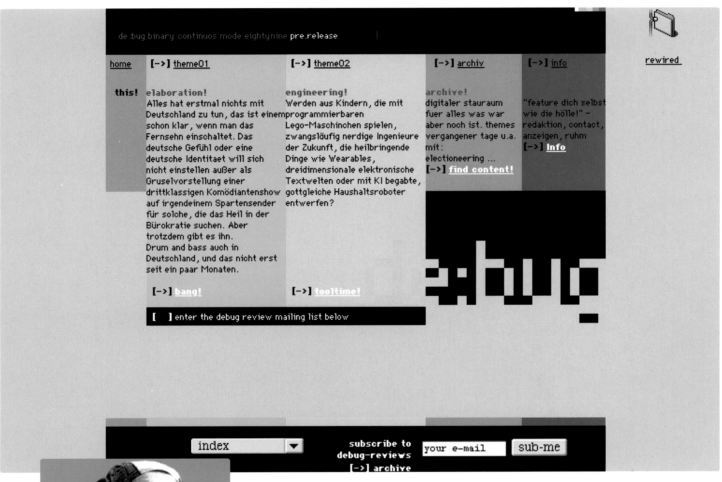

From the visual design of the **homepage**, it is immediately clear that the site consists of four different sections, each with its own background colour. The section headings are actually the navigation bar which is used on every page. The lower frame, with **the pop-up** links and the possibility of subscribing to De:bug's discussion list, is also used throughout the site.

View source

Anyone who wants to see just what **frames**, **tables** and **binhex colours** can create need look no further than De:bug. It takes some time, as well as a few thorough perusals of the source code, to work out where the frames end and the tables begin, but with these simple elements the De:bug designers create a site that is a delight to use. It displays a good sense of the issues facing designers who are involved in sites for online publishing, where there will inevitably be extensive content and many different pieces of information that the user will need to navigate through. Simple devices include colour-coding of different sections and using frames so that changes generally occur within the larger framework of the homepage. These small aids help users to understand where they are within a potentially confusing amount of information. And, of course, it also helps the designers to maintain a site which is constantly being supplemented with new content.

TITLE OF THE SITE De:bug binary continuous mode ➤ **PLACE AND DATE OF DESIGN** Berlin 1998 ➤ **CLIENT** de:bug verlagsgesellschaft mbh, de:bug, zeitung für elektronische lebensaspekte (de:bug, newspaper for electronic life aspects) ➤ **COPYRIGHT OWNERS** de:bug verlagsgesellschaft mbh ➤ **PRODUCTION** Sascha Koesch, Jan Rikus Hillmann, Gerold Liere ➤ **PLATFORM USED FOR DESIGNING THE SITE** Macintosh 100%

OFFICIAL URL http://www.de-bug.de (version 2.3 beta) ➤ **LANGUAGE** German, parts in English ➤ **INTERACTION DESIGN** Jan Rikus Hillmann ➤ **SCREEN DESIGN** Jan Rikus Hillmann ➤

EDITORIAL Sascha Koesch ➤ **CONTRIBUTORS** all the de:bug editors and writers ➤

APPLICATIONS USED Photoshop, BBedit

DE:BUG BINARY CONTINUOUS MODE

http://www.de-bug.de

The electronic version of the German magazine De:bug, published monthly as a newspaper, is a surprising exception among the many thousands of text-based webzines. As a newcomer (it started its print version in 1997 and it's been on the Web since 1998), De:bug shows that even a simple webzine that republishes print material can be good-looking and a joy to use.

De:bug is all about electronic lifestyles. The editors claim it's 'the result of a synthesis between urban youth culture and the aesthetic and intellectual expedition into the wasteland of digital media'. In a typical issue, you'll come across articles on the German drum 'n' bass scene, descriptions of synthesiser emulators and computer games, essays on biotechnology and robots, and of course loads of music reviews.

The electronic De:bug stands out because of the attention paid to layout and navigational design. It pushes simple html to extremes, without denying that it's anything more than 'just' a text-based site. Through its consistent use of minimal, very simple design tricks, De:bug becomes an easy-to-navigate and visually taut website that very effectively makes use of the Web's advantages (linking to e-mail, different ways of navigating through the content, use of outward-bound links).

First of all, there's the very definite colour palette of greens, blues and oranges (even used for images) which visually holds the site together. De:bug's textual nature is emphasised through the scarce use of images (with the few illustrations that do exist being loaded in a separate window) and the lack of animation and buttons. De:bug has a flat approach to Web design. It 'misuses' the widely hated frames concept to create a layout grid on top of a Netscape grey background that conspicuously alludes to the early days of Web publishing. Frames are dynamic insofar as new data is loaded into them. De:bug's use of frames allows the flat screen, or the layout, to become dynamic without letting it take on depth.

That the navigation is easy and clear is not a logical given for a site which is structured in different sections and which also makes an archive of older issues available within the current issue's framework. This clarity is achieved by a combination of pop-ups (the only java-scripted element in the site), a navigation bar and the consistent use of background colours. Any page within the site is just two clicks away, but since the general frames (with titles, pop-ups and navigation) remain on screen, there's no chance of getting lost. The background colours designate the different sections. These colours are repeated in the navigation bar — a simple procedure by which the navigation bar also functions as a means of orientation and, although it's in a separate frame, visually becomes part of the page as a whole. As for typography, De:bug has chosen to use a rather small sans serif font that remains readable because the screen design is sober and, as mentioned, lacks images and animations.

Of course there are weaknesses as well. When the site is viewed using a higher resolution, there's a good change it will not fit the screen. And the Web interface to the discussion list — the interactive part of the site — is ugly: it's hosted by another organisation, and these pages' design, while quite reserved, is harsh to the eye compared to the neat De:bug pages.

This site may look unspectacular for those in search of the latest tricks, but the (deceptive!) simplicity fits the content very well and makes for an enjoyable read.

by Arie Altena

The suitcase, with the link to a website

which is associated with De:bug, can be understood as an allusion to pre-WWW gopher sites. The link automatically changes so that, during a first visit, one is tricked into believing that changes are based on one's clicking behaviour. The link is in a separate frame with a meta-tag that links to a page with yet another link. A beautiful example of minimal tagging with maximal result.

The **pop-ups** are doubled in the archive section: one for the current issue, and one for the archive. The archive thus becomes visually embedded in the current issue.

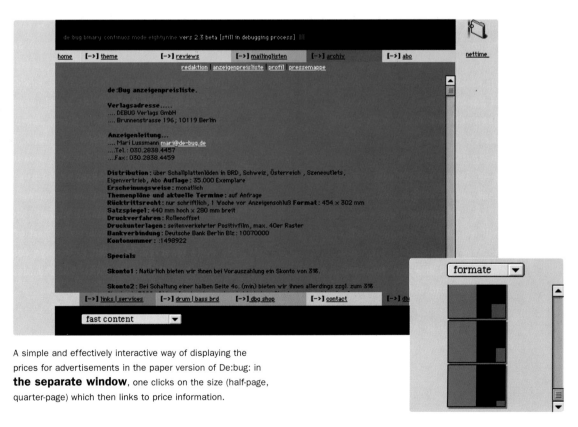

A simple and effectively interactive way of displaying the prices for advertisements in the paper version of De:bug: in **the separate window**, one clicks on the size (half-page, quarter-page) which then links to price information.

The **images** in De:bug are all displayed in a separate window with fixed sizes
so that they don't interfere with the webpage's layout. The site's colour palette
is used for all the images (except black and white ones), which results in a
tight fit between text layout and illustration. The separate window is also used
for linking to related material on the WWW.

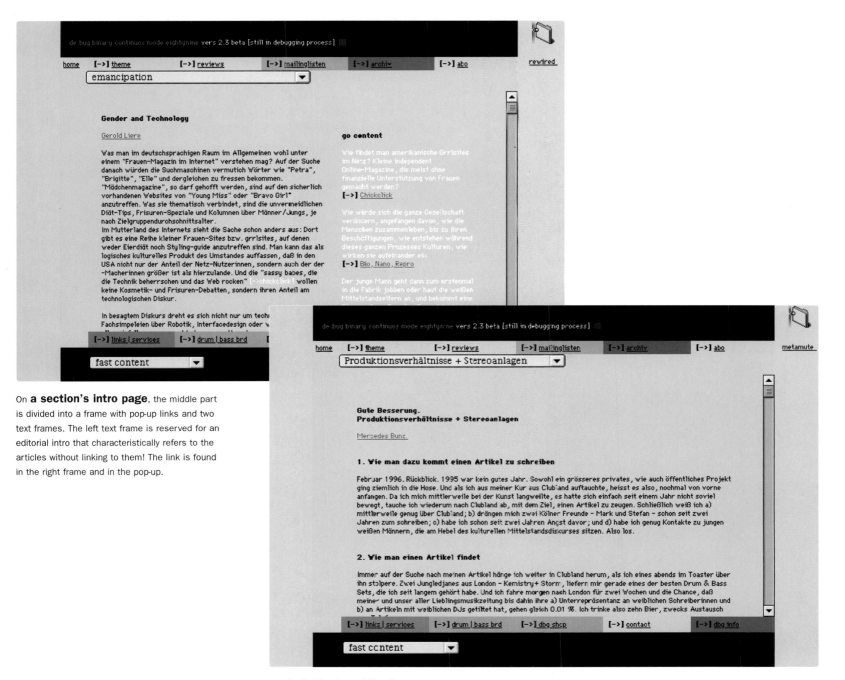

On **a section's intro page**, the middle part
is divided into a frame with pop-up links and two
text frames. The left text frame is reserved for an
editorial intro that characteristically refers to the
articles without linking to them! The link is found
in the right frame and in the pop-up.

The **individual contributions** always occupy one
whole frame in the middle part of the screen amid the
navigation frames and a background of Netscape grey.

The opening screen for the **Death issue** sets the tone for the eerie actions you'll soon be undertaking. Going in, you'll have to scan this man's body by 'feeling' your way across the image. Scanning backwards and forwards across the body calls up the texts in the lower half of the screen, dealing with matters of the soul or the possibilities of resuscitation.

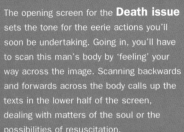

what is death?   loading

Shhhhh !

the

        man **you**
                    are
        about
                to see
        looks
                dead

Ron Mueck's *Dead Dad*. Silicone and acrylic sou[...]
Courtesy of the Saatchi Collection, London, [...]

○brain death   ○what is death?   CO[...]

Has his soul departed?

To measure the soul, says Dr. David Jones of New Scientist magazine, attach piezolelectric transducers, inertial-navigation accelerometers and other instruments to a dying person. Theoretically, this could measure the direction and speed of the soul as it leaves the body. Although that theory is as yet unproven, one doctor in Germany, has had more success. In repeated experiments, he placed highly sensitive scales under the legs of dying patients' beds. At the moment of death, he consistently noted a loss of 21 grams of weight.

Ron Mueck's *Dead Dad*. Silicone and acrylic sculpture.
Courtesy of the Saatchi Collection, London, UK.

○brain death   ○what is death?   **COLORS24**

Is his heart beating?

The heart pauses for a fraction of a second after every beat (during 70 years of life, it has actually been at rest for the equivalent of 40 of them). After a cardiac arrest, the heart can be motionless for up to six minutes. Even though the blood stops circulating, the corpse isn't breathing, and there's no sign of life, full resuscitation is still possible.

Ron Mueck's *Dead Dad*. Silicone and acrylic sculpture.
Courtesy of the Saatchi Collection, London, UK.

○brain death   ○what is death?   **COLORS24**

"Home is where I can scream at the top of my lungs and no one cares." Natalie, USA

COLORS

i   21   22   23   24   25   TIME   27   YP

This **homepage** for COLORS Magazine covers the Home issue. Built up from a number of frames, it uses a continuously reloading topframe to display statements about what 'Home' means to various people. The numbers at the bottom open up a new window for each issue.

TITLE OF THE SITE COLORS, eine website que parle about el resto del mondo ➤ OFFICIAL URL http://www.colorsmagazine.com ➤ PLACE AND DATE OF DESIGN Treviso, Oct '97 – Sept '98 ➤ CLIENT COLORS magazine, Oliviero Toscani (United Colors of Benetton) ➤ EDITORIAL COLORS Magazine, Editor in Chief: Oliviero Toscani, Creative Editor:

LANGUAGE English (other language inclusion forthcoming) ➤ COPYRIGHT OWNERS COLORS Magazine S.r.L, United Colors of Benetton ➤ PRODUCTION New Media Department, Fabrica, project coordination: Tom Hobbs ➤ EDITORIAL COLORS Magazine, Editor in Chief: Oliviero Toscani, Creative Editor: Adam Broomberg, Managing Editor: Claudine Boeglin, Executive Editor: Carlos Mustienes, Senior Editor: Rose George, Art Director: Thomas Hilland (Printed magazine only, Time-Touch) ➤ CONTRIBUTORS N/A Screen design, Steve Bowden (Fat-Touch), Tom Hobbs (Fat-Touch), Lloyd Thomas (Fat-Home), Spencer Higgins (Fat-Time), Interaction design Steve Bowden (Fat-Touch), Tom Hobbs (Fat-Touch), Lloyd Thomas, Lloyd Thomas (Fat-Home), Spencer Higgins (Fat-Time) ➤ SOUND DESIGN Lloyd Thomas (Fat-Home), Spencer Higgins (Fat-Time) ➤ ANIMATION/GRAPHICS Steve Bowden (Fat-Touch), Tom Hobbs (Fat-Touch), Tom Hobbs (Fat-Touch), Lloyd Thomas (Fat-Home) ➤ APPLICATIONS USED Adobe Photoshop 4.01, Adobe Illustrator 6, Macromedia Director 6 (6.5), Macromedia Flash 2 & 3, Macromedia Dreamweaver 1, Macromedia SoundEdit 16 version 2, Macromedia Freehand 8, BB Edit 4.5 ➤ AWARDS Communication Arts 'site of the week' April '98 Digital Thread 'advent 11 Gallery' May '98 amongst others... ➤ PLATFORM USED FOR DESIGNING THE SITE Macintosh 100%, (wintel for testing only)

COLORS MAGAZINE

http://www.colorsmagazine.com

In the seven years of its printed existence, COLORS Magazine has established international renown for the controversial visual statements initiated by photographer Oliviero Toscani and designer Tibor Kalman. Positioning themselves as a global magazine on local cultures, it was only a matter of time before they would make the move to the Internet. So what should you expect from the online version of this infamous magazine? How would the largely photography-based issues translate to the dynamic environment of the Web? Contrary to your expectations, the editors and designers of COLORS Magazine online have chosen not to go for the abundance of visual material so characteristic of the magazine. Instead they have created a highly condensed version of each printed issue's theme.

From the outset, it is clear that the designers have been looking for Web equivalents for the powerful visual communication forged by the image and text combinations. Relying heavily on the two main tools, Shockwave and, more recently, the vector-based animations of Flash, the chosen topics are turned into poignant online statements.

One initial decision that was made was to create one page as a home-base. From there, each theme issue is presented in a new pop-up window. Even though this feature is a Web trick on the rise, it has been put to good use here. It allows the designers to create a specific format for each issue, regardless of the users' settings for their browser windows. In this way, the Home issue is set within a square window, the Time issue in a horizontally-oriented timeline, and so on. It also allows the user to browse through several issues at once, as several windows can be open at the same time.

Each of these online issues generally consists of two or three items which were also featured in the printed version. But here these items present opportunities to test new ways of browsing through image and text combinations, developing even more engaging means of communication. The editors and designers constantly perform various interface experiments, ranging from innovative approaches to tired gimmicks. In the Smoke issue, a 3D smoke cloud provides the main navigation through statements about its toxic contents. In its design, this interface comes surprisingly close to current designs for associative information browsers. Its subtle use of substance names, which come up or disappear in the cloud, coupled with text which pops up at a twist of the mouse, make for an almost seamless interface. At least as impressive is the example from the Death issue, where you need to 'scan' the corpse of a naked man to call up questioning statements on the nature of death. This almost tactile interface adds an extra eerie dimension to the subject, not suited to the weak at heart!
The Fat issue and the Time issue stand out among the more light-hearted contributions. In the Fat issue, for instance, 'The Ideal Body' utilises Shockwave to allow the users to experiment with the images of naked bodies, varying their ideal proportions in width and height. 'How Fat is your World?' uses the zoom option in Flash to visualise the imbalance of world food consumption. Some continents swell to enormous proportions which represent their abundance, while others shrink to represent their shortage. In the Time issue, your patience is tried when you are presented with a large scrolling text, which begins by announcing that you have to brace yourself to vertically scroll through X-amount of pixels if you want to read the entire text. The text subsequently launches into a rant about the brevity of your attention span, telling you that your chances of making it to the end of this boring flat text are nil.

It is this immediate addressing of the users, as well as the attempt to engage them, that is striven for in most of the items in COLORS online. Though not always successful due to the present tools' limitations, I have the feeling that, with the rise of java programming and active server pages, we can expect a lot more enticing pieces of work from these designers in the near future.

by Geert J. Strengholt

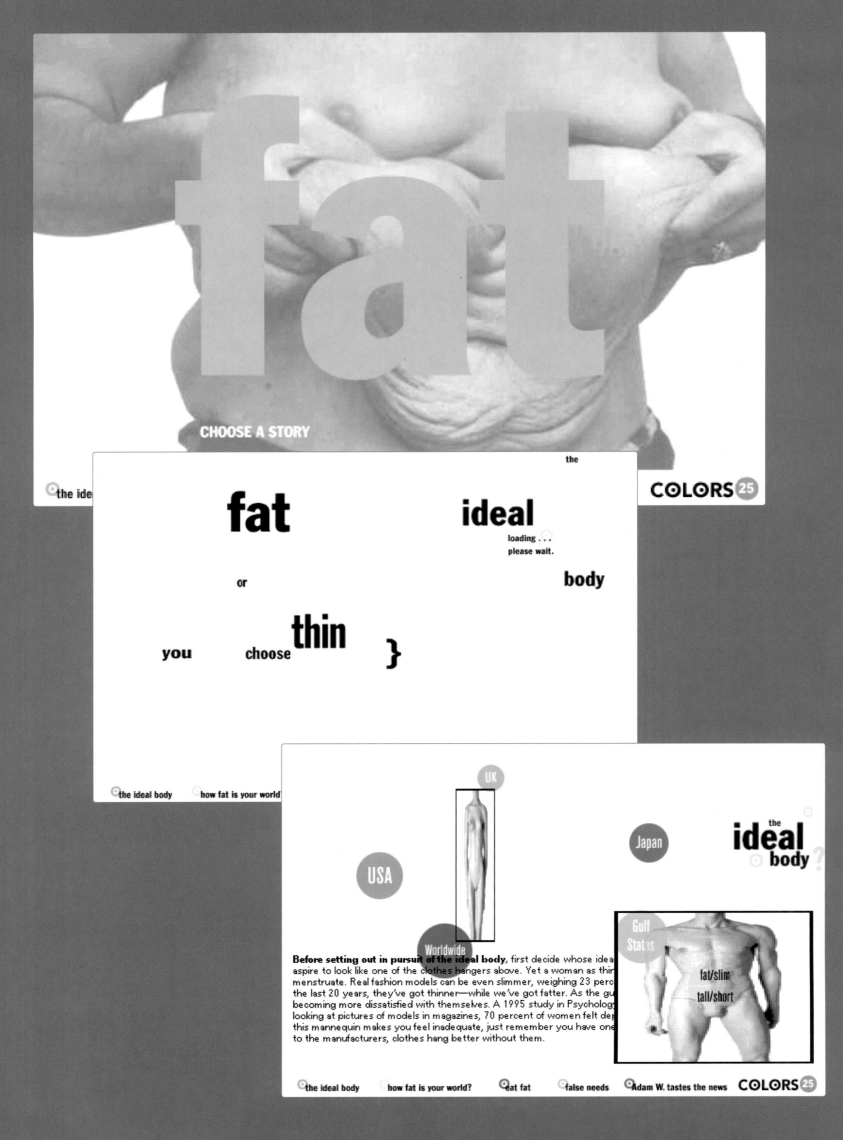

fat

CHOOSE A STORY

the ideal

COLORS 25

the

fat   ideal

loading . . .
please wait.

or   body

you   choose thin   }

the ideal body   how fat is your world

UK

USA

Japan

the
ideal
body ?

Worldwide

Gulf
States

fat/slim

tall/short

Before setting out in pursuit of the ideal body, first decide whose idea
aspire to look like one of the clothes hangers above. Yet a woman as thin
menstruate. Real fashion models can be even slimmer, weighing 23 perc
the last 20 years, they've got thinner—while we've got fatter. As the gu
becoming more dissatisfied with themselves. A 1995 study in Psycholog
looking at pictures of models in magazines, 70 percent of women felt de
this mannequin makes you feel inadequate, just remember you have one
to the manufacturers, clothes hang better without them.

the ideal body   how fat is your world?   eat fat   false needs   Adam W. tastes the news   COLORS 25

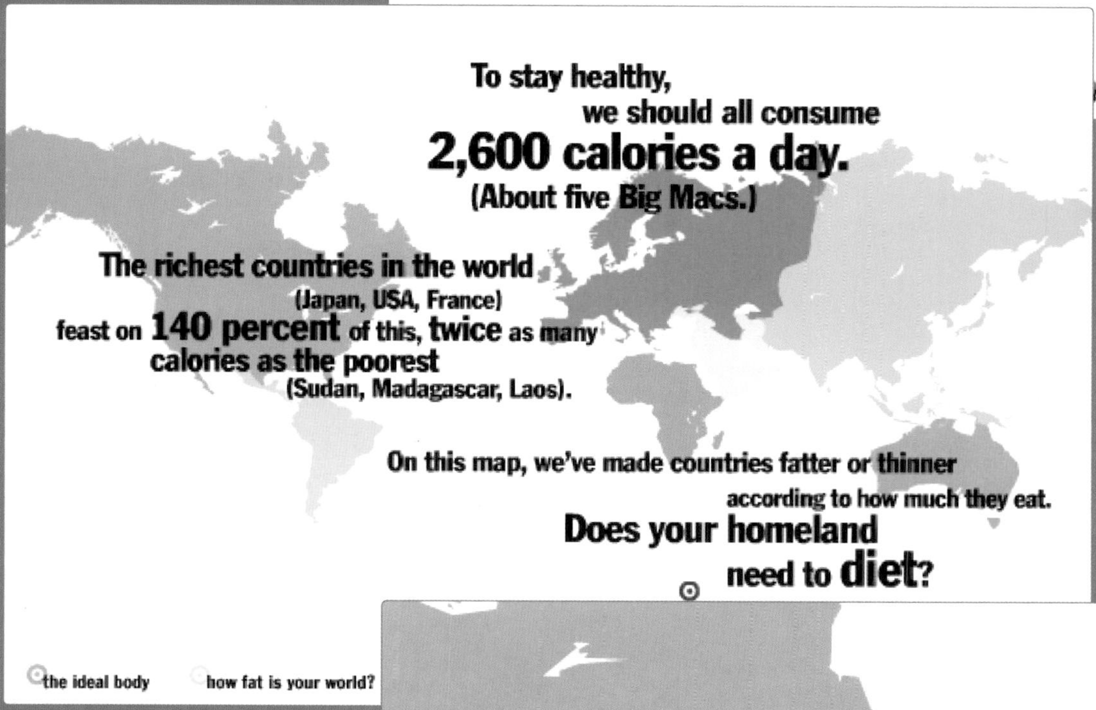

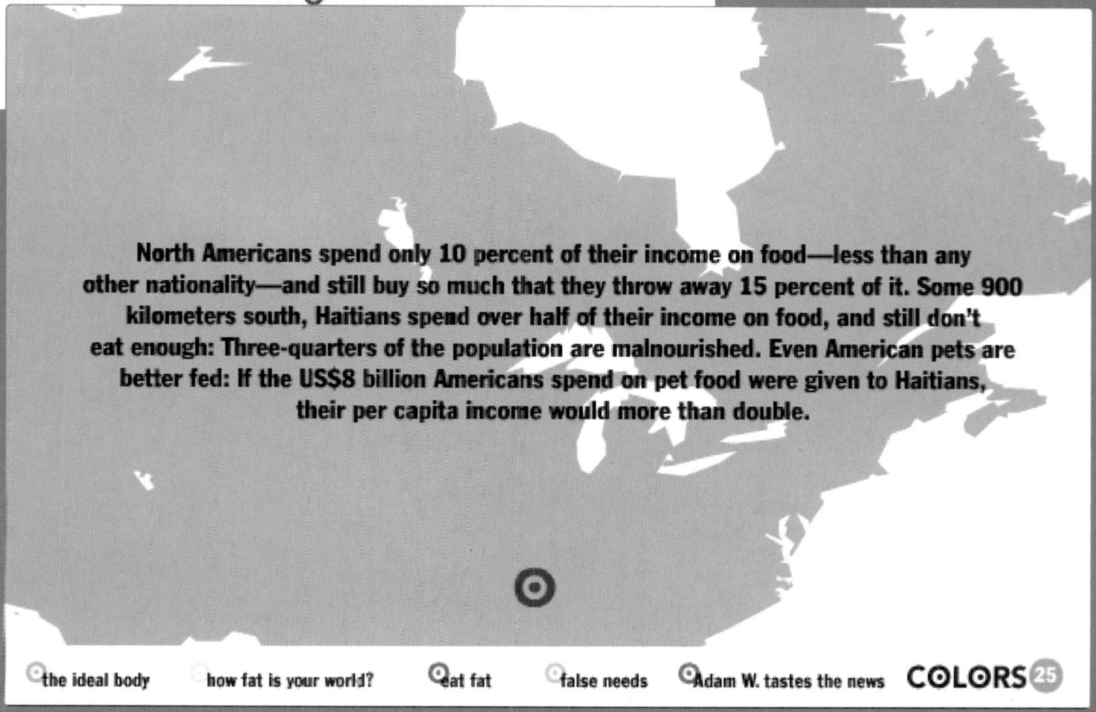

How Fat is your World?

To stay healthy,
we should all consume
2,600 calories a day.
(About five Big Macs.)

The richest countries in the world
(Japan, USA, France)
feast on **140 percent** of this, **twice** as many
calories as the poorest
(Sudan, Madagascar, Laos).

On this map, we've made countries fatter or thinner
according to how much they eat.
**Does your homeland
need to diet?**

the ideal body   how fat is your world?

This obviously is the **Fat issue**, where a Shockwave animation fades-in this impressive image. After playing around with the opening statements — the typography jumbles up when you move your mouse across — you enter a graphic playground of nudes. Once you get the hang of it, you can inflate or deflate these figures to preposterous proportions, making the notion of the ideal figure obsolete.

North Americans spend only 10 percent of their income on food—less than any other nationality—and still buy so much that they throw away 15 percent of it. Some 900 kilometers south, Haitians spend over half of their income on food, and still don't eat enough: Three-quarters of the population are malnourished. Even American pets are better fed: If the US$8 billion Americans spend on pet food were given to Haitians, their per capita income would more than double.

the ideal body   how fat is your world?   eat fat   false needs   Adam W. tastes the news   COLORS 25

Some of these people say the world will end this year.
If it doesn't, there are plenty of other deadlines to look forward to

APOCALYPSE WHEN?

The Church of the SubGenius Reverend Steve Bevilacqua: "At 7am on July 5, members will be teleported in what we call 'rapture' up to the space vessel where every member receives their personal vision of paradise. Those left behind on earth will die slowly. The Xists (from the Planet X) will grant their alien technology to humans, who will abuse it and wipe themselves out in a very bad way. Membership of the Church of the SubGenius is only US$30. We could be wrong, but for $30 isn't it worth your life to find out?" Pictured is SubGenius founding father J. R. "Bob" Dobbs.

Take a deep breath. You'll have to scroll roughly 2,559 pixels to read the 1,483 words will appear on this screen. That's fewer than in the average COLORS story But this time we've done nothing whatsoever to make you want to read them No moving captions. No big pictures. No pretty colors. No enhanced download time. Nothing In fact, the chances that you will take the time to read to the end of the story are virtually ni

In the **Time issue**, you find this
Flash feature about doomsday
prophets, entitled 'Apocalypse When'.
Literally zooming in through the
'celestial' menu in the second screen,
you can access information on cults
and sects like the Church of the
Subgenius.

What's in  your

SMOKE

?

loading

cadmium   phosphorous

formaldehyde

Formaldehyde "We inject formaldehyde into the veins and the cheeks," says a spokesperson for the Association Française d'Information Funéraire (French Funeral Information Association). "It preserves a dead body for up to a week." In living people, however, formaldehyde causes cancer as well as respiratory, skin and gastrointestinal problems. That's why—until Canada's Tobacco Control Act was struck down in 1995—Canadian cigarette packs legally had to list formaldehyde as one of tobacco's toxic constituents.

COLORS21

methoprene

phosphorous

Methoprene "Just like any vegetable product, tobacco naturally gives off a complex variety of chemicals when you burn it," says Dr. Murray Kaiserman. But methoprene isn't one of them. An "insect growth regulator" that stunts larvae development, methoprene appears on the list of tobacco additives released in 1994 by the US tobacco industry. It also appears in flea spray.

COLORS21

Good question! Let's find out. In the
screens that follow, you seem to be able to
move through a cloud of smoke, turning it
around, analysing it and identifying its toxic
components. By bringing forward components
like formaldehyde and linking them to
explanatory text, while submerging others in
the smoke, this image is turned into a great
interface for browsing information.

130

View source

One of the key techniques used in the Colors website is **Shockwave**. *Its foremost function here is to provide an engaging interface to textual or image material. By using Shockwave, this can basically be contained within the single window set up for each issue, whether the text is in plain html or incorporated into the Shockwave movie.*

The designers have created a range of small animated sequences and engaging interactions with a focus on **'tactile' quality interactions** *— the user needs to 'take hold of the image'. Whether controlling a scrolling piece of text, exploring a cloud of smoke or scanning a body, it's the tactility that engages the user.*

In more recent issues, **Flash**, *the vector-based animation program, is used to create enticing, almost cinematic experiences. Especially in the Fat issue, its ability to draw the user in with Flash's* **zoom-in function** *works extremely well. The flow from the satellite view towards ever more detailed information about consumer habits is supported by the fact that the resolution of its imagery remains the same at any stage.*

RETIREMENT HOME

Harry Auty, 82, has been living in a retirement home in West Yorkshire, UK, since 1991, when his leg was amputated.

07:00
09:00
12:00
16:30
18:00
21:00

RETIREMENT HOME   ORPHANAGE   HOSPITAL   HOUSE ARREST   REFUGEE CAMP

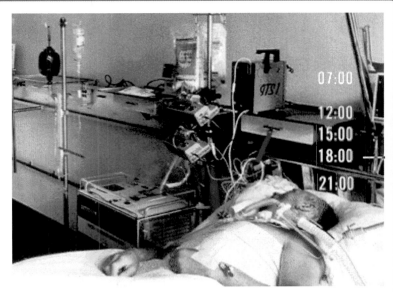

I'm too weak to eat by myself: My husband feeds me dinner. I look forward to going back to the hospital every month, it's my second home.

07:00
12:00
15:00
18:00
21:00

RETIREMENT HOME   ORPHANAGE   HOSPITAL   HOUSE ARREST   REFUGEE CAMP

COLORS may be the future, but **they have to sell magazines too**, so here's the information on how to buy or subscribe. The endless horizontal scroll in the bottom frame presents the covers of all issues which have been printed so far.

The latest issue is about **Toys**, with Flash animations by George Larou.

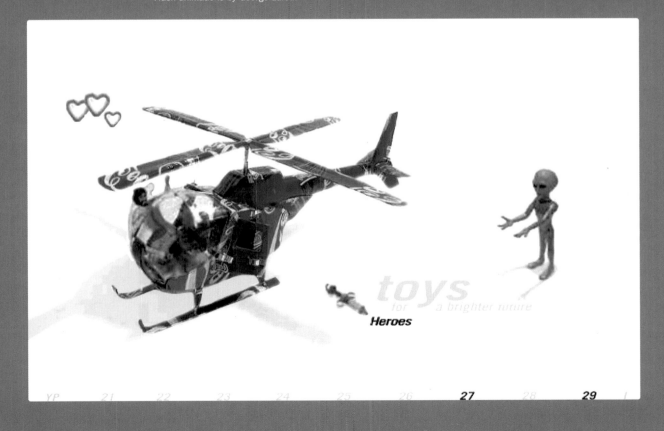

All the **index pages** have the same design, but differ in their use of colour and choice of image, which set the mood for the content. They can be updated easily by adding a button that links to a new issue.

Volumeone also has **samples from their commercial work** for print and screen. Clicking the sample image links to a higher resolution image or a remote website; both are opened in a new window.

VOLUMEONE

http://www.volumeone.com

Volumeone is a quarterly webzine put together by the Brooklyn-based 'visual communications studio' founded by Matt Owens. The purpose of this zine is to explore the new narrative possibilities of the World Wide Web and to find out how visual communication functions online.

The URL www.volumeone.com brings you to the title page of the most recent issue. From here you can access the three different parts of the site: four buttons lead to the contributions in the current issue, numbers on the left lead to the title pages of the other issues, and a button at the right gives access to information about the company.

Choosing to see one of the contributions makes a new window with fixed sizes appear. This creates the feeling that you're going to see a finished piece of work. And the contributions are indeed a mixture of text, image, animation, buttons and, sometimes, audio, that are integrated into a complete experience. Mostly these consist of a few screens which can be accessed by clicking on a button. Here the elegance of Volumeone shines through: the buttons are part of the page's visual design, though you find them immediately; to go back you have to close the window.

Each issue of Volumeone is thought of as an experiment in using the latest browser or plug-in capabilities. It would be a mistake, though, to think that Volumeone is just full of weird experiments. Every single screen of Volumeone looks simple and elegant. 'Sprezzatura' seems to be the core of their aesthetic ideology: no matter how complicated a page is technically, no matter how experimental the use of Flash or java script, make it look elegant and easy to do.

Cars from the '70s show up everywhere on this site, as do Japanese toy fighter robots, and what look like heroic illustrations from '50s children's books. Pop culture and technology are clearly a favourite topic. The signs of the achievements of technology and wealth abound: space flight, '60s SF, plastics and fast food. Yet these are not used as images of optimism, but rather as signs of nostalgia or estrangement. Typically, a lot of the contributions can seem to have a slight political edge, but it seems that they're just using political themes because they have the right 'feel', rather than for any critical reasons.

Volumeone stands out for the clarity and effectiveness of its design. Exploring the site is a pleasant and rewarding enterprise; something worth discovering lies behind every button. At Volumeone they're very good at visual communication, but they're even better at creating narrative flow. Yet Volumeone is not about a content that is communicated, although you can get this impression given the recurrent theme of estrangement in modern society. It is about how to communicate a message.
In the end, Volumeone is nothing more and nothing less than a showcase of what Matt Owens and his company can do with the World Wide Web, and that's a lot.

by Arie Altena

TITLE OF THE SITE Volumeone ➣ **OFFICIAL URL** http://www.volumeone.com ➣ **PLACE AND DATE OF DESIGN** Brooklyn, NY (updated quarterly) ➣ **CLIENT** Volumeone ➣ **LANGUAGE** English ➣ **COPYRIGHT OWNERS** Matt Owens ➣ **PRODUCTION** Matt Owens
➣ **EDITORIAL** Matt Owens, Danielle Aubert, Mark Owens ➣ **CONTRIBUTORS** Matt Owens ➣ **SCREEN DESIGN** Matt Owens ➣ **INTERACTION DESIGN** Matt Owens ➣ **SOUND DESIGN** Matt Owens ➣ **ANIMATION/GRAPHICS** Matt Owens
➣ **AWARDS** ACD web 100, Shocked Site of the Day, Highfive Award, AXIS Web 100, Communication Arts Site of the Week ➣ **PLATFORM USES FOR DESIGNING THE SITE** 100% Macintosh ➣ **APPLICATIONS USED** Adobe Photoshop, Adobe Illustrator,
Macromedia Flash 2 and Flash 3, Ray Dream Designer, Adobe Image Ready, BBEdit

playground polemics

playground polemics

Volumeone is **masterful at making use of simple elements of Web design** in a way so effective that you forget its conventionality or simplicity. For instance, in this page it's nothing more than two brilliantly timed, animated GIFs.

This series consists of four examples of expressions signifying **'unspoken elocution'**. The letters of the text are animated, continually appearing and disappearing.

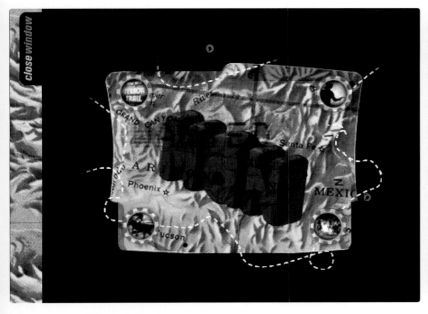 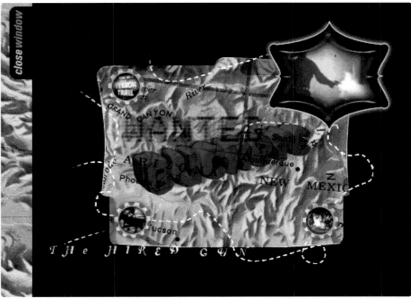

'**Wanted Man'** tells the short story of an outlaw in the days of the Wild West.
It's a good example of the integrated use of animated GIFs. Clicking on one of the
four corners of the image of Arizona starts a small black and white animation.

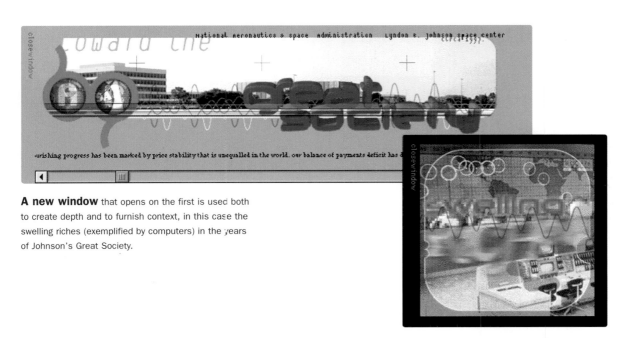

A new window that opens on the first is used both
to create depth and to furnish context, in this case the
swelling riches (exemplified by computers) in the years
of Johnson's Great Society.

Some contributions look like flyers to a SF
party, like this one about Japanese robot
the Great Mazinga. The image on
the upper left is animated; note how the
buttons are integrated in the design.

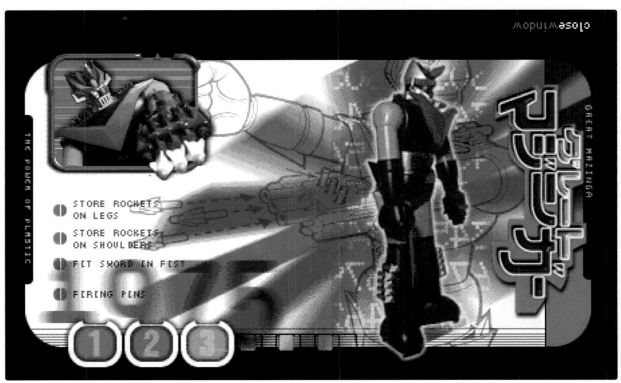

'One Goes There, Yes' is a great contribution made in Flash. Images superimposed upon animated letters fly around and text begins to scroll by when you move your mouse over the pointing hand.

View source

Volumeone uses the various means that Web technologies offer to create dynamic narratives. The most conventional way of doing this, of course, is to create a flow using links that make images and text open within the same window. Yet what's just as simple, and used very effectively in Volumeone, are **animated GIFs** which are integrated into the design of a page, or which start when you click on the appropriate section.

Using **java script** to open every part of a contribution in a new, **fixed-size window** is a third way of generating narrative connections (or disjunctions) and depth. Making intelligent use of text in the browser's status bar adds to the significance of the link, as does using the title of the page that opens in a new window. **Narrative dynamics** can also be created by letting text scroll by, or by animating the text using Flash and making it flow over the image so that image and text become integrated.

Tarmac.

The mechanisms of weaponry.

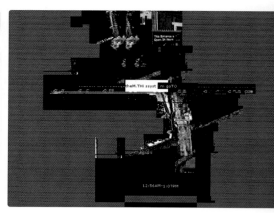

UNTITLED.html
An experimental trip through the East Village of NYC, designed in DHTML and Shockwave.
Follow the E and discover the sounds and images of e12 street.
You'll need a 4.0 browser to view this piece.

E-Z Rider
Follow the adventures of Abdellah Osman as he travels up
the Nile through Egypt, Sudan and Eritrea, culminating in
a bizarre encounter with a lunatic from East LA.
Photographs by Abdellah and Ibrahim.
Additional design by Nadia Beliveau.

La Carretera de Informacion
Mexico City in a multimedia context.
TERRY LALO S brings us images from the streets of the world's largest
city, and devises a metaphor for the Information Superhighway.
Shockwave Flash 3.0 required.
Click on the thumbnails and fragments of images
to access the annotated photography.

The front page of Scroll: this page, a good reminder of the fact that simple, bold design does work on the Web, deploys the familiar java script roll-over routine for its chief effect — as your mouse moves over the titles, they are brought out of their Gaussian blur, into sharp focus.

138

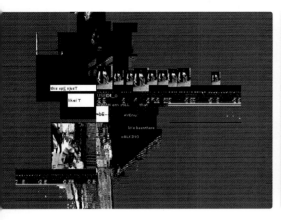

An experimental trip through the East Village of NYC, designed in dhtml and Shockwave. Follow the E and you'll discover the sounds and images of E13 street

SCROLL

TITLE OF THE SITE Scroll ⚑ **OFFICIAL URL** http://scroll.behaviour.com ⚑ **PLACE AND DATE OF DESIGN** Montreal, May 1997 ⚑ **CLIENT** Behaviour Communications ⚑ **LANGUAGE** English, some French ⚑ **COPYRIGHT OWNERS** Behaviour Communications ⚑ **PRODUCTION TEAM** Producer: Theo Diamantis. Contributing Editor: Will Aitken. Art Direction: Ray Wood. Interface Design: Claude Labrie. Inhouse Design: Hoover Chung, Claude Labrie, Catherine Leconte, Ray Wood. Contributing Designers: David Opp, Vinnie Ray, Eric Rosevear, Michiel Schriever, Marina Zurkow. Contributing Photographer: Diana Shearwood. Programming: Marilyn Aziz, Nicolas Leduc, Sean Terriah, Catherine Leconte. Technical Manager: Simon Piette. Production Director: Daniel Gagnon ⚑ **AWARDS** Silver Medal, Interactive Design, New Art Director's Club Gold Medal, Interface Design, New Media Invision Awards Silver Medal, Best General Interest Magazine/Young Adult, New Media Invision Awards Silver Medal, Streamline, Macromedia Director, Flash, Dreamweaver/BBEdit, Freehand. ⚑ **PLATFORM USED FOR DESIGNING THE SITE** Macintosh 50%, Wintel 50% ⚑ **APPLICATIONS USED** Macintosh: Photoshop, Illustrator, Premiere, After Effects, Image Ready, Streamline, Macromedia Director, Flash, Dreamweaver/BBEdit, Freehand, Debabelizer. Wintel: Photoshop, Illustrator, Premiere, After Effects Image Ready Streamline, Macromedia Director, Flash, Dreamweaver/BBEdit, Freehand, Debabelizer. SoundEdit 16 Gifbuilder, Nodester, Debabelizer, Sgi Alias-Maya.

http://scroll.behaviour.com

Scroll, a website by Behaviour New Media, is intended to showcase contemporary culture online. It certainly has a very contemporary look and feel, complete with distressed, motion-blurred typography, phonetic titles and a modishly garish palette; indeed, the site is in every way a paradigm of '90s graphic design conventions. It's also an extremely well-built site, robust and bug-free throughout — qualities that are surprisingly rare in this age of WYSIWYG editors and cowboy coding. That, of course, is why Scroll has already been the recipient of a number of awards, as well as a series of excellent reviews from various sources.

Content in Scroll is split into six categories: 'Trip', a series of travelogues and visits to places falling under the dubious banner of 'Analogue Ghettos of the Global Village'; 'En Macchina', which examines the mechanics of media, with one piece focusing on Goebbels' propaganda machine; 'Studio', a showcase for conventional art and media projects; 'Garage', a series of web-specific projects; 'Story', a collection of fiction featuring new (though perhaps somewhat lacklustre) work by Douglas Rushkoff; and 'Editorial', a group of essay-style incursions into contemporary media issues.

Certain projects stand out: UNTITLED.html, in 'Trip', is a exploration of New York's East Village. It uses dynamic html and Shockwave to move the visitor through an engaging montage of animated images and sounds. Without attempting to be exhaustive, the project manages to convey a sense of the chaos and disorder of New York's streets, and it excels because of its commitment to playing up the Web's strengths, rather than rehashing old design ideas in the new medium. While this is not true of every project housed in Scroll (which would be remarkable indeed), the sensitivity with which the designers deploy frames and new windows, and the attention paid to clarity and layout, ensures that Behaviour's site remains an eminently enjoyable experience. Other projects worthy of mention are the particularly amusing Sex Slave Rebels, which makes excellent use of Shockwave's proprietary Flash platform to tell the story of an escaping gimp (we await further instalments!); editor Theo Diamantis's article on the homepage as self-styled schlock; and the strange, inscrutable Solipsistic Universe of Happy Smackett.

One of the most recent additions is Azimuth 360°, a multimedia extravaganza about Frank Gehry's Guggenheim Museum in Bilbao. Made in Flash, this non-linear exploration offers three 'angles' on Gehry's shiny creation on the banks of the Nevrion river. Against the background of a cross-section of the museum building, a personal account by Will Aitken of his amusement at and appreciation of Gehry's architectural design serves as an introduction. The 90° angle presents a collection of photographs of the building and its surrounding city, along with anecdotes by the photographers who spent five days in Bilbao documenting their experience. The 180° angle presents a short musing called Daedalus, illustrated with stylised photography. In the 360° section, the museum is shown through a series of Quicktime VR movies, containing links to quotes from Gehry himself. All in all, the Azimuth 360° project tries to convey the experience of exploration and wonder that the Guggenheim Museum evokes among its real-life visitors.

In summary, Behaviour's Scroll project distinguishes itself as a paragon of cutting-edge design and fresh, funky content on the Web. If it can keep up the pace, Scroll looks to become a formidable online presence.

by Jamie King

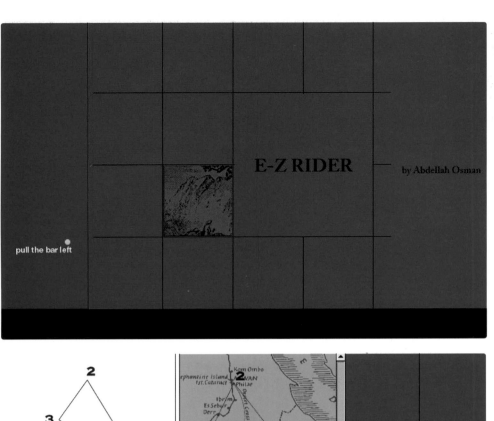

Sex Slave Rebels: Naoki Mitsuse uses Flash to tell us the story of one gimp who rebels against his oppressors.

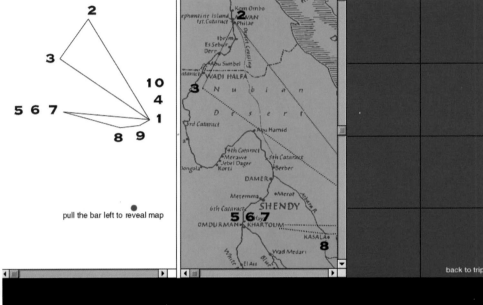

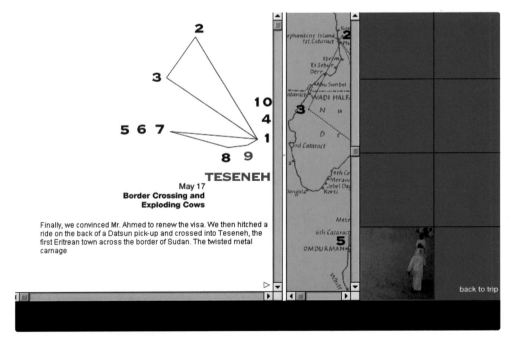

Another example from the **'Trip' section**. Follow the adventures of Abdellah Osman as he travels up the Nile through Egypt, Sudan and Eritrea. Note the use of frames here: you can pull open or close the frames by pulling their border, thus revealing or hiding the map and the grid where photographs are displayed.

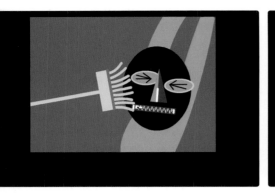

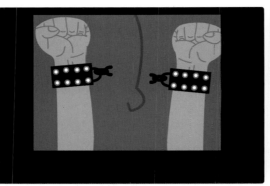

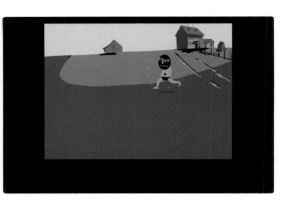

Two lawyers examine the principles behind copyright and intellectual property laws. Their question is: **shall the first idea be the last?** by Anonymous Barristers.

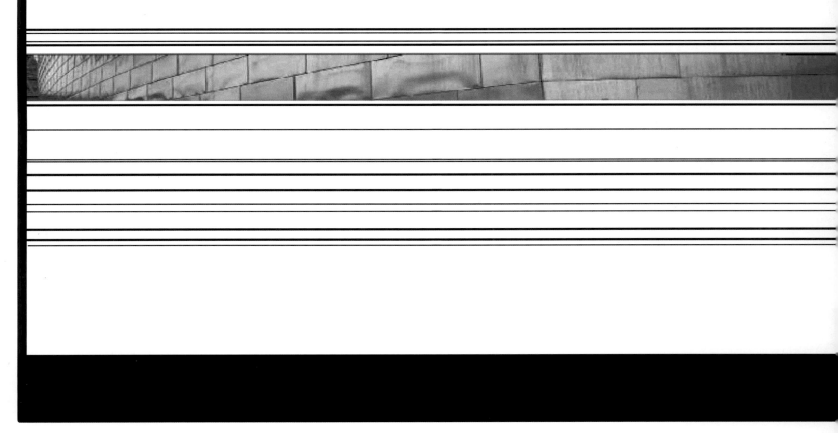

This Flash-based combination of text, photography and animation attempts to convey the experience you'll have as a visitor to Gehry's **Guggenheim Museum in Bilbao**. The small cube provides the main navigation through the three 'angles' of perspective. The small squares below allow you to navigate through a series of texts.

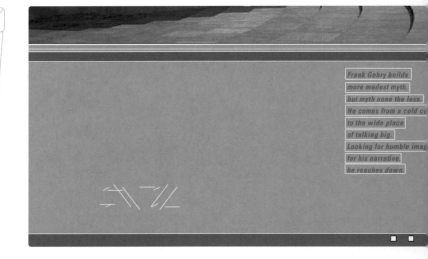

View source

In its many contributions, Scroll obviously features a range of special techniques and applications. Take a look at the homepage. Designed in **dynamic html**, it layers and animates its menus by **moving and replacing images** using roll-over scripts. For example, one of the menus moves into view from behind the Scroll logo in a separate layer, commanded by a roll-over java script. Recent additions make extensive use of Flash for simple animations (the escaping gimp) or multimedia experiences (Azimuth 360°).

In contrast to these state-of-the-art design techniques, the use of the old 'flaw' of **resizable frames** in EZ-rider stands out as an old but very effective trick. When frames were first applied in html design to break up the browser window in order to display multiple documents, it was impossible to set a fixed width for them. The user could always resize them at will. This is put to good use here, creating the illusion of uncovering the hidden map and photo-documentary by simply 'brushing' one frame aside. Continuously shifting and resizing the frame borders allows you to move your attention from text to map, to photographs, and back again.

Frank Gehry builds more modest myth, but myth none the less. He comes from a cold c[...] to the wide place of talking big. Looking for humble imag[...] for his narrative, he reaches down.

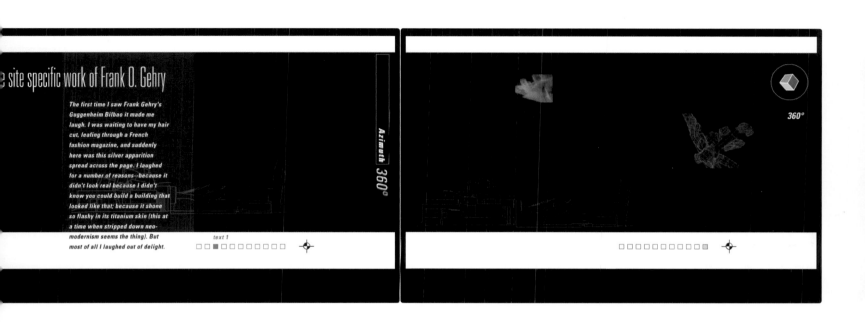

e site specific work of Frank O. Gehry

The first time I saw Frank Gehry's Guggenheim Bilbao it made me laugh. I was waiting to have my hair cut, leafing through a French fashion magazine, and suddenly here was this silver apparition spread across the page. I laughed for a number of reasons--because it didn't look real because I didn't know you could build a building that looked like that; because it shone so flashy in its titanium skin (this at a time when stripped down neo-modernism seems the thing). But most of all I laughed out of delight.

Azimuth 360°

text 1
□ □ ■ □ □ □ □ □ □ □ □

360°

□ □ □ □ □ □ □ □ □ □ ▣

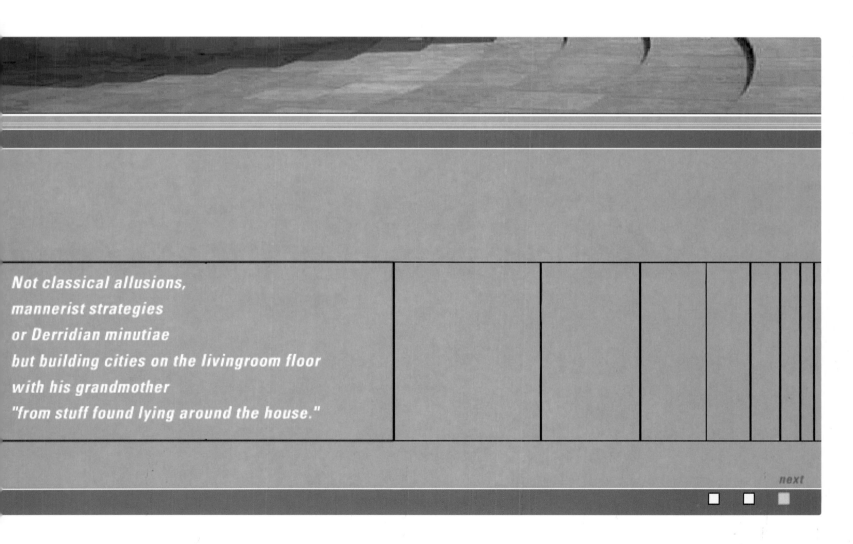

Not classical allusions,
mannerist strategies
or Derridian minutiae
but building cities on the livingroom floor
with his grandmother
"from stuff found lying around the house."

next

The **main music interface** for
the site looks like this. Shifting the
'sliders' with the mouse changes the
track selected in the fake window
display. Once selected, clicking the
'play' icon starts the track. Users
are given two options: new releases
offering around 20 tracks, and the
back catalogue, with a more extensive
choice. Once selected, the tracks play
happily as the soundtrack to your visit.

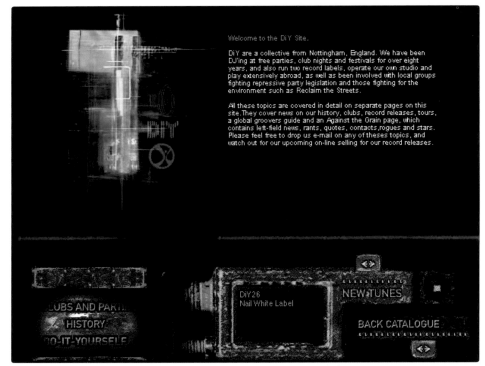

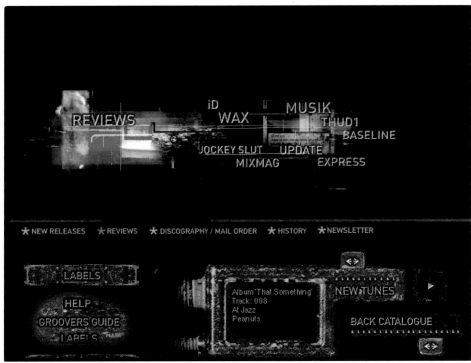

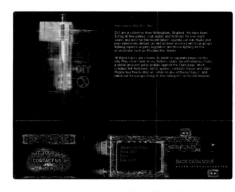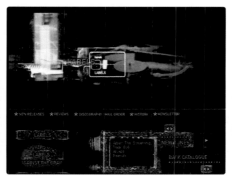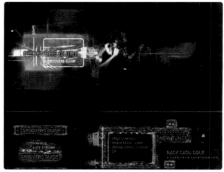

Here's an example of the **attractive images** that adorn each section's title screens. These montages have a look that suggests that they're amalgamations of a personal collection of dance-related memorabilia.

DIY RECORDS

http://www.digit1.com/diy

Coming to life in the highly charged atmosphere of the UK's early '90s free party/club culture, with its attendant criminalisation by the notorious Criminal Justice Act, DIY made their mark on the scene via a number of events and festivals, including involvement in the notorious Avon Free Festival at Castlemoreton Common, Gloucestershire in 1992, where 40,000 revellers clashed with the police, making front-page news and in the process becoming a landmark in the UK's anti-establishment rave history.

Designers Digit1's website for DIY takes this history on board and represents it for the Web audience, and just like its real-life counterpart, this is all done to a constant soundtrack of 'repetitive beats' ensuring that if this website were a party, it would certainly be under arrest!

Yes, this website has been designed to engage viewers with DIY's music as they browse the site. The interface, a dirty metallic console that sits in the bottom third of the fixed-size browser window, has two selectors that can be dragged left and right. These can play tunes either from current releases on DIY's label or tracks from the back catalogue. The music interface stays constant during the browsing of the site, and essentially provides a mini-hi-fi of DIY tunes. If using a good connection, it works smoothly and with a reasonable audio quality, one that isn't interrupted by the surfing going on in the rest of the browser window's upper frame.

Users are given a number of sections to browse, all of which are accessed from a scrolling menu that shares the bottom frame with the music selector. Double-clicking your selection can take you to standard sorts of website information: contacts, help, links, etc., while other sections take a more in-depth look at DIY, its artists, personalities and history. Bearing in mind how the collective came into being, it is perhaps unsurprising that the most interesting and comprehensive parts are the 'History' and 'Against the Grain' sections. In 'History', the text is by default both a history of DIY and a mini-history of the rave scene, giving a good idea of how the scene built up and then diversified into a number of different strands. 'Against the Grain' contains a number of interesting sections, including a tour history of the DIY sound system that takes in several diverse locations across the world. A series of short essays about the politics of the free party movement and a selection of shockwave movie 'quotes' from various luminaries such as David Toop and John Cage dynamically build, fade and come together on the screen in front of you.

Digit1 say that the 'look and feel of DIY was very much inspired by regenerating and recycling objects, giving them new life and purpose within new media'. Of course, some media can be regenerated more easily than others. In the case of collectives such as DIY, who already take a principled stand on utilising the democratic potential of electronic ways of making music, much can be gained as Net access becomes more widespread. The principled creativity of collectives such as DIY can make use of network technology to extend existing connections and find new areas to spread the word, while simultaneously circumventing and confronting the structures of the music industry and society alike — online music being already one of the most hotly contested areas in the independent versus corporate battles for the future of the Web. And with this site soon to accommodate live webcasts and transactions, it could provide a vital key to the growth and strength of such an oppositional culture — do-it-yourself indeed.

by Noel Douglas

TITLE OF THE SITE DIY Records ➣ OFFICIAL URL http://www.digit1.com/diy ➣ PLACE AND DATE OF DESIGN London, June/July 1998 ➣ CLIENT DIY Records ➣ LANGUAGE English ➣ COPYRIGHT OWNERS DIY Records, Digit1 Digital experiences LTD

PRODUCTION Nick Cristea, Henry Brook ➣ EDITORIAL Sascha Koesch ➣ CONTRIBUTORS Drew Hemnet ➣ SCREEN DESIGN Simon Sankarhyya, Brad Smith ➣ INTERACTION DESIGN Nick Cristea, Simon Sankarhyya

SOUND DESIGN Owen Lloyd, Digs & Woosh ➣ ANIMATIONS AND GRAPHICS Henry Brook, Brad Smith ➣ PLATFORM USED FOR DESIGNING THE SITE Macintosh 50%, Wintel 50% ➣ APPLICATIONS USED Macintosh: Photoshop, Director, Freehand.

Wintel: Director, Dreamweaver, Flash, Soundforge

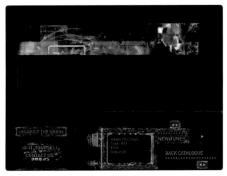

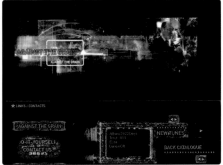

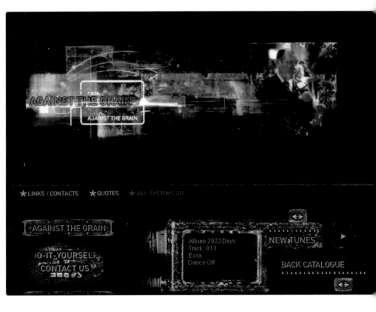

This shows how **one of the title screens and selection buttons fade in** when selected from the scrolling menu in the bottom frame.

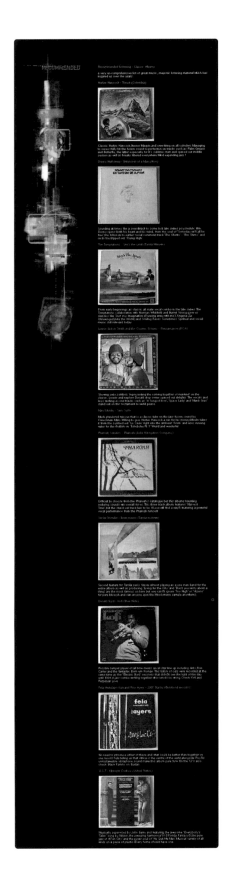

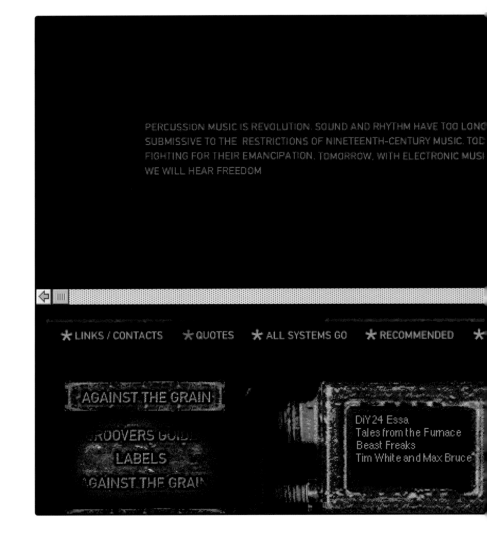

PERCUSSION MUSIC IS REVOLUTION. SOUND AND RHYTHM HAVE TOO LONG
SUBMISSIVE TO THE RESTRICTIONS OF NINETEENTH-CENTURY MUSIC. TOD
FIGHTING FOR THEIR EMANCIPATION. TOMORROW, WITH ELECTRONIC MUSI
WE WILL HEAR FREEDOM

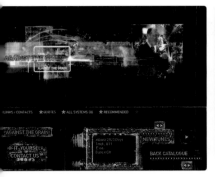

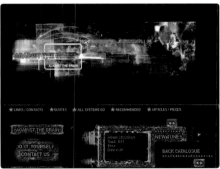

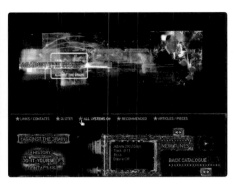

THE CULT OF THE DJ IS THE RETURN OF THE
NUREMBERG SHUFFLE. DANCERS NO LONGER
EQUAL UNDER THE GROOVE, PASSIVE FIXATION
REPLACING RAPTURE. 'EYES FRONT!'

DOCTOR ROGAS

★ LINKS / CONTACTS   ★ QUOTES   ★ ALL SYSTEMS GO   ★ RECOMMENDED   ★ ARTICLES / PIECES

AGAINST THE GRAIN

HELP

GROOVERS GUIDE

DiY 24 Essa
Tales from the Furnace
Beast Freaks
Tim White and Max Bruce

NEW TUNES

BACK CATALOGUE

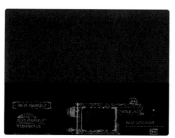 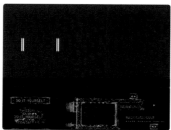  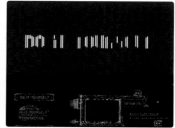 

This sequence is the **introductory screen** to a small Shockwave music toy.

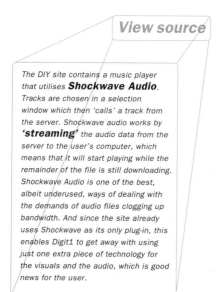

View source

The DIY site contains a music player that utilises **Shockwave Audio**. Tracks are chosen in a selection window which then 'calls' a track from the server. Shockwave audio works by **'streaming'** the audio data from the server to the user's computer, which means that it will start playing while the remainder of the file is still downloading. Shockwave Audio is one of the best, albeit underused, ways of dealing with the demands of audio files clogging up bandwidth. And since the site already uses Shockwave as its only plug-in, this enables Digit1 to get away with using just one extra piece of technology for the visuals and the audio, which is good news for the user.

 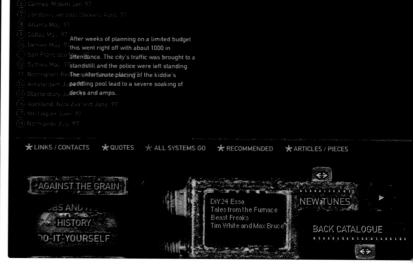

All Systems Go is an umbrella organisation set up to link together different sound systems fighting anti-party legislation. Contained within the site section bearing the same name is a Shockwave itinerary for the DIY system during 1997. Click on a location and a different tale from the events is told in a window graphic that fades into the foreground. Click it again and it fades away, as the menu returns to the front.

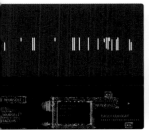
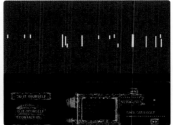
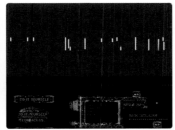

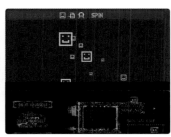

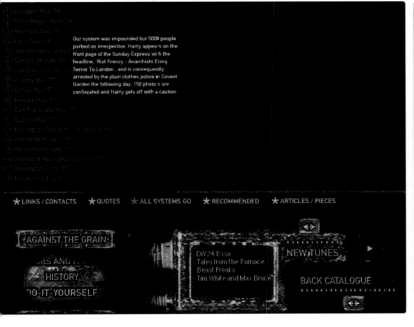
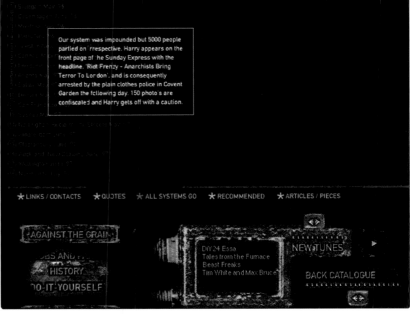

From the FUSE98 section in the menu, the user can call up a series of quotes and comments left by attendees. Two triangular buttons set the text scrolling up or down. Note how the **scrolling text** exposes the use of layers when it moves underneath the menu.

 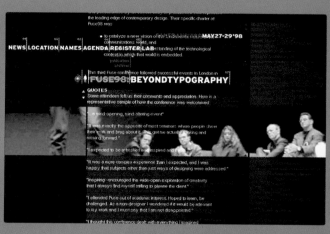

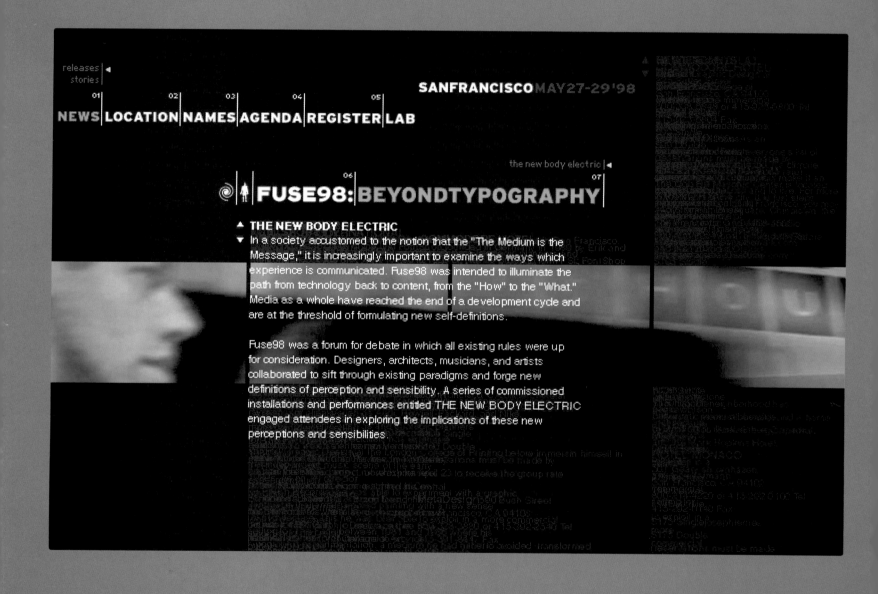

releases
stories

01	02	03	04	05

SANFRANCISCO MAY27-29'98

NEWS LOCATION NAMES AGENDA REGISTER LAB

the new body electric

06   07

FUSE98:BEYONDTYPOGRAPHY

▲ **THE NEW BODY ELECTRIC**
▼ In a society accustomed to the notion that the "The Medium is the Message," it is increasingly important to examine the ways which experience is communicated. Fuse98 was intended to illuminate the path from technology back to content, from the "How" to the "What." Media as a whole have reached the end of a development cycle and are at the threshold of formulating new self-definitions.

Fuse98 was a forum for debate in which all existing rules were up for consideration. Designers, architects, musicians, and artists collaborated to sift through existing paradigms and forge new definitions of perception and sensibility. A series of commissioned installations and performances entitled THE NEW BODY ELECTRIC engaged attendees in exploring the implications of these new perceptions and sensibilities.

FUSE98

http://www.fuse98.com

Over the past few years, the FUSE conferences have established a name for themselves among the international design community. As an international platform, the FUSE conferences explore the future of graphic design in both practice and theory. For FUSE98, MetaDesign, in conjunction with Fontshop International and Neville Brody, proposed the theme 'Beyond Typography', in an attempt to 'catalyse' a new vision of the fundamental nature of the communications world and the technological context in which it is embedded. For several days, designers, architects, musicians and artists explored existing paradigms in order to forge new definitions of perception and sensibility. In view of the emphasis on technology which has dominated design in recent years, FUSE98 tried to find a way back from technology to content, from the 'how' to the 'what and why' of graphic design in the digital domain.

No wonder, then, that such a prestigious conference prides itself on setting up a state-of-the-art information website. Moving the technology almost literally to the background, co-organisers MetaDesign in San Francisco created this subtle and very functional site, which explored the advanced possibilities of dynamic html.

The FUSE98 site is divided into two interlinked sections, one for the conference information and one for the presentation of online graphic experiments in the FUSElab. Both sections are characterised by the same sparse, elemental design and layout, mainly distinguished by the use of complementary background colours. The conference site provides all the necessary information for those of us who were planning to attend. Basic information on the city of San Francisco, the Nob Hill Masonic Center, transportation and accommodation is presented with the same elegance as the extensive information on speakers and participants. The FUSElab section presents a continuous flow of submitted work by leading or up-and-coming designers, mostly in Shockwave or Flash. Supplemented by some basic information, like title, file size and necessary plug-ins, the work itself is either presented in a newly opened window or within the context of the designer's site.

In both sections, navigational menus form an integrating and structuring element in the layout of the page(s). Doing away with the 'traditional' separate bar of buttons along the top or side of the page — as well as your browser's complete tool and location bars, for that matter — it is an exceptionally strong feature of the design. This basic menu of options is always present as a complete site map, offering more detailed options when touched upon by the mouse. All the available information is added and built around the expanding menus. You'll realise this specifically once you experience the textual information scrolling away underneath the title and navigation elements.

This layering and repositioning of graphic elements and information seems to be the running theme in the FUSE98 site. Each screen is built from composed layers, from the nearly illegible texts that serve as a background grid element to the crossbar of images that runs underneath some of the textual information. It is an almost formal play on the main technique used to create this site, the layers in dhtml.

One of the frequent drawbacks of websites that accompany international conferences is that they freeze after the event. This partly holds true for the FUSE98 site as well. Those who missed out on the event will search the site in vain for conference proceedings. Aside from some press clippings, the site remains as it was. However, the FUSElab has remained open to submissions, keeping the spirit of the event alive a while longer.

by Geert J. Strengholt

TITLE OF THE SITE FUSE98 ➤ OFFICIAL URL http://www.fuse98.com ➤ PLACE AND DATE OF DESIGN MetaDesign San Francisco, Dec. 1997 – Feb. 1998 ➤ CLIENT FUSE Conferences ➤ LANGUAGE English ➤ COPYRIGHT OWNERS MetaDesign SF

DIRECTION Rick Lowe (Design direction), David Peters (Producer) ➤ SCREEN DESIGN Olivier Chetelat, Shawn Hazen, Eva Walter ➤ INTERACTION DESIGN Olivier Chetelat, Shawn Hazen, Joseph Ternes ➤ PRODUCTION Joseph Ternes (DHTML/JavaScript).

EDITORIAL Christopher Myers, Shel Perkins, David Peters ➤ CONTRIBUTORS Ken Coupland (editorial), Rhonda Rubinstein (editorial), Jon Wozencroft (editorial), Ligia Dias (photography), Mark Eastman (photography). Various designers for the FUSE98LAB submissions

AWARDS American Center for Design Web 100, 1998. Macromedia DHTML Spotlight, April 6 1998. Macromedia Shocked Site of the Day, April 21 1998. Webmaster Central DHTML site of the Week, February 1998. Digital Thread One Page Wonder, March – April 1998

PLATFORM USED FOR DESIGNING THE SITE Macintosh 95%, Wintel 5% ➤ APPLICATIONS USED Macintosh: Illustrator 7, Photoshop 4, Photoshop 4.5, Fetch, GifBuilder. Wintel: Netscape, for testing only

The **long scrolling list** of participants on the left calls on further personal info to be displayed below the menu.

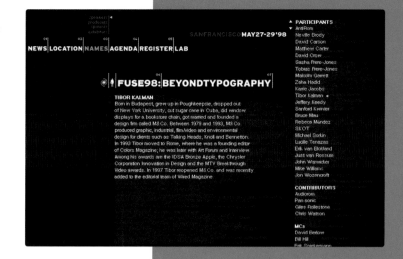

These page details show how the **navigation menu** is built up. The first two images feature the fade-in and fade-out title sequence that previews the layout of the main menu. The expanding submenus appear from the main items by means of roll-over scripts. The submenus are mutually exclusive.

View source

*The experimental version of the FUSE98 site was created entirely in **dynamic html**. Basically this makes it possible to hide most of the information in invisible layers, waiting for the user to call on it from the menu. What could previously only be done by using frames — the loading of various bits of information from a menu in a specified frame — can now be solved simply by bringing information to the surface with a **click or roll-over** of the mouse. This is how MetaDesign realised these expanding menus which in turn give access to further textual information. Note that both the FUSE98 site and the FUSElab section each consist of one large html file which contains all the textual information and coding needed to display it interactively.*

*Dhtml also pre-empts the usual problems associated with fixing layouts, by providing the possibility of **absolute positioning of image and text**. This becomes especially evident in the FUSElab section, where java script roll-overs on the contributors' names load information and an image representing their submissions in the grid-like space below. This grid-like structure is fixed, predetermining where pieces of information should be displayed.*

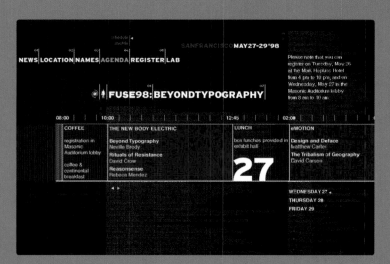

The **conference timeline** is featured as a lengthy horizontal scroll moving in both directions.

Information about the city of San Francisco and the **location** of the conference centre.

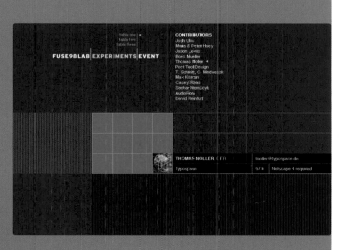

The FUSElab shows the clearest **example of absolute positioning** within a dhtml layout. The grid-like layout basically designates the space where images and text will dynamically be displayed. Based on the user's actions in the menu, information on the designers and their entered work is displayed in the grid which is prepared in the lower part of the screen.

COMMUNITY BASED SITES

In the **'Fuel' section** an interview about the film Slam shows some of the strong, bold graphic layouts and texts within the site.

In the **main screen** layout, tables provide structure to diverse information which is then permanently framed by the top and bottom frames of the window.

Platform uses a number of **pop-up menus** that can be floated onscreen to control the main screen content, this helps make navigation clearer for the user.

TITLE OF THE SITE Platform ➤ **OFFICIAL URL** http://www.platform.net ➤ **PLACE AND DATE OF DESIGN** Williamsburg, Brooklyn, 1997 ➤ **CLIENT** Platform Network ➤ **LANGUAGE** English — though the site are currently being translated into German, Japanese, and French ➤ **COPYRIGHT OWNERS** Platform Network (Platform LLC) ➤ **PRODUCTION** Tina Imm and Ben White, Creative Directors (and Partners); Frank Zuber, Art Director ➤ **EDITORIAL** Stephen Greco, Editorial Director (and Partner) ➤ **CONTRIBUTORS (EDITORIAL)** Tom Constable, Jon Caramanica, Lizzie Simon, Kem Poston, Amanda Ricken, Anicee Gaddis, Dimitri Ehrlich, Julia Szabo, Jil Derryberry, Andre Pinces, Brendan Biddlecom, Tony Le, Saidah Blount ➤ **SCREEN DESIGN** Frank Zuber, Tina Imm, Ben White, Miguel Hurtado, Ron Croudy ➤ **INTERACTION DESIGN** Ben White, Tina Imm, John Lianoglou ➤ **SOUND DESIGN** Ben White, Tom Constabile ➤ **ANIMATION/GRAPHICS** Ben White, Frank Zuber, Miguel Hurtado ➤ **PLATFORM USED FOR DESIGNING THE SITE** Macintosh 100% ➤ **APPLICATIONS USED** BBEdit, Photoshop, Ilustrator, Streamline, Freehand, GoLive Cyberstudio, Netscape

PLATFORM

http://www.platform.net

Based in New York, Platform tags itself as a site for 'Transglobal Urban Living'. Its content is aimed squarely at a global audience that likes its music sampled and bassy, engages in active sports such as snowboarding and wears small designer 'streetwear' labels. Its design in some ways reflects the hectic, densely packed atmosphere of its geographical home, New York. But beneath the apparent chaos is a complex and multifaceted website which manages to kill more than two birds with one stone.

The homepage initially seems top-heavy with options, animated GIFs and menus, but the tightly packed html table is in fact logically laid out, with adverts on the right, features in the middle and site control on the left. Sometimes the site's complexity makes this navigation seem a little confusing, but, handily enough, the ever-present bottom part of the screen is always devoted to selectors for the site's main areas. There's also a small Shockwave audio player in this part of the screen that plays tracks on demand from a playlist accessed via a pop-up window. The 'urban' theme is reflected in small details throughout the site(s): the use of flat greys in the background colours (which enhance text legibility in such a small space), the use of utilitarian, military fonts and background graphics that often resemble the kind of aluminium sheets found in industrial club interiors. The site is very rich in content and, as its name suggests, Platform supports other sites as a means of fostering a community based on common interests. For instance, the 'Megazine' section pulls together eight different 'partner' magazines, all of whose websites can be accessed directly; subscriptions and back issues from all of them are available online. As a sort of portal site, Platform sometimes 'frames' other sites within itself, both literally and conceptually. The range of material on the generic Platform site is very diverse. In the 'Fuel' section, there are features including a report on a political demonstration (the Million Youth March), advice on helping to treat depression and some reflections on Buddhist teachings. It must be said, though, that these items sit rather strangely with some of the other sections such as 'Balls', which focuses on a range of extreme sports including an interview with 'extreme fighter' Ivor Zinoviev (who is quoted as saying that when he fights, 'You're allowed to do everything but gouge your opponent's eyes out or punch their spinal column!').

Despite the range of material on the site, it generally all holds together well graphically. Most sections have original titles and layouts that rarely clash with the main Platform 'look', and the 'feel' of the graphics is contemporary without being too fashion-led. Platform is also a heavily commercial site in many ways. Like the 'Megazine' section, 'Rocketshop' also contains links to ten small designer clothes labels which sell a range of streetwear. This section operates using a virtual 'shopping basket' which can be filled with the desired choices and ordered securely over the Net. Much like with the business empire of those other famous New Yorkers, the Beastie Boys, you get the feeling that this is just a bunch of like-minded friends trying to help each other out. Consequently, 'business' is put firmly in its place, as a means to an end rather than an end in itself, mainly because there's a notion of community at work here that goes beyond consumer purchases. As such, the site manages to stay on the right side of the credibility fence. Ultimately, Platform succeeds in its intention: its busy, tightly organised design and diverse content reflect both the lifestyles of its audience and the pace of modern urban living, and at the same time act as co-ordinators which both foster and facilitate an online community.

by Noel Douglas

Fridge magazine is a good example of the quality of the rest of the 'partner' sites available via Platform's selectors.

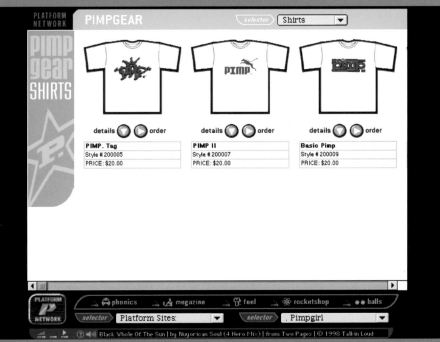

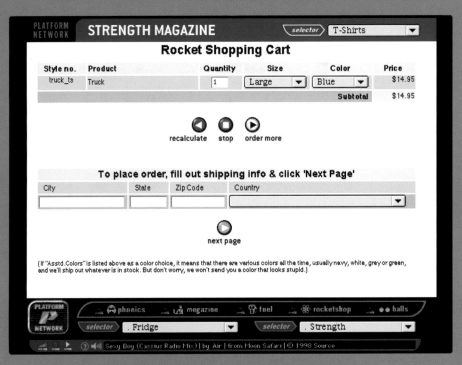

Online shopping for all the latest streetwear available internationally.

View source

An intrinsic part of Platform.net in helping the various designers to sell their clothes in the Rocketshop is the use of the **SSL protocol for secure online transactions**. That your information is being transmitted securely via SSL is indicated by the fact that your browser will have an unbroken key or padlock in the lower left-hand corner of the status bar. SSL (Secure Socket Layer) is a widely used Internet security protocol that provides data encryption (so that no one except the recipient can read the information being sent), authentication (so that you're sure the information is going where you intended) and message integrity (so that the information is correct when it arrives at its destination). SSL uses public key encryption to exchange a session key between the user and server; this session key is used to encrypt the http transaction (in both directions). Each transaction uses a different session key so that if someone manages to decrypt a transaction it doesn't mean that the server's secret key has been decoded; if you want to decrypt another transaction, you'll need to spend as much time and effort on the second transaction as you did on the first.

As the site relies on sustaining a sense of community, **the 'Links' section** can be added to by users of the site. There is also a mailing list which includes the option of having daily record reviews sent to you via e-mail.

COMMUNITY BASED SITES

ADDRESSES

Art and Design experiments

The Remedi Project
Josh Ulm
435 2nd avenue, #4
San Francisco, CA 94118
USA
Tel +1 415 221 5411
ulm@theremediproject.com
Contributors:
Annette Loudon, annette@construct.net
George Larou, glarou1@maine.rr.com
John J. Hill, jinn@52mm.com
Jimmy Chen, jimmy@typographic.com
Shannon Rankin, srankin@maine.rr.com

Fork Unstable Media V3.3
Fork Unstable Media
Manuel Funk
Juliusstrasse 25
22769 Hamburg
Germany
Tel +49 (0)40 432 948 0
Fax +49 (0)40 432 948 11
info@fork.de

Jodi.org
jodi@jodi.org

Lateral
Lateral Net Ltd
Winchester Wharf
Clink Street
London SE1 9DG
UK
Tel +44 (0)171 378 1011
Fax +44 (0)171 403 4586
studio@lateral.net

Hygeia Revisited
Tapio Mäkelä
Lapinrinne 4 D 30
00180 Helsinki
Finland
GSM +358 (0)40 5071965
Fax +358 (0)10 2905004
tapio@projekt.net
Susanna Paasonen
Lapinrinne 4 D
00180 Helsinki
Finland
suspaa@utu.fi

Some of my Favourite Web Sites are Art
Rhizome Communications Inc.
c/o Postmasters Gallery
459 West 19th Street
New York, NY 10011
USA
Tel +1 212 727 7024
Info@rhizome.org

The Secret Garden of Mutabor
Jens Schmidt (yenz)
Via Mercadante 8
20124 Milano
Italy
Tel +39 (0)2 29404538
yenz@micronet.it

Educational sites

National Geographic
National Geographic Society
P.O. Box 98199
Washington, D.C. 20090-8199
USA
Tel +1 813 979 6845

Design for Life: A Centennial Celebration
Elisabeth Roxby
roxx.com
9 East 13th St.
Suite 2J
New York, NY 10003
Tel +1 212 243 3501
Fax +1 212 243 4918
elisabeth@roxx.com

BBC Windrush
BBC Education
Michael Bedward
Web Producer
3&6 Langham Place
London W1A 1AA
UK
Tel +44 (0)181 752 6086
Fax +44 (0)181 752 7353
Windrush@bbc.co.uk

Promotional sites

Dorado.net
Dorado Records
Fabian Sasson
76 Brewer Street
London W1R 3PH
UK
Tel +44 (0)171 287 1689
Fax +44 (0)171 287 1684
webmaster@dorado.net

Levi Strauss & Co. Europe
Lateral Net Ltd
Winchester Wharf
Clink Street
London SE1 9DG
UK
Tel +44 (0)171 378 1011
Fax +44 (0)171 403 4586
studio@lateral.net

Gispen
Sander Kessels
Nieuwe Keizersgracht 58
1019 DT Amsterdam
The Netherlands
Tel +31 (0)20 422 9210
Fax +31 (0)20 422 9212
Kessels@xs4all.nl

G-Shock.com: Time for the 21st Century
Razorfish Inc.
107 Grand Street 3rd Floor
New York, NY 10013
USA
Tel +1 212 966 5960
info@razorfish.com

Mercedes-Benz A-Class
Icon Media Lab Spain
Juan Mantilla
calle Toledo, 94 6-dcha
28005 Madrid
Spain
Tel +91 365 60 56
juan@iconmedialab.es

Heathrow Express
Crown Digital
Bee Thakershi
United House
9 Pembridge Road
London W11 3JY
UK
Tel +44 (0)171 565 6346
Fax +44 (0)171 727 9940
thakershib@crowndigital.com

LundstromARCH.com
Juxt Interactive
Todd Purgason
2201 Martin St., Suite 203b
Irvine, CA 92612
USA
info@juxtinteractive.com

Transaction based sites

Fabric8
Fabric8
Olivia Ongpin
P.O. Box 420794
San Francisco, CA 94142
USA
Tel/Fax +1 415 487 9702
ooo@fabric8.com

24h Cinema Service
VPRO Digitaal
Bruno Felix, Petra Schrevelius
P.O. Box 11
1200 JC Hilversum
The Netherlands
Tel +31 (0)35 671 2738

Rabobank Internetbankieren
Mediamatic Interactive Publishing
Willem Velthoven
P.O. Box 17490
1001 JL Amsterdam
The Netherlands
Tel +31 (0)20 626 6262
Fax +31 (0)20 626 3793
desk@mediamatic.nl

E-publishing sites

Atlas Magazine
Futurefarmers
1201 B Howard Street
San Francisco, CA 94103
USA
Tel +1 415 552 2124
Fax +1 415 552 6328
ame@sirius.com

De:bug binary continuous mode
De:bug Verlags gmbh
Jan Rikus Hillmann
Brunnenstrasse 196
10119 Berlin
Germany
marketing@de-bug.de

COLORS Magazine
New Media Department
Fabrica S.p.A
Via Ferrezza,
31050 Catena Di Villorba, Treviso
Italy
Tel +39 422 6161
contact@colors.it

Volumeone
Matt Owens
654 Metropolitan Ave. 3rd floor
Brooklyn, NY 11211
USA
Tel +1 718 384 5521
Fax +1 718 302 9511
info@volumeone.com

Scroll
Behaviour Communications Inc
Theo Diamantis
10 Duke
Montreal, H3C 2L7
Canada
theod@behaviour.com

Community based sites

DIY Records
Digit1 - Digital Experiences Ltd
Nicolas Critea
6 Flitcroftstreet
London WC2H 8DJ
UK
Tel +44 (0)171 681 0110
Fax +44 (0)171 691 2233
studio@digit1.com

FUSE98
MetaDesign San Francisco
Mark Goldman
350 Pacific Avenue
San Francisco, CA 94133
USA
Tel +1 415 627 0790
Fax +1 415 627 0795
mgoldman@metadesign.com

Platform
Platform Inc.
Stephen Greco
67 Metroploitan Ave.
Brooklyn, NY 11211
USA
mail@platform.net

GLOSSARY

ActiveX ActiveX is the name Microsoft has given to a set of 'strategic' object-oriented program technologies and tools. ActiveX is Microsoft's answer to the java technology from Sun Microsystems. An ActiveX control is roughly equivalent to a java applet.

animated GIF An animated GIF is a graphic image on a webpage that moves simply by running through a sequence of separate images. An animated GIF can either loop endlessly, or present one or a few sequences and then stop the animation.

applet An applet is a small application program. Used on the Web together with java (the object-oriented programming language), an applet is a small program that can be sent to a user along with a webpage. Java applets can perform interactive animations, immediate calculations or other simple tasks without having to send a user request back to the server.

browser A browser is a program that provides a way to look at, read and even hear all the information on the World Wide Web. New generations of the most commonly used browsers, Netscape and Microsoft's Internet Explorer, provide enhanced and dynamic capabilities for animations and streaming multimedia.

Cascading Style Sheet (CSS)
A Cascading Style Sheet, or CSS, is a simple mechanism for adding style to html documents. With CSS, you can specify styles such as the size, colour, and spacing of text, as well as the placement of text and images on the page. Cascading Style Sheets allow an author to specify how a page should look, and also allow readers to attach a personal style sheet in order to adjust the appearance of the page to allow for human or technological handicaps.

database A database is a collection of data organised so that its contents can be easily accessed, managed and updated. The most prevalent type of database is the relational database in which data is defined so that it can be reorganised and accessed in a number of different ways. In the context of a website, information can be retrieved from the database and presented in a browser by means of templates.

dynamic html (dhtml)
Dynamic html is a collective term for a combination of new html tags, style sheets and programming that will let you create webpages that are more animated and more responsive to user interaction than previous versions of html. Dynamic html can allow webdocuments to look and act like desktop applications or multimedia productions.

dynamic fonts Dynamic fonts are a feature of Netscape's Communicator and enable website designers to specify special font styles for a webpage or site. A font file is downloaded as a plug-in from the Web server along with the first page that uses it.

frames Frames are an html option for splitting up the browser window into discrete sections, each displaying a different html document.

java A programming language developed especially for use in the distributed environment of the Internet. Using java, programmers can create complete applications that run either on a single computer or among servers and clients in a network. Java is also used to build small applications or applets for use as part of a webpage.

java script Java script is a programming or script language from Netscape.

layers Layers are a feature in 4.x browsers where, in contrast to frames, multiple sources of content can be stored in the same document. The information in separate layers can be controlled, moved and displayed by means of java script

log-on and log-in Log-on generally describes the procedure used to gain access to an operating system or application on a remote computer. A log-on usually requires the user to provide a user ID and a password. An increasing number of websites require the user to register before entering or logging onto the site.

pop-up A pop-up is a Graphical User Interface (GUI) element, usually a small window, that appears ('pops up') in response to a mouse click or roll-over. It is commonly used to display extra information, or to expand an existing menu.

Quicktime Quicktime is a multimedia format developed by Apple which combines sound, text, animation and video in a single file. A Quicktime player installed in a browser makes it possible to play short multimedia sequences. Quicktime VR is the spatially enhanced version.

roll-over (or mouse-over) A roll-over (or mouse-over) is a technique which employs java script to allow the user to change a page element (buttons or graphic images) when the user rolls the mouse over it.

site map A visual representation of a website, revealing its main or complete structure and layout.

Shockwave A multimedia player created by Macromedia which makes it possible to play interactive Director movies in the WWW environment. The user's browser needs to be enhanced with the Shockwave plug-in. The latest version is a combined plug-in that also plays Flash movies.

source code General term for all html coding and java scripting involved in determining the presentation and layout of an html document.

view source 'View source' is the name of one of the browser menu options which allows the user to take a look at the source code, or html coding, that makes up a page on the Web.

COLOPHON

Editors Noel Douglas, Geert J. Strengholt, Willem Velthoven (Mediamatic, Amsterdam)

Editorial Production Noel Douglas, Geert J. Strengholt (Mediamatic, Amsterdam)

Translations and Final Editing Douglas Heingartner / hotline@xs4all.nl

Selection The selection of sites was made by the editors in close co-operation with the contributors and other international correspondents

Contributors Arie Altena / arie@mediamatic.nl, Peter Gorgels / peter@mediamatic.nl, Noel Douglas / noeld@ndirect.co.uk, Paul Kahn / paul@dynamicdiagrams.com, Jamie King / jamie@jamie.com, Noortje Marres / n.s.marres@mail.uva.nl, Nina Pope / nina@somewhere.org.uk, Harry Roumen / roumen@knoware.nl, Nathan Shedroff / nathan@vivid.com, Susanna Speier / suzspeier@aol.com, Erik Spiekermann / erik@metadesign.de, Geert J. Strengholt / geertjan@mediamatic.nl, Alex Wilkie / a.wilkie@rca.ac.uk

Design Bobbert van Wezel BNO / bvwezel@iae.nl

Thanks to Lou Rosenfeld, Jennifer Fleming, Robin Verdegaal, Dick Rijken, Sander Kessels and of course to the entire staff at Mediamatic